Children, Philosophy, and Democracy

John P. Portelli and Ronald F. Reed
Editors

Detselig Enterprises Ltd.

Calgary, Alberta, Canada

Canadian Cataloguing in Publication Data

Main entry under title:
Children, philosophy, and democracy

Includes bibliographical references
ISBN 1-55059-115-0

1. Children and philosophy. 2. Philosophy—Study and
teaching (Elementary) 3. Critical thinking in children. I.
Portelli, John Peter. II. Reed, Ronald, date.
B105.C45C54 1995   108'.3'4   C95-910162-4

© 1995 Detselig Enterprises Ltd
210-1220 Kensington Rd. N.W.
Calgary, Alberta, Canada, T2N 3P5

Detselig Enterprises Ltd. appreciates the financial assistance received
for its 1995 publishing program from the Department of Canadian
Heritage, the Canada Council, and the Alberta Foundation for the Arts,
a beneficiary of the Lottery Fund of the Government of Alberta.

Cover Design by Bill Matheson

Printed in Canada   ISBN 1-55059-115-0   SAN 115-0324

Table of Contents

SECTION III

Pedagogical Possibilities in Philosophy for/with Children

To

Our Wives,

Anna and Ann

Acknowledgments

We are grateful to the contributors who made their material available, accommodated our suggestions, and patiently waited for the publication of this collection.

We are also grateful to the following journals, publishers, and organizations for permission to reprint in this collection those essays which have been previously published: *Thinking* for "Text Characters and Lump Characters" (Chapter 3); Dialog Books for "Whole Language and Philosophy with Children: A Dialog of Hope" (Chapter 5); *Analytic Teaching* for "Peirce, Feminism, and Philosophy for Children" (Chapter 7); the organizing committee of the Second World Congress on Violence, University of Montreal (1992) for "Educating for Violence Reduction and Peace Development: The Philosophical Community of Inquiry Approach" (Chapter 6).

We are indebted to our institutions: Mount Saint Vincent University for a research grant; Texas Wesleyan University (in particular Mark Wasicsko, provost of the University, and Allen Henderson, Dean of the School of Education) for continued support and help. In every respect, this project has been a joint effort of both editors.

Finally, our very sincere thanks to Ted Giles of Detselig Enterprises Ltd. who generously continues to encourage and support such projects.

John P. Portelli and Ronald F. Reed

Halifax and Fort Worth

January, 1995

Paul Bitting began his professional career in the public schools of New York city serving as a classroom teacher, counsellor, and administrator. He is presently an assistant professor in the College of Education and Psychology at North Carolina State University. He has published in the areas of critical thinking, Philosophy for Children, and multicultural philosophy in the schools in journals such as *Thinking, Educational Studies* and *Urban Education Review.*

Susan Church is superintendent of educational and student services with the Halifax County–Bedford District School Board, Nova Scotia, Canada. She has worked as both a classroom and a support teacher in elementary and junior high schools. She has published widely in professional books and journals. She is particularly interested in the politics of educational change.

David Kennedy, formerly of Northern Michigan University, is a professor of education at Western Carolina University. He is the author of numerous articles on Philosophy for Children and early childhood education.

Matthew Lipman is the director of the Institute for the Advancement of Philosophy for Children, Montclair State College, New Jersey, and the creator of the original Philosophy for Children curriculum.

San MacColl is a professor of philosophy at the University of New South Wales, Australia, and co-author (with Chris de Haan) of *Kinder Kit.*

Reenie Marx teaches Moral and Religious Education at Laurentian Regional High School in Lachute, Quebec, Canada. She is the author of two books: *Love and Justice: More than Just Words* and *Freedom and Dignity.*

Gareth Matthews is a professor of philosophy at the University of Massachusetts at Amherst. His publications include *Philosophy and the Young Child* (1980), *Dialogues with Children* (1984), and *Philosophy of Childhood* (1994).

Linda Nowell is the assistant director for the Creative and Critical Teaching Center and the Center for Professional Development and Technology at Texas Wesleyan University. Her work has appeared in *Analytic Teaching, Inquiry*, and *Thinking.*

Sharon Palermo, formerly a preschool teacher in the Boston area, is currently a resource teacher with the Halifax County–Bedford District School Board, Nova Scotia, Canada. Her publications include a novel for young readers, *Chestnuts for the Brave* (Nimbus Publishers, Halifax, 1991), and an award winning short story, "I am Hilda Burrows" (in *The Blue Jean Collection*, Thistledown Press, Saskatoon, 1991).

John P. Portelli, a former elementary school teacher, is presently a professor of education at Mount Saint Vincent University, Halifax, Nova Scotia, Canada, where he has taught since 1986. His research has focused primarily on philosophical issues in the curriculum and developing critical/philosophical discussions in schools.

Michael Pritchard is the chair of the Philosophy Department at Western Michigan University. His books include *Philosophical Adventures with Children* (1985) and *On Becoming Responsible* (1991). He co-authored (with James Jaksa) *Communication Ethics: Methods of Analysis,* and co-edited *Profits and Professions* (with Wade L. Robison and Joseph Ellin) and *Medical Responsibility* (with Wade L. Robison).

Ronald F. Reed teaches philosophy, education, and humanities at Texas Wesleyan University where he is director of the Creative and Critical Teaching Center. He is the author of *Rebecca* and *Talking with Children,* the editor of *When We Talk,* and the co-editor (with Ann Margaret Sharp) of *Studies in Philosophy for Children.*

Glynis Ross, formerly a high school teacher for 14 years, is presently a Grade 6 teacher with the Halifax County–Bedford District School Board in Nova Scotia, Canada. Her M.A. thesis (Dalhousie University), *Gadflies in School: The Role of Philosophy in the Classroom of a Democracy,* recounts her efforts to do philosophy with students in high school.

Ann Margaret Sharp is the associate director of the Institute for the Advancement of Philosophy for Children. She has worked with Matthew Lipman since 1978 in the creation of the Philosophy for Children Program and has been primarily reponsible for its dissemination abroad. As director of the graduate program in Philosophy for Children at Montclair State College, she has been involved in the preparation of future teacher-educators in Philosophy for Children.

Children, Philosophy, and Democracy represents an attempt to deal with the evolution of one of the leading critical thinking movements to emerge in the 1970s and 1980s in North America, and some of the issues (primarily ethical, political, and pedagogical) that arise from this evolution. Philosophy for Children, along with its dominant "creation" – the community of inquiry – has been "practised" by thousands of students, teachers, educators, and philosophers over the past two decades. That practice, in turn, has generated serious reflection about the very nature of the educational enterprise.

Philosophy for Children began in the late 1960s when Matthew Lipman, who at the time was a professor of philosophy at Columbia University, became seriously concerned with some fundamental educational problems. Put into the contemporary language of education, Lipman was upset with a cognitive and an affective problem. The former related to a perceived diminution of children's ability to reason and to solve problems. The latter, a more diffuse and equally upsetting one, was concerned with how children felt about schooling and about the academic endeavor. Stated simply, the longer children were in school, the less they seemed to like and to value it.

At first, Lipman toyed with the idea of writing a story that individual children might chance upon in a library or bookstore, which would model a cooperative community of inquiry with children, and would, in effect, invite children into the fictional world giving them a place where they would practise and hone the art and craft of thinking. Over the course of the next few years (1970-74), as Lipman field-tested his novel, now known as *Harry Stottlemeier's Discovery*, in schools around the Columbia campus, that idea was modified and expanded. The quality of happenstance – the individual child stumbling over the volume on a library shelf – was jettisoned. In its place, especially as Lipman left Columbia in 1974, moved to Montclair State College in New Jersey, and with Ann Margaret Sharp formed the Institute for the Advancement of Philosophy for Children (I.A.P.C.), came the notion that *Harry* would be the first element in a conscious process of reforming and reconstructing the educational enterprise. Between 1973 and 1988, six more programs (ranging from grades K through twelve) were constructed by Lipman and his associates at I.A.P.C.

At this point, Philosophy for Children is being taught in some 5 000 schools in the United States. The program has been translated into eighteen languages, and there are Philosophy for Children Centers throughout the United States and in Chile, Costa Rica, Brazil, Mexico, Nigeria, Spain, Portugal, Guatemala, Iceland, Denmark, Canada, Austria, Australia, England, and Taiwan. Experimental research in the U.S. and in many of the countries cited above has demonstrated that children exposed to philosophy by well-prepared teachers gain significantly in reasoning, reading comprehension, and mathematical performance.

There has been a quiet explosion (if explosions can be quiet) in Philosophy for Children over the course of two decades. Philosophy for Children is no longer the creation of one person. It has been changed, expanded, restructured, and transformed as it has passed through different hands and different cultures. Especially when Philosophy for Children went overseas, it changed and, in many ways, the change has been dramatic. Philosophy for Children today may be a family of practices and practitioners, but as in the case with many large families, individual members may not even be recognizable to others.

Given that diversity, it is helpful to recall what was, circa 1974-1988, standard Philosophy for Children methodology. One begins with a philosophically rich text which serves as a sort of "springboard" to dialog. That text contains a series of gems, a series of interesting, important philosophical problems. It does not follow that children have to discover all of the gems. It does not follow that teachers should be in the business of leading the children to discover now this gem, and now that one. What is important to remember is that *Harry*, or others in the Lipman corpus or other philosophically rich texts, is an exercise in philosophy. The task, once one begins with this narrative, is how to unpack it and enable it to yield what it contains.

Ultimately, Philosophy for Children is about that which is the most private of events, that is, thinking, and most explicitly the improvement and enhancement of the child's ability to think. Since that which is private is inaccessible to direct contact, one has to find indirect means to reach it. This happens most obviously at the beginning of a typical philosophy-for-children session. Each child, or perhaps each couple or trio of children, has a copy of the text. The children, in the best of all educational worlds, are sitting in a circle where they can see each other. The session begins with a child reading a paragraph of the text aloud. The next child picks up where the previous child has finished, continuing to read aloud. The process continues around the circle until a chapter – typically four or five pages – has been read. The reading, and depending on the skill level of the readers it may be a rather long and, at times, labored reading, allows individual children to personalize the text by bringing their inflections and their emphasis to individual paragraphs. It allows their thought to determine what will be stressed and what will receive most attention. At the same time, the community is looking at one, shared text and hearing and sharing a series of different verbal interpretations of the text. The reading, if it goes well, if it is more than a simple preamble to the talk which comes next, serves as a bridge step between the public and private. It brings the child out of herself or himself, gives the child something to do, that is, read a text, so that the child does not have to make thought out of whole cloth, but it is respectful of, indeed dependent on, that which is most personal to the child, that which the child deter-mines to be worth stressing in the reading.

When the reading is complete, the teacher asks a deceptively simple question or family of questions. That question or questions, combined with the existence of the text, provides a ready way to place Philosophy for Children within the political-educational spectrum that has developed in North America. Where the romantic teacher might be said to rely exclusively on student interest, and the more conservative teacher might be said to ignore interest and focus on a pre-existing curriculum that all students must know regardless of their feelings about it, Philosophy for Children steers a middle ground. The question asked by the philosophy-for-children teacher relies on interest. The teacher says, in effect, "What did you find interesting in the selection we have just read? What do you want to talk about? What do you find curious, problematic, and so on about the selection?" The discovery of interest is necessary for the process to continue, but it should be pointed out that even though the questions the children have about the text may be very free-form, un-predicted and unpredictable, bizarre, or tangentially related to the text, the discovery that is being attempted is *about* or *into* the text. One starts with the text and it is the text that provides a coherent whole, a meaningful starting point from which students may develop their own interests.

The teacher then records the children's interest, typically phrased as a question, and those questions provide the agenda for further discussion. The teacher facilitates that discussion by using her or his preparation and knowledge to ask philosophically significant questions (questions that will help the inquiry grow) and, even more important, by indirectly creating an environment which will encourage the children to search for meaning and inquire cooperatively, that is, create a community of inquiry.

There is something deceptively simple about Philosophy for Children. One imagines a potential critic reducing the pedagogy down to a three-stage process, that is, get a group of children together, read something, and then talk about it. Although that reduction may be accurate, it masks the complexity that appears as soon as the teacher puts it into practice. As stated earlier, teachers around the world have been putting the theory into practice for two decades now. *Children, Philosophy, and Democracy* attempts to capture that complexity by reflecting the diverse possibilities and variations that have been developed.

In Section I, the focus is on the dynamic which occurs in the educational environment when philosophy for children encounters other movements and ideas. In "Responsible Children," Michael Pritchard goes beyond the thinking skills movement to suggest a broader, more holistic understanding of intelligence. San MacColl reacts against the fashionable claim that education should make children feel good about all their activities. Ronald Reed, in "Text Characters and Lump Characters," extends Philosophy for Children into a postmodern era. Gareth Matthews looks, once again, at the relationship of Piaget and other developmentalists to Philosophy for Children's view of the child. Concluding the section, John Portelli and Susan Church compare Philosophy for Children to the movement with which it is most frequently aligned – Whole Language.

In Section II, the writers look at the community of inquiry as the instantiator and nurturer of many democratic values. Matthew Lipman sees the community of inquiry as one way of dealing with the violence endemic to the urban scene. Ann Margaret Sharp offers a Peircean conception of the community of inquiry and critically reflects on its value to philosophy for children and feminist philosophy. David Kennedy makes explicit many of the connections between Dewey's democratic theory and the community of inquiry in philosophy for children. Paul

Bitting contemporizes the discussion by focusing on the multicultural characterization of democratic communities. And Ronald Reed in "Critical Theory, Postmodernism, and Communicative Rationality," looks at the community of meaning that must occur if democracies are to be healthy.

Section III deals with significant questions of pedagogy and practices developed by teachers. Linda Nowell reflects on educational reform and the possibilities of creating a "meaning-centred environment." Glynis Ross, Reenie Marx, and Sharon Palermo discuss, respectively, their attempts to do philosophy with children in high school, middle, and elementary school.

Ronald F. Reed and John P. Portelli

Section I

Character of Philosophy for Children

CHAPTER 1

Reasonable Children*

Michael Pritchard

The seeds, as it were, of moral discernment are planted in the mind by him that made us. They grow up in their proper season, and are at first tender and delicate and easily warped. Their progress depends very much upon their being duly cultivated and properly exercised. (Reid, 1788)

Introduction

Aristotle warns us that children are not ready for lectures in moral philosophy. They lack experience and they are more subject to unruly passions than reason. This suggests that the title of my paper is an oxymoron. Can children be *reasonable*? On such questions I am what children's writer and illustrator William Steig calls a *hopist* (as expressed in a CBS News interview). A pessimist would insist that children cannot be reasonable. An optimist would say either that children actually are reasonable or that becoming so is readily within their reach. A hopist attempts to avoid being overwhelmed by the empirical evidence either way. Instead, he or she simply clings to the hope that children *can* be reasonable and sets about seeing what can be done to help bring this possibility into reality. Of course, thinking that something is so doesn't make it so; but, as William James points out, believing you can maintain your balance walking along the edge of a cliff is essential to being able to do so.

In any case, what follows are some of my hopist reflections on the prospects for the existence of reasonable children. As a sidenote for the pessimists, I will simply add that if we are to have any hope that children will become reasonable *adults*, we need to attend carefully to those aspects of childhood that hold out some prospect for such an outcome. As a sidenote for the optimists, I offer a word of caution. "Reasonableness" is not an all-or-nothing concept. There are degrees of reasonableness. Just as Thomas Reid mentions the need to nurture the "seeds of moral discernment," the same must be said of the "seeds of reasonableness" in children. (Since they are interconnected, this should come as no

---

* Copyright 1995, Michael Pritchard

surprise.) I have no interest in trying to convert children into adults. But I am interested in the extent to which children, as children, can be reasonable, as well as the bearing this might have on their becoming reasonable adults.

My point of entry in this paper is moral education. Reasonableness applies to much more than morality, but if I can make some inroads in the controversial area of moral education, the rest of the task should be somewhat easier.

It is often asked whether morality can be *taught*. In higher education this question is commonly converted to the question of whether morality can be *studied*.[1] Instead of viewing students as subjected to passive indoctrination, our attention shifts to students as actively striving to develop and refine their abilities to think through moral concerns. This, at any rate, seems to have been the consensus view of a large and diverse group of educators brought together by the Hastings Center some years ago to discuss the appropriate goals of teaching ethics in higher education.

The Hastings Center group agreed on five major goals (Callahan, 1980).

Courses in ethics should:

1. Stimulate the moral imagination of students.

2. Help students recognize moral issues.

3. Help students analyze key moral concepts and principles.

4. Elicit from students a sense of responsibility.

5. Help students to accept the likelihood of ambiguity and disagreement on moral matters, while at the same time striving for clarity and agreement insofar as it is reasonably attainable.

Intended for college-age students, this set of goals presupposes that students are not moral neophytes. Students are regarded as a basic resource in the sense that they are assumed already capable of moral imagination (which needs further stimulation), already capable of understanding moral issues (even though they sometimes need help recognizing their presence), already possessing moral concepts and principles (which need more careful analysis), already having a sense of responsibility (which can be further activated by studying ethics), and already somewhat experienced at attempting to negotiate unclarities and disagreements. Seriously pursued, these goals can be expected to enhance the capacity for reasonableness in students as they encounter moral issues surrounding them.

Just as it is presumed that college students have some basic logical sensitivities and abilities prior to taking their first college course in logic, it is presumed that college students have some basic moral sensitivities and abilities. If this could not be presumed, one might ask, how could one even begin to teach a course in ethics? But, it might be thought, matters are quite different at the pre-college level, especially in the elementary schools: there such presumptions have no place. Particularly at the elementary school level, moral education is commonly regarded as a matter of "instilling" or "implanting" moral values. This is why many fear placing moral education on the public schools' agenda. *Whose* values, it may be asked, are to be implanted? And *what* values will they be?

In this essay I will argue that although the dangers of indoctrination are very real, they are not nearly as formidable as is commonly thought. This is because helping even young children nurture their "seeds of moral discernment" need not involve indoctrination. To conclude that it does is to underestimate the already considerable moral abilities children typically have by the time they enter school. In fact, as I will try to show, the Hastings Center goals are suitable for elementary school students as well as college students. Of course, adjustments for the more limited understanding and experience of young children must be made. But enhancing the capacity for reasonableness is as realistic an objective for young children as for college students. In fact, insofar as children's capacity for reasonableness is neglected, we should lower our expectations for the reasonableness of college students.[2]

Moral discernment is highly valued. We value it in ourselves and others as a mark of reasonableness.[3] To understand fully what Thomas Reid means by the seeds of moral discernment "being duly cultivated and properly exercised," we must view children as agents, not merely patients. In some contexts "cultivated" implies passivity. For example, a field is cultivated by a farmer. It does not cultivate itself. In an educational context, teachers might attempt to cultivate appreciation and judgment in their students. However, children can be encouraged to do this for themselves. If moral discernment is a mark of reasonableness, it is clear that at some point children themselves must begin to exercise their powers of judgment – that is, to develop their capacity to think for themselves. In this they cannot remain passive.[4]

Civic Education and Critical Thinking

I want to discuss two major areas of popular concern in the public schools that provide entering wedges for moral education: civic education and critical thinking. Public education in our society is sustained by a political system committed to certain individual liberties and democratic decision making.[5] In turn, public education is legitimately expected to help sustain that system by preparing children for citizenship. This is the function of civic education, which aims at helping students acquire the necessary understanding and skills for effective, responsible participation in a constitutional democracy. What, then, are the values civic education should emphasize? Robert Fullinwider (1991) suggests the following:[6] the capacity to make independent, rational judgments about civic matters; respect for the rights of others; and the capacity to discuss and defend political views that may differ from theirs. However, as Fullinwider (1991) amply shows, the dispositions that civic education encourages do not, in fact, confine themselves to the civic arena. For example, the ability to discuss and defend political views is not an ability to discuss and defend *only* that. Once encouraged, the critical thinking skills exhibited in the civic arena are likely to show up anywhere. And, just as these skills are assets in the political arena, they are assets in other areas of life as well.[7]

The kind of critical thinking encouraged in civic education is a form of reasonableness. Such reasonableness is a social virtue. (Hence, the title of this paper is "Reasonable Children," rather than, say, "The Reasonable Child.") But reasonableness in all of its forms is a social virtue. Criteria for reasonableness are not simply conjured up by an individual. Insofar as one is reasonable, one is prepared to reason *with* others, even if the object of concern is basically oneself (for example, "Am I brave?"). What does reasoning with others involve? Minimally, it can be understood to include those skills and dispositions encompassed by what educators refer to as *critical thinking*. Robert Ennis (1987) succinctly defines critical thinking as "reasonable reflective thinking that is focused on deciding what to believe or do" (p. 1).[8] Although admirably brief, Ennis's definition may be too narrow. Critical thinking can also be used to make sense of what we read, see, or hear and to make inferences from premises with which we may disagree or about which we have no particular view. Such critical thinking may lead one to decide what to believe or do, but it need not.[9]

In addition to his definition of critical thinking, Ennis provides an elaborate taxonomy of critical thinking skills. This taxonomy is much broader than his definition would suggest. It includes dispositions to seek clear statements of questions, to be open-minded, to seek as much precision as the subject permits, to think in an orderly manner, and to be sensitive to the feelings and level of understanding of others. It also includes abilities such as focusing on the context of an argument, detecting unstated assumptions, clarifying arguments, making inferences from premises, and interacting with others in a reasonable manner.

It is clear from this list that critical thinking involves more than the employment of "higher level" thinking skills, and more than clever or skillful argumentation. It requires sensitivity to the needs, interests, and ideas of others as well as intellectual skills. Critical thinking does include thinking for oneself. But it also includes thinking well, that is, exercising good judgment. This means having reasons for one's judgments, or, as Matthew Lipman puts it, having reliable *criteria* for one's judgments (Lipman, 1991).

The idea of thinking for oneself deserves more attention than it will receive here.[10] But at least this much should be said. Thinking *for* oneself is not the same as thinking *by* oneself. Humpty-Dumpty claims that words mean what *he* says they mean – nothing more and nothing less; and he is, therefore, free to make them mean whatever he wishes. This view of language doesn't work. Neither does a Humpty-Dumpty view of critical thinking. Humpty-Dumpty cannot make something become a good reason by deciding, for himself, that it is a good reason. What makes something a good reason, in morality or elsewhere, is a difficult, and perhaps controversial, matter. But individual fiat does not make something a good reason. Neither does consensus of the majority. Although reasonableness requires a willingness to have one's reasons subjected to public scrutiny, reasonable people can disagree with one another; and the number of people on either side does not settle the question of who, if anyone, has the most reasonable view. This much is clear, I think, from any comprehensive taxonomy of critical thinking skills.

Reasonableness and Morality

It should be noted especially that reasonableness in the context of morality is not to be equated with rationality. Someone can be unreasonable without necessarily being irrational. A selfish person may (unreasonably) take more than his or her fair share, likely at the expense of others. Yet, from the standpoint of self-interest, this is not necessarily irrational. A person may make excessive (unreasonable) demands and yet not be irrational. A person might be unwilling to reason with others about an issue or refuse to listen to others' points of view without being irrational. But we may regard this as unreasonable. It is only when rationality is combined with fair-minded regard for the views and interests of others that reasonableness is present. As W.H. Sibley (1953) puts it:

> *If I desire that my conduct shall be deemed <u>reasonable</u> by someone taking the standpoint of moral judgment, I must exhibit something more than mere rationality or intelligence. To be reasonable here is to see the matter – as we commonly put it – from the other person's point of view, to discover how each will be affected by the possible alternative actions; and, moreover, not merely to "see" this (for any merely prudent person would do as much) but also to be prepared to be disinterestedly <u>influenced</u>, in reaching a decision, by the estimate of these possible results. I must justify my conduct in terms of some principle capable of being appealed to by all parties concerned, some principle from which we can reason in common. (p. 557)*

Sibley's account calls for several comments. First, it is clear that, from a moral point of view, a reasonable person tries to be responsive to the perspectives of others. Minimally this requires trying to understand what others' perspectives are – noting significant differences from one's own. That this is not an easy task for young children is evidenced by Piaget's pioneering work in cognitive development. Although he seems to underestimate younger children's capacity to engage in non-egocentric thinking (see, for example, Margaret Donaldson, 1978), getting beyond egocentric thinking is especially difficult in social relations, particularly for those with limited experience. However, it seems only fair to add that this is a lifelong struggle. Adults, too, are susceptible to a great deal of egocentric thinking.[11]

Second, Sibley's reasonable person not only tries to understand what matters to others, he or she is prepared to be *influenced* by this. Of course, even those who make use of their understanding of others' perspectives for manipulative or exploitive purposes can be said to be influenced by that understanding. Clearly this is not what Sibley has in mind, for he refers to being *disinterestedly* influenced. This requires *respecting* others, acknowledging that their interests matter too – and that one must try to justify one's behavior by appealing to principles or considerations from which all can reason in common. Third, a point that Sibley does not discuss, reasoning from common principles or considerations does not imply that reasonable people will always agree with one another. There are many reasons why this is not a realistic expectation. There may be some disagreement or confusion about just what these common principles or considerations mean (for example, "fair," "safe," "health," "well-being") and how they apply to particular circumstances. There may be disagreement about facts, and about inferences made from facts. (For example, there may be disagreement about the chemical properties of asbestos in the schools, as well as about the long-term risks to those exposed to it.) There may be differences in personal values (some may prefer reading novels to watching television, playing sports to walking in the woods, living in the city to rural life, and so on). Although reasonable people can be expected to reject many interests as unacceptable (for example, those violating basic considerations of respect and regard for the well-being of others), this leaves much about which to differ. Furthermore, like-mindedness is no aim of reasonableness. Some rather significant mutual acceptance, or at least tolerance, of differences is itself a mark of reasonableness.

Fourth, Sibley's passage concentrates on other-regarding attitudes and behavior. However, we also speak of reasonableness of self-regarding attitudes and behavior. For example, although the presence or absence of willpower and bravery in an individual often has important consequences for others, our attention is first drawn to the individual in question. For that individual, it is primarily a matter of self-struggle, a concern for a kind of self-mastery. Here, too, we can talk about reasonable and unreasonable attitudes and behavior – and the criteria for evaluation are sharable rather than simply conjured up by the individual engaged in struggle.

Finally, reasonable people remain open to the possibility that their favored conceptions may require alteration or revision. Ronald Dworkin (1977) provides a good illustration of this:

> Suppose I tell my children simply that I expect them not to treat others unfairly. I no doubt have in mind examples of the conduct I mean to discourage, but I would not accept that my 'meaning' was limited to these examples, for two reasons. First, I would expect my children to apply my instructions to situations I had not and could not have thought about. Second, I stand ready to admit that some particular act I had thought was fair when I spoke was in fact unfair, or vice-versa, if one of my children is able to convince me of that later; in that case I should want to say that my instructions covered the case he cited, not that I had changed my instructions. I might say that I meant the family to be guided by the concept of fairness, not by any specific conception of fairness I might have had in mind. (p. 133)

It should be noted that Dworkin is not inviting just any kind of challenge to his conception of fairness. Presumably it will have to be one capable of *convincing* him that he was mistaken; and this implies that the challenge is accompanied with good reasons. Thus, both parent and child are subject to the constraints of reasonableness. Like any parent, Dworkin would like to believe that the examples of unfairness he has in mind at any given time are reasonable. But he is not willing to hold this belief in the face of convincing reasons to the contrary. As a reasonable parent, he is open to the possibility that he might be wrong about some of his examples. To deny this possibility (and reject evidence to the contrary) is to be willing to be wrong *twice* – and to wish that for his child as well.

Of course, reasonableness and unreasonableness are not our only terms of appraisal. Our values have many different sources, and there is great diversity among them, both between persons and within the same person. Not all values are specifically moral values, and there is no reason to insist on uniformity across persons. But even within morality there may be many different ways of satisfying plausible criteria for being a well-developed, moral person; and reasonable people might even disagree about some of the criteria. Nevertheless, the range of possibilities is not limitless. It is important to recognize the earliest appearance of those affective and cognitive capacities that are essential to the development well-developed, moral persons;[12] and whatever else is emphasized, those capacities that contribute to reasonableness need special attention.

As already noted, getting beyond egocentric thinking is essential for reasonableness. In his studies of the development of empathy, psychologist Martin Hoffman (1970, 1976) provides convincing evidence that very young children are capable of genuinely empathic responses to the distress of others.[13] These responses indicate some awareness of the very different perspectives of others. They also seem to manifest a genuine concern for the distress of others. William Damon (1988) presents further evidence of this from recent research on the moral development of children. So, there is good reason to suppose that non-egocentric and non-egoistic behavior is possible at a very early age. Since both are essential to later moral development, it is important for parents to be attentive and responsive to early manifestations.

Recall Thomas Reid's observation on the "seeds of moral development," whose "progress depends very much upon their being duly cultivated and properly exercised" (Reid, 1788, p. 595). If parents believe their children are not ready to accept non-egoistic reasons for behaving or not behaving in certain ways, they will not cultivate the "seeds of moral discernment" in that direction. In fact, by substituting egoistic reasons in their stead, parents may actually contribute to the warping of those "seeds." If children are capable of non-egocentric thinking at a very early age, then parents would do well to reinforce this and provide opportunities for their children to develop this capacity. By assuming that their children are not capable of non-egocentric thinking until well into their school years, parents may actually reinforce and prolong the "tunnel vision" that so often impedes the development of moral sensitivity.

Of course, it is implausible to suppose that an eighteen month old child's empathic response to the distress of another child incorporates moral conceptions. However, the responsiveness and caring that are present can be expected eventually to contribute to that child's moral outlook – *unless this is otherwise discouraged*. Furthermore, the wait will not be long. Richard A. Shweder, Elliot Turiel, and Nancy C. Much (1981) provide evidence that children as young as four have an intuitive understanding of differences among prudential, conventional, and moral rules:

> *In fact, at this relatively early age, four to six, children not only seem to distinguish and identify moral versus conventional versus prudential rules using the same formal principles (e.g., obligatoriness, importance, generalizability) employed by adults; they also seem to agree with the adults of their society about the moral versus conventional versus prudential status of particular substantive events (e.g., throwing paint in another child's face versus wearing the same clothes to school every day). (p. 288)*

Of course, this is only the beginning. Gareth Matthews (1980) nicely outlines how we might expect conceptual change to occur in children as their experience broadens and deepens:

> *A young child is able to latch onto the moral kind, bravery, or lying, by grasping central paradigms of that kind, paradigms that even the most mature and sophisticated moral agents still count as paradigms. Moral development is then something much more complicated than simple concept displacement. It is: enlarging the stock of paradigms for each moral kind; developing better and better definitions of whatever it is these paradigms exemplify; appreciating better the relation between straightforward instances of the kind and close relatives; and learning to adjudicate competing claims from different moral kinds (classically the sometimes competing claims of justice and compassion, but many other conflicts are possible). (p. 28)*

This may seem to place too much emphasis on the cerebral. What about the will, one might ask? What about matters of the heart? What about behavior? However, what must be borne in mind is that typically the kinds of reflection Matthews describes take place in contexts in which it very much matters to the participants how issues are understood. There may be concerns about sharing toys, distributing dessert fairly, doing household chores, or helping an elderly neighbor who is too ill to care properly for her pet. There might also be concerns about all sorts of issues at school – sharing materials, taking turns, school government; privileges and rights, punishments and rewards, social relationships, and so on. That is, sorting through and refining paradigms is not typically just an intellectual exercise.

"That's just it," an objector might say, "the problem is that these things do matter to children – too much, in fact. Children aren't ready for reasonable discussion of such issues. Aristotle is right, first they need to be *habituated* – their passions have to be brought under control by good habits. Give them firm rules and reinforce them. Then, much later, such matters can be discussed."

This underestimates children in two respects. First, it assumes that they do not already have some rather stable moral dispositions by the time they enter school. Second, it assumes that reflection and discussion can contribute little to the refinement of dispositions that are already somewhat in place. It is, again, to view children as patients rather than agents.

Fortunately, there is now a great deal of empirical evidence that these acknowledgements are warranted. Ask any group of five- to ten-year old children what they think about lying or fairness, for example, and marvel at the range of thoughtful responses.[14] For example, favoritism, taking more than one's fair share, not taking turns, listening to only one side of the story, jumping to conclusions, not treating equals equally (and unequals unequally), and the like are readily volunteered as kinds of unfairness. These are common concerns in the lives of children from a very early age – within their family structures, on the playground, and in school.

Illustrations

Earlier I indicated that the Hastings Center statement of goals for teaching ethics in higher education can also be applied to the pre-college curriculum, including elementary school. It is now time to explain more fully why I think this is so. I will do so by providing suitable illustrations.

One effective way to *stimulate the moral imagination* is through stories. For example, what child has not had serious thoughts about being brave – whether this involves putting one's head under water for the first time, going to the dentist, speaking in front of an audience, standing up to a bully, or staying home alone for the first time?

Frog and Toad (Lobel, 1971) also wonder about bravery. Here is how Arnold Lobel's (1971) "Dragons and Giants" begins.

Frog and Toad were reading a book together. "The people in this book are brave," said Toad. "They fight dragons and they are never afraid."

"I wonder if we are brave," said Frog. (p. 42)

How can they tell if they are brave? Toad suggests two conditions that must be met. They must do the sorts of things brave individuals do. And they must not be afraid when they do them (or at any other time).

They discover that telling whether these two conditions are met is not easy:

Frog and Toad looked into a mirror. "We look brave," said Frog.

"Yes, but are we?" asked Toad. (p. 42-43)

So, Frog and Toad set out on an adventuresome hike. They begin climbing a mountain. They come upon a dark cave:

A big snake came out of the cave.

"Hello, lunch," said the snake when he saw Frog and Toad. He opened his wide mouth. Frog and Toad jumped away. Toad was shaking.

"I am not afraid!" he cried. (p. 45)

As if to prove their fearlessness, Frog and Toad continue climbing. Then they hear a loud noise and see large stones rolling toward them:

"It's an avalanche!" cried Toad. Frog and Toad jumped away. Frog was trembling.

"I am not afraid!" he shouted. (p. 47)

They reach the top of the mountain, only to find themselves under a shadow cast by a hawk. They jump under a rock. After the hawk flies away, Frog and Toad scream out, "We are not afraid!" At the same time they begin running as fast as they can back to Toad's house. After arriving safely, Toad says: "Frog, I am glad to have a brave friend like you." Frog replies, "And I am happy to know a brave person like you, Toad" (p. 50). Then Toad jumps into bed and pulls the covers over his head. Frog jumps into the closet and shuts the door. The story concludes: "They stayed there for a long time, just feeling very brave together" (p. 51).

What should the *reader* conclude? Were Frog and Toad brave? Remember, Frog and Toad set down two conditions for bravery. First, they had to do the sorts of things brave individuals do. Climbing the mountain and not turning back seem to be the right sort of thing, although running back home and hiding may raise some doubts about just *how* brave they were. The second condition, doing these things without being afraid (in fact, *never* being afraid), seems to fare much worse. After all, Toad shook, Frog trembled, and they both ran down the mountain as fast as they could and hid under covers and in the closet. How can they say they were not at least a little bit afraid? And doesn't that spoil their bravery?

But, a young reader might say, they did do some things that they had been afraid to try before. Didn't that take at least a little bravery? Still, another young reader might reply, they shook and trembled and ran home and hid. So, they must have been afraid. Yes, another reader replies, but weren't some of the things they did really dangerous? "Hello, lunch," said the snake. Was that just a bluff? Wouldn't even a brave frog have reason to fear such a snake? What else could Toad do – stay for lunch? But, the first reader counters, Toad didn't just run away – he *shook.*

We adults might now recall Aristotle's distinction between bravery and foolhardiness – a distinction that makes fear an integral part of bravery. And Aristotle distinguishes bravery from cowardice. What if Toad had not moved, we ask? Aristotle might say that he was either foolhardy (lacking proper fear) or cowardly (paralyzed by fear).

Can young children appreciate these distinctions? One way to find out is to try some variations on the Frog and Toad story. This invites children to *analyze key moral concepts.* Suppose that Frog and Toad are next time accompanied by some other friends, say Turtle and Mouse.[15] This time when the snake says "Hello, lunch," neither Turtle nor Mouse move. Turtle doesn't move because he has fallen asleep inside his shell while they have paused in front of the dark cave. He is awakened by the snake saying "Hello, lunch." But he simply thinks they are being invited to lunch and decides he'd rather extend his nap instead. Mouse doesn't move because he is too terrified. Does it matter how Frog and Toad behave? Suppose Toad quickly runs to safety, but Frog first yanks on Mouse's tail to get him to move to safety. Was Turtle brave because he wasn't afraid of Snake? Was Mouse brave because he didn't move? Who was more brave, Frog or Toad? Do we have to suppose that Frog wasn't afraid when he stayed to help Mouse?

We usually think that being brave is a good thing. Is it? Why? Is it better to be brave and fearless than brave and fearful? Arnold Lobel doesn't complicate his story by directly raising such questions. Frog and Toad present themselves in such a way that the young reader is invited to challenge their claims to be brave. But it is only a short step from this to questioning Frog and Toad's early characterization of bravery as requiring fearlessness. If bravery is, indeed, a desirable quality, then reflecting on what it means to have it can be a valuable exercise – one that calls on the use of reason, and one that may contribute to one's reasonableness in both attitude and behavior.[16]

Other Frog and Toad stories (Lobel, 1971) similarly invite young readers' reflections. "A List" humorously portrays Toad compiling a "List of things to do today," only to become frozen into inaction because his list is carried away by the wind. Toad does not chase it down because that's not something on his list of things to do. This story raises questions about rational planning. Can one ever expect to be able to list everything one might need to do? Should one even try? How is it reasonable to proceed when unexpected events interfere with planned events?

"The Garden" addresses both the virtue of patience (waiting for seeds to grow into flowers) and the irrelevance of many of our well-intentioned efforts to help other things grow. "Cookies" is a delightful story about willpower: "trying hard *not* to do something that you really want to do" (p. 35). If Frog and Toad give away all their cookies to the birds, does this show that they now have the willpower not to eat any more cookies? Or do they have to be able to resist eating cookies while they still have some within reach? Once again, young readers are invited to analyze an important moral concept, willpower. Do Frog and Toad really have lots and lots of willpower after they give the cookies to the birds? Is Frog and Toad's strategy reasonable, even if it doesn't actually exhibit will-power? Here's another possible strategy. Frog and Toad could keep on eating cookies until they feel sick (something Frog offers as a reason for stopping now). Then they could resist eating more cookies even if several were left. Of course it would no longer be true to say that they really want to eat more – and they wouldn't have to try hard at all not to eat them. Would this be a reasonable strategy?

What some might want to say is that Frog and Toad use a reasonable strategy for dealing with situations in which they don't have willpower. If the temptation is too great, remove it. But are there times when it might be really important to be able to do better than this – that is, to be able to resist cookies even when they are within reach and you really do want another one? What if you can't really get rid of what you want (for example, they aren't *your* cookies to give away to the birds, or every time you try to get rid of something tempting, more of it shows up)? Is it important to have willpower in situations like that?

The last story in *Frog and Toad Together* (Lobel, 1971), "The Dream," is quite interesting from a developmental standpoint. Since Lobel's stories are in the I CAN READ series, the primary audience constitutes an age range (4-8) that Piaget and Kohlberg would say is dominated by egocentric thinking. If they are right, most of the intended audience will fail to grasp much of what "The Dream" is about. Toad dreams that, as he becomes more and more impressed with himself, Frog gets smaller and smaller. "Why do you think Frog gets smaller and smaller?" we might ask a four year old. Our answer is that this is how Frog seems to Toad in the dream – and this is because Toad keeps "puffing himself up" in comparison to Frog:

> *"Frog," cried Toad, "can you play the piano like this?"*
>
> *"No," said Frog. It seemed to Toad that Frog looked even smaller. (p. 55)*
>
> *"Frog," cried Toad, "can you do tricks like this?"*
>
> *"No," peeped Frog, who looked very, very small. (p. 57)*
>
> *"Frog, can you be as wonderful as this?" said Toad as he danced all over the stage. There was no answer. Toad looked out into the theater. Frog was so small that he could not be seen or heard. (p. 59)*

Toad dreams he is spinning in the dark, shouting "Come back, Frog. I will be lonely" (p. 60).

> *"I am right here," said Frog. Frog was standing near Toad's bed.*
>
> *"Wake up, Toad," he said.*
>
> *"Frog, is that really you?" said Toad.*
>
> *"Of course it is me," said Frog.*
>
> *"And are you your own right size?" asked Toad.*
>
> *"Yes, I think so," said Frog. Toad looked at the sunshine coming through the window.*
>
> *"Frog," he said, "I am so glad that you came over."*
>
> *"I always do," said Frog.*

Toad seems to have learned much from this dream. Can a four-year-old? Seemingly, no, if the estimation of developmental psychologists such as Jean Piaget and Lawrence Kohlberg are right – for Toad has learned something about immodesty, loneliness, and friendship that he could not appreciate if he were trapped totally within an egocentric perspective.[17] But Toad can appreciate this, and I'll bet many of his four-year-old friends can, too.

Sometimes a short passage from a story can illustrate a young child *recognizing a moral issue* that had only moments before gone unnoticed. J.D. Salinger's short story, "Down at the Dinghy," is a case in point

(Referred to in Diller, 1978). Four-year-old Lionel is upset and threatening to run away:

> *"Well, will you tell me from there why you're running away?" Boo Boo asked. "After you promised me you were all through?"*
>
> *A pair of underwater goggles lay on the deck of the dinghy, near the stern seat. For answer, Lionel secured the headstrap of the goggles between the big and the second toes of his right foot, and, with a deft, brief leg action, flipped the goggles overboard. They sank at once.*
>
> *"That's nice. That's constructive," said Boo Boo. "Those belong to your Uncle Webb. Oh, he'll be so delighted." She dragged on her cigarette. "They once belonged to your Uncle Seymour."*
>
> *"I don't care."*
>
> *"I see that you don't," Boo Boo said.*
>
> *Boo Boo then takes a small package from her pocket. "This is a key chain," she says, "Just like Daddy's. But with a lot more keys on it than Daddy's has. This one has ten keys."*
>
> *Lionel leaned forward in his seat, letting go the tiller. He held out his hands in catching position. "Throw it?" he asked. "Please?"*
>
> *"Let's keep our seats a minute, Sunshine. I have a little thinking to do. I should throw this key chain in the lake."*
>
> *Lionel stared up at her with his mouth open. He closed his mouth. "It's mine," he said on a diminishing note of justice.*
>
> *Boo, looking down at him, shrugged. "I don't care."*
>
> *Lionel slowly sat back in his seat, watching his mother, and reached behind him for the tiller. His eyes reflected pure perception, as his mother had known they would.*
>
> *"Here." Boo Boo tossed the package down to him. It landed squarely on his lap.*
>
> *He looked at it in his lap, picked it off, looked at it in his hand, and flicked it — sidearm — into the lake. He then immediately looked up at Boo Boo, his eyes filled not with defiance but tears. In another instant his mouth was distorted into a horizontal figure-8, and he was crying mightily.*

Salinger's little episode cries out for analysis. Just what is Lionel's perception? Is it that one bad turn deserves another – and best of all is for the wrong-doer to administer self-punishment? Has Lionel engaged in a bit of Golden Rule reasoning – or is this a misreading of the Golden Rule, since it is not clear that anyone is being done unto as they would have others do unto them? However Lionel's reasoning is to be characterized, it is clear that, through coming to appreciate a perspective other than his own, he learned a lesson in responsibility (*eliciting a sense of responsibility*) – and it is clear that this lesson will not be lost on many young children who hear a story like this.

Lionel seems to be expressing some sort of recognition of the moral importance of *reciprocity*. Adults know that this is a very complex area of moral life. To what extent are children capable of appreciating such complexities? Lionel seems to have begun to catch onto some of it at age four. What is it reasonable to expect down the road a bit? Some years ago I had the privilege of participating in a 40-minute discussion of just such matters with a group of ten-year-olds. I began the discussion by reading an episode from Matthew Lipman's (1983) children's novel, *Lisa*. Timmy accompanies Harry to a stamp club meeting at which Harry trades stamps with other children. Timmy is deliberately tripped by a classmate as he and Harry are leaving the classroom. Timmy immediately knocks his classmate's books off his desk and runs out of the room. Later, as Harry buys Timmy an ice cream cone, Timmy comments, "But I had to get even. I couldn't let him get away with it, tripping me like that for no reason."

Harry and his friends are perplexed by all these examples. Is it right to retaliate against someone who trips you? How is this like or unlike a fair exchange of stamps? If someone does you a favor, should you return the favor someday? The 10-year-olds with whom I shared the story were eager to help sort out these matters. They discussed at great length possible alternatives to Timmy's retaliation (thus exercising *moral imagination*). Larry challenged the basic idea of "getting even" (*analyzing key moral concepts*).

> *Sometimes you do need to get even. Well, actually there's no such thing as even, because then he'll get even.*

Having raised the problem of what it means to "get even," Larry went on to distinguish between *wanting* to do something (strike back) and *having* to do it. Several children suggested ignoring the offender as a tactic for discouraging him (since he would have failed to get the desired response from the victim). Pressed by the example of an offender who stays on the attack, Carlen said:

> *If he were to, like Emily said, chase after you and hit you or something like that, then you defend yourself. I mean, maybe then you've got to get him back. Not really get him back, but you have to defend yourself and hit him if he's hitting you.*

So, a basic distinction was made between trying to get even ("get him back") and self-defense. Further, the children distinguished both of these ideas from attempting to teach someone a lesson. Finally, they carefully distinguished exchanges involving harms from exchanging favors, insisting that the Golden Rule applies in the latter cases but not the former.

Although this discussion was limited to problems that are familiar to children, the ten-year-old participants uncovered an impressive variety of considerations that need to be brought to bear on those problems. I have often asked myself what other kinds of considerations adults might wish to bring up in that context. I always come up empty. Furthermore, the principles and concepts discussed by the children serve adults rather well when applied to analogous problems in adult life.

In between Arnold Lobel and J.D. Salinger's fictional four-year-olds and my actual group of ten-year-olds are many examples of actual six- to eight-year olds displaying readiness for serious moral reflection. For example, philosopher Clyde Evans (1978) reports a discussion he once had with a group of kindergarten and first graders about the following dilemma: A father has promised to take his daughter to the carnival on her seventh birthday. Just before arriving at the ticket window the father discovers he has forgotten his wallet, and there is not time to return home for it. The sign says that children under seven get in at half-price. The father counts the money in his pocket and realizes that if his daughter lies about her age, there will be enough money to get them into the carnival and go on some rides. If she tells the truth about her age, there will be enough money to get into the carnival but none for any rides. He leaves the choice up to her.

As might be expected, the children had divided opinions. A boy said that lying in this case might lead the girl to become a habitual liar. Others replied that this was just one little lie. Then came a response in the form of a striking analogy:

> The first boy then provided further support. He said that lying is just like pollution. To say that it's only one little lie is like saying it's only one little candy wrapper. But all the little candy wrappers add up. The first thing you know you have a big pollution problem. Likewise, the first thing you know you'll have a big lying problem. (Evans, 1978, p. 168)

This is an impressive instance of analogical reasoning. It might be thought to be just a reiteration of the first worry – that the girl might end up becoming a habitual liar. But the pollution analogy suggests another angle. One person habitually dropping candy wrappers is not going to result in a big pollution problem. But *everyone* (or lots of people) dropping candy wrappers (popcorn boxes, soda cans, and so forth) might. Now attention shifts from what one person does to a *kind of act* performed by everyone ("What if everyone did that?") – that is, now attention shifts to the collective consequences of many people telling lies.[18]

Gareth Matthews (1980) reports this example:

> *IAN (six years) found to his chagrin that the three children of his parents' friends monopolized the television; they kept him from watching his favorite program. 'Mother,' he asked in frustration, 'why is it better for three children to be selfish than one?' (p. 28)*

This question would be a challenge for any adult. Matthews decided to write a little story around Ian's comment and present it to a group of eight- to eleven-year-olds (Matthews, 1984, pp. 92-93). The lively discussion that followed elicited comments about the inconsiderateness of the three visiting children, the desirability of working out a solution that would satisfy all four children, the importance of respecting people's rights, and how one might feel if one were in Ian's place. Matthews then outlined a possible utilitarian analysis: "What about this argument, that, if we let the three visitors have their way, three people will be made happy instead of just one?" (Matthews, 1984, p. 95). Martin replied, "It's not really fair if three people get what they want and leave one person out. That one person will feel very hurt." This was followed by children's comments about very specific considerations, such as the types of TV programs involved and relationships among the children (for example, relative ages, whether they are siblings, friends, or strangers). In short, by examining various possibilities, the children tried to work out a reasonable resolution of a very difficult problem.

Ian's question, like many other questions children will eagerly discuss if given the chance, may not readily lend itself to a solution that all reasonable people will agree upon. One mark of reasonableness is recognizing that this is so in a way that does not destroy mutual inquiry. This is why the Hastings Center group of educators emphasize a fifth goal of ethics in higher education: *Helping students learn to accept ambiguity and disagreement while at the same time continuing to try to reduce it through further attempts to clarify ideas and to engage in reasonable discussion.*

Here is a story that illustrates the importance of this fifth goal. It is taken from materials prepared by Lipman et al. (1984):

> *A teacher comes into her classroom one day with a large bag of candy. She explains that the candy is a gift to the class, and she's been told that she must distribute it fairly.*

Now, she says, "What is fair? Would the fairest thing be for me to give the most to those who deserve the most? Who deserves the most? Surely it must be the biggest and strongest ones in the class who deserve the most, for they probably do most things best."

But the teacher is greeted by a large outcry from the class. "What you propose is most unfair," they tell her. "Just because this one is better at arithmetic or that one at baseball, or still another at dancing, you still shouldn't treat us all differently. It wouldn't be fair to give some members of the class, say, five pieces of candy where others might get one piece or none at all. Each of us is a person, and in this respect we're all equal. So, treat us as equals and give us each the same amount of candy."

"Ah," the teacher answered, "I'm glad you've explained to me how you feel about this. So, although people are very different from each other in many respects, fairness consists of treating them all equally."

"That's right," the pupils answer. "Fairness is equal treatment!"

But before the teacher has a chance to distribute the candy, the phone rings, and she's called down to the office. When she gets back some minutes later, she finds that the children have all been fighting over the candy. Now each of the biggest and strongest children have a big handful of candy, while the remainder have varying amounts, and the smallest children have only one each.

The teacher demands order, and the class becomes very quiet. Obviously she is very disturbed about what the children have just done. But she's determined to be fair, and fairness, they've all agreed, is equal treatment. So, she tells the children, "You've taught me what fairness is. Each of you must give back one piece of candy." (p. 63)

As might be expected, most children who hear this story immediately object that this is *not* fair. Adults might think that what ten-year-olds are likely to do is dwell on various ways of more fairly handling the distribution of the candy. And they would be correct in thinking this. However, this is not *all* that ten-year-olds discuss – at least not the group to whom I read this story (Pritchard, 1985).

Adults realize that this story is about more than the fair distribution of candy. It is about fairness generally – and especially about the ideas of desert and treating people equally. But ten-year-olds realize this, too. In the space of fifteen minutes the group with whom I met discussed the fair grading: Should those who are less able get higher grades because they try harder? Should grades be awarded for group accomplishments rather than just on an individual basis (for example, 90% of the class performing at a certain level)? They discussed the importance of having special opportunities for students with disabilities to receive awards, as in the Special Olympics. At the same time, many insisted that the most able should have special opportunities, as well. They discussed group punishment as an alternative to individually differentiated punishment (both of which they had undoubtedly experienced). In short, in just a few moments, they displayed an understanding of different, and often competing, bases for awards and punishments. While appreciating the importance of equality, they realized that this is complicated by differences in opportunities, experiences, abilities, efforts, and actual accomplishments. They shunned simplistic solutions and seemed gain satisfaction from articulating complicating factors. They wanted to leave nothing out that might affect a reasonable determination of fairness.

Admittedly, they did not discuss the fairness or unfairness of various taxation schemes (for example, flat versus graduated rates). Such concerns will come in due time. Meanwhile, ten-year-olds (as well as younger children) have a wealth of examples that they can usefully discuss – not only to prepare them for difficult issues they will have to face later, but also to help them cope with difficult issues they face now.

Conclusion

Two tenth-graders, David Benjamin and Jeremy Scott (Benjamin & Scott, 1989) complain:

> In high school there is a common system of "learning" that goes something like this: listen, take notes, memorize, and regurgitate facts. Each high school subject seems to show the world through a distinct window unconnected to the window presented by other classes. (p. 29)

Five years earlier David Benjamin and Jeremy Scott had been introduced to *Harry Stottlemeier's Discovery* (Lipman, 1982). They enjoyed this introduction to philosophical inquiry. Unfortunately, nothing like this was encouraged in their subsequent school years. So, they decided to take matters into their own hands, seeking out David's father, Martin Benjamin, who had discussed *Harry Stottlemeier's Discovery* with them five years earlier. At Martin Benjamin's suggestion, they read Thomas Nagel's *What Does It All Mean?* (1987). Their review of this book continues:

> Philosophy, on the other hand, attempts to look through all windows at once. The method of reasoning we acquired through *What Does It All Mean?* is not introduced in high school. We feel that a high school philosophy course would benefit interested students. Not only does philosophy deal with abstract concepts, but it is also concerned with everyday decisions. As we reached high school age, we realized that we were facing

some difficult problems involving ethics and justice. Philosophy encour-
aged us to gain a better understanding of these questions and to reach an
objective position, on which we might base our actions. (Benjamin &
Scott, 1989, p. 29)

I would urge that there is no need for philosophy to wait until high school. Obviously David Benjamin and Jeremy Scott would agree – so, I suspect, would the group of 10-year-olds with whom I met in an after-school program in a public library (Pritchard, 1985). However, the kind of critical thinking philosophy encourages is bound to spill over into areas of controversy, particular in regard to morality. Of course, it is not just the study of philosophy that is bound to encourage moral reflection. Any subject (for example, history, government, biology, and literature) that seriously encourages the critical thinking of students is an open invitation for moral reflection. For those who welcome the schools helping children become reasonable persons, this is not unwelcome news. However, many fear what the schools might do if they make moral education part of their business, and they may wish to draw the line at this point.

The cost of keeping moral education out of the schools is likely to be high. It requires endorsement of the model of education that David Benjamin and Jeremy Scott decry. So, assuming that many students share their view, this advocates the continuation of schooling that many find uninteresting, unchallenging, and only marginally relevant to many of the issues they find most important to them outside the confines of school. However, deliberately or not, moral values are reinforced (or under-mined) in the schools. Cheating is discouraged, respect for students and teachers is encouraged, and so on. In short, educational institutions depend for their viability on the acceptance of basic moral values, values that may or may not match up well with values found in the corridors, the playgrounds, and the streets between home and school – or even in the homes of some children. To expect all of this to work out well without moral education being in any explicit way placed on the educational agenda is quite optimistic.

It might be replied that these moral values are reinforced only to enable schools to get on with their main business – educating students. These are ground rules for the schools to function effectively. Distinct from this, however, is the question of whether moral values should be discussed *within* the curriculum itself. But, attempting to keep moral content out of the curriculum is equally hopeless. As Fullinwider (1991) says, a school that attempted this would probably have to close down:

It could not teach children their native language since so much of any natural language is about how to be and not to be. It would have to deprive its students of all stories of human affairs, since those stories are structured by evaluative concepts — by ideas of success and failure, foresight and blindness, heedfulness and heedlessness, care and negligence, duty and dereliction, pride and shame, hope and despair, wonder and dullness, competition and cooperation, beginning and ending. But without stories of human affairs, a school could not effectively teach non-moral lessons either. It could not teach about inflation, log-rolling, scientific discovery, coalition-building, paranoia, ecological niches, deterrence of crime, price controls, or infectious disease. (pp. 206-7)

Worse, anything resembling *critical thinking* would need to be eliminated from the schools, too. Reid (1788) notes that our "power of reasoning, which all acknowledge to be one of the most eminent natural faculties of man, . . . appears not in infancy" (p. 595). This capacity, like that of moral discernment, also needs to be duly cultivated and properly exercised. The recent hue and cry that the schools are failing to help students develop critical thinking skills echoes Reid's observation. So, there is a nation-wide call for getting beyond rote learning. Hardly anyone would oppose critical thinking in the schools – as long as it can stay away from the moral domain. But it cannot be kept away.

An anecdote will illustrate the problem. A few years ago I visited a 4th grade class. I spent the half hour discussing assumptions with the students. I gave them several "brainteasers" that can be solved only if one examines unwarranted assumptions that block our ability to proceed. For example, 6 toothpicks can be placed end-to-end to form 4 equilateral triangles only if we construct a three-dimensional pyramid, rather than lay them all on a flat surface.[19] As long as we assume we are restricted to a two-dimensional, flat surface, we will not be able to solve the problem.

After class, one of the students told me a story. A father and son are injured in a car accident. They are rushed to separate rooms for surgery. The doctor attending the son announces, "I cannot perform surgery on this boy. He is my son." The student then asked me to explain how the boy could be the doctor's son. I had heard the story several years earlier. So I quickly answered the question. Some of today's 4th graders still struggle with this question for a while ("The first father was a priest," "The doctor was his step-father"). But when this was first aired on television's "All in the Family," Archie Bunker was not the only one who was stumped. A significant percentage of adult viewers were, too.

Why did this 4th grader come up with this example? We had been talking about assumptions, but none of my examples had any social content. Here was an example resting on an unwarranted assumption – an assumption that contains gender stereotypes. The student apparently understood very well the basic point about assumptions. Then, like any good critical thinker, she *applied* it in a novel way – a way that has everything to do with moral education. So, even critical thinking about seemingly innocuous "brainteasers" threatens to get out of control.

Given this, it seems best simply to face up to the task of moral education, rather than act as if it could be avoided altogether. However, something interesting happens when moral education is put on the main agenda, rather than remaining on the hidden agenda. If schools explicitly acknowledge they are in the moral education business, how will they defend themselves against the charge of indoctrination? Fullinwider (1991) suggests that we see moral education as something like learning a vocabulary, learning how to use words and concepts. As Fullinwider puts it, "A moral education supplies tools of evaluation (a vocabulary) rather than a doctrine for adhesion (dogma)" (p. 207). To this we should add that students need to be encouraged to *use* these tools in the class-room. That is, they need to be encouraged to engage in evaluative thought – with each other.

When this is done in a mutually supportive atmosphere, what evolves is a *community of inquiry* (Sharp, 1988). In such a classroom each student is regarded as having the potential to make valuable contributions to the issues discussed. Students are expected to give reasons in support of what they say, to listen to one another carefully, and to be responsive to one another. This kind of learning environment can be expected to help develop and refine the reasonableness of students. Such a community of inquiry, Reid might agree, affords students opportunities to "duly culti-vate and properly exercise" their "seeds of moral discernment." And this is what *empowers* students eventually to go on responsibly, on their own, rather than under the watchful eye of teacher or parent.

To deprive students of such opportunities in the schools is to deprive them of an educational right as basic as any other. No one seriously suggests that students should be legally required to go to school, but that math and science education have no place there. Why should it be any different if we substitute "moral education" for "math and science edu-cation?" If the answer is that most parents cannot handle the math and science education of their children all by themselves, the same is true of moral education. Admittedly, unless it is a form of moral indoctrination, moral education in the schools is not like math and science education – at least not as these subjects are described by David Benjamin and Jeremy Scott. But this is not an objection for hopists like me, who hold out hope that the schools can contribute significantly to the reasonableness of children – and that this would be a good thing.

Notes

1. For example, see Callahan (1980). There the emphasis clearly is on students as active learners rather than passive recipients of moral instruction.

2. This worry is precisely what prompted Matthew Lipman to undertake the project of presenting logic to elementary school students. The resulting success of Philosophy for Children no doubt exceeded his initial expectations, but it confirms his insight that logic cannot wait.

3. What I take reasonableness to consist of will be discussed below.

4. This does not mean that children are to be regarded as adults. Moral discernment requires experience as well as judgement. And there is much that young children are not experientially or emotionally ready to confront. However, as will be shown later, many have already developed a surprisingly sophisticated understanding of morality by the time they enter school.

5. The civic education argument that follows is based on Robert Fullinwider's (1991) work.

6. Fullinwider (1991) cites Gutmann (1987), Crittenden (1988), and Galston (1989).

7. How else are we to understand the nation-wide call for greater emphasis on developing critical thinking skills? This is not simply a call for critical thinking in civic education.

8. Robert Ennis and Stephen P. Norris (1989, p. 3) offer the same definition. There they claim that their definition is a close approximation of what educators generally mean by critical thinking.

9. This paragraph and the next are based on my "STS, Critical Thinking, and Philosophy for Children" (1991). There I discuss critical thinking at much greater length. See especially pp. 220-228.

10. For an especially helpful discussion, particularly in regard to the social aspects of thinking for oneself, see Guin (1992).

11. One of my favorite illustrations: I once spent a fair amount of time trying to explain to a class the role of egocentricity in the

early stages of Lawrence Kohlberg's theory of moral development. A student then announced that she thought she understood what is meant by 'egocentric.' Pleased, I asked her to explain. She smilingly replied, "You find Kohlberg's work interesting. So, you assume we do, too."

12. Roughly speaking, affective capacities are capacities for emotion and feeling, whereas cognitive capacities are capacities for rational and logical thought. Just what relationships these capacities have to one another in the moral domain is subject to much debate. I address many of these issues in my *On Becoming Responsible* (1991). See especially Chapters 4-8.

13. According to Hoffman (1970, 1976), even infants give evidence of empathic responses to the crying of other infants. However, at this stage infants apparently have no clear sense of the distinction between themselves and others. So, he refers to this as "global empathy." Still, as young children develop their understanding of the perspectives of others, empathy becomes differentiated. This is not an escape from egoism, for it is only at this point that ego itself clearly emerges. So, now there can be concern both for others and self. Equally important, non-egocentric understanding begins to develop much earlier than theorists such as Jean Piaget and Lawrence Kohlberg suggest. Hoffman's earliest example is an 18-month old child comforting another toddler. There is little reason to suppose that very young children cannot respond to overt expressions of adult distress as well. However, the understanding of more subtle and complex forms of suffering no doubt must await appropriate cognitive development.

14. For detailed examples, see, for example: Lipman and Sharp (1978), especially the selections by Martin Benjamin, Ann Diller, Clyde Evans, and R.M. Hare; Matthews (1984); Pritchard (1985).

15. Lobel's Frog and Toad are both male. My Turtle and Mouse are also male. It might be interesting to tell these stories with a mix of male and female characters, or with only female characters.

16. Frog and Toad seem to think of bravery in terms of physical courage – facing physical dangers. However, there are other forms of bravery, too – such as moral courage. For example, in Judy Varga's (1961) *The Dragon Who Liked to Spit Fire*, Darius the friendly dragon is banished from the King's castle after accidentally setting fire to the royal banners. Although forbidden from ever seeing little Prince Frederic again, Darius later saves Frederic from a wild boar. Readers might regard this as another instance of physical bravery (depending on whether the wild boar

is seen as posing danger to Darius, too). But, since Darius was acting contrary to the king's orders, it seems also to be an instance of moral courage. An even clearer instance of moral courage is supplied by the king, who now has to summon up the courage to admit he was mistaken.

The king cleared his throat three times. He did not know how to begin, for kings don't like to admit they are wrong. But he was a very just king, so he cleared his throat a fourth time. "It is rather nice to have a dragon around the castle," he said. "Frederic could never have a better, more faithful friend than Darius." He took off his own medal and hung it on the little dragon's neck.

17. Piaget and Kohlberg claim that children do not get beyond predominantly egocentric thinking until well into their school years.

18. In fact, Clyde Evans is reporting on a session that was videotaped. In the videotape, "No Clearcut Answers," one of the children uses the very words, "What if everyone did that?" Another comments that the carnival might have to go out of business.

19. The pyramid will have an equilateral triangle as its base, with each side of the triangle being a toothpick. Each of the remaining three toothpicks can then have one of its ends placed at one of the angles of the base triangle, while the other ends are brought together at a single point. The result is a four-sided pyramid.

References

Aristotle. (1985, 1095a). *Nicomachean ethics* (p. 4). T. Irwin (trans.).

Benjamin, D. & Scott, J. (1989). Review of *What does it all mean? Thinking*, 7(4), 29.

Callahan, D. (1980). Goals in the teaching of ethics. In D. Callahan and S. Bok (Eds.), *Ethics teaching in higher education* (pp. 61-74). New York: Plenum.

Carroll, L. (1986). *Alice's adventure in wonderland and Through the looking glass*. New York, NY: Airmont Publishing Co., p. 198.

Crittenden, B. (1988). *Parents, the state and the right to educate*. Melbourne: University of Melbourne Press.

Damon, W. (1988). *The moral child*. New York: MacMillan.

Diller, A. (1978). On a conception of moral thinking. In M. Lipman & A. M. Sharp (Eds.), *Growing up with philosophy* (pp. 326-338). Philadelphia: Temple University Press.

Donaldson, M. (1978). *Children's minds*. London: Fontana.

Dworkin, R. (1977). *Taking rights seriously*. Oxford: Oxford University Press.

Ennis, R. (1987). A conception of critical thinking – with some curriculum suggestions. *Newsletter on Teaching Philosophy.* (Available from the American Philosophical Association.)

Ennis, R. and Norris, S. P. (1989). *Evaluating critical thinking.* Pacific Grove, CA: Midwest Publications.

Evans, C. (1978). The feasibility of moral education. In M. Lipman & A. M. Sharp (Eds.), *Growing up with philosophy* (pp. 157-173). Philadelphia: Temple University Press.

Fullinwider, R. (1991). Science and technology education as civic education. In P. Durbin, (Ed.), *Europe, America, and technology: Philosophical perspectives* (pp. 197-215). Netherlands: Kluwer Academic.

Galston, W. (1989). Civic education in the liberal state. In N. L. Rosenblum (Ed.), *Liberalism and the moral life* (pp. 89-101). Cambridge, MA: Harvard University Press.

Guin, P. (1992). Thinking for oneself. In A. M. Sharp and R. Reed (Eds.), *Studies in philosophy for children* (pp. 79-86). Philadelphia: Temple University Press.

Gutmann, A. (1987). *Democratic education.* Princeton, NJ: Princeton University Press.

Hoffman, M. (1970). Moral development. In P. A. Mussen (Ed.), *Carmichael's manual of child psychology*, vol. 2 (pp. 261-369). New York: Wiley.

Hoffman, M. (1976). Empathy, role-taking, guilt, and the development of altruistic motives. In T. Lickona (Ed.), *Moral development and behavior* (pp. 124-143). New York: Rinehart & Winston.

James, W. (1948). The will to believe. In W. James, *Essays in pragmatism* (pp. 88-109). New York: Hafner Publishing Co.

Lipman, M. & Sharp, A. M. (Eds.). (1978). *Growing up with philosophy.* Philadelphia: Temple University Press.

Lipman, M. (1982). Harry Stottlemeier's discovery. Upper Montclair, NJ: First Mountain Foundation.

Lipman, M. (1983). *Lisa.* Upper Montclair, NJ: First Mountain Foundation.

Lipman, M. et al. (1984). *Philosophical inquiry.* Montclair, NJ: I.A.P.C.

Lipman, M. (1991). *Thinking in education.* New York: Cambridge University.

Lobel, A. (1971). *Frog and Toad together.* New York: Harper & Row.

Matthews, G. (1980). *Philosophy and the young child.* Cambridge, MA: Harvard University Press.

Matthews, G. (1984). *Dialogues with children.* Cambridge, MA: Harvard University Press.

Matthews, G. (1987). Concept formation and moral development. In J. Russell (Ed.), *Philosophical perspectives in developmental psychology* (pp. 175-190). Oxford: Basil Blackwell.

Nagel, T. (1987). *What does it all mean? A very short introduction to philosophy.* New York, NY: Oxford University Press.

Pritchard, M. S. (1985). *Philosophical adventures with children.* Lanham, MD: University Press of America.

Pritchard, M. (1991). STS, critical thinking, and philosophy for children. In P. T. Durbin (Ed.), *Europe, America, and technology: Philosophical perspectives* (pp. 217-246). Netherlands: Kluwer Academic.

Pritchard, M. (1991). *On becoming responsible.* Lawrence, KS: University Press of Kansas.

Reid, T. (1788, 1895). *Essays on the active powers of the mind in philosophical works,* vol 2, with notes by Sir William Hamilton. Hildesheim: Gekorg Olms Verlagsbuchhandlung.

Sharp, A. M. (1988). What is a community of inquiry? In W. Hare and J. P. Portelli (Eds.), *Philosophy of education: Introductory readings* (pp. 207-218). Calgary, AB: Detselig Enterprises.

Shweder, R. A., Turiel, E. & Much, N. C. (1981). The moral intuitions of the child. In H. H. Flavell and L. Ross (Eds.), *Social cognitive development: Frontiers and possible futures* (pp. 288-305). Cambridge: Cambridge University Press.

Sibley, W. M. (1953). The rationale and the reasonable. *Philosophical Review, 62*: 554-560

Varga, J. (1961). *The dragon who liked to spit fire.* New York: William Morrow .

CHAPTER 2

What is the Value in Self-Esteem?

San MacColl

Introduction

Self-esteem is a notion much appealed to in education and in philosophy for children, where its cultivation is claimed as a significant success. The improvement in self-esteem in particular is marked both in reports from teachers and in recent studies (Sasseville, 1992). Yet the notion of self-esteem is not all that clear even at an intuitive level. Construing it broadly as our own estimation of our self, I want to draw attention to two crucial dimensions of self-esteem which should not be overlooked. These are the value dimension of self-esteem, that what is esteemed must be valued; and the social dimension of self-esteem, that self-evaluation needs to be socially reliable.

Not only does self-esteem lack a concise usage, but the self is also a problematic concept. The nature of the self has long been contentious in theory, and these days theories of the self and the subject have proliferated (Taylor, 1989). A brief survey of this history is useful to situate current theoretical trends. In traditional philosophy, theories of the self have been dominated by epistemological interest, the relation between subject and object, and the quest for certainty. A consolidated view of the subject derived from various sources in the philosophical tradition gives us an abstract human subject who is autonomous and independent, and identified by a rational mind. The focus varies from concerns with an essential nature and metaphysical substance, to the self-containedness and unity of the subject, to autonomy and free will, to the rationality of the knower. In this view of the subject, the body does not figure nor the emotions, except to be controlled. But on further analysis this universal human subject turns out to have only qualities associated with the male. So it is not a generic human subject, but an implicitly gendered one. There has been strong criticism of this tradition in philosophy especially by feminists recently (for example, Gatens, 1983; Gross, 1986; Gilligan, 1988; Lloyd, 1980, 1989). The autonomy and solidity of the self-directed individual has been exposed as sexless and bodiless.

The sources amalgamated to form this "traditional" view of the subject occur in different areas of philosophical concern. Some of the major ones are found in the consideration of the nature of mind and self (for example, Descartes' emphasis on the role of reason, and the distinction of the spiritual from material substance); in political theory (for example, in Rousseau and Locke, the notion of the liberal individual who is autonomous, and self-directed, is developed); and in epistemology (such as in Descartes, or Locke, the knowing subject is separated from the object known). This is just a selection from a wide range of philosophers who have contributed, endorsed, or varied the amalgam, but its variations have not diminished its power or influence.

The limitations of the abstract human subject in such theories of the self are amply shown by a consideration of social, cultural, and historical influences on the development of the self and through the notion of the self-constitution of the subject as it has been explored in the late work of Michel Foucault (1985, 1988). These considerations are importantly connected to the question of the self as agent, an issue we neglect at our peril (Smith, 1988). Contemporary interest in what we are as subject, and how we are constituted as subjects of experience has changed the questions asked of a theory of the subject and accounts of subjectivity. In particular the sovereignty of reason and the individual subject as knower have been displaced, so that the traditional relation of subject and object does not retain its former significance. The issues of the social construction of the subject, the importance of psychoanalytic theory, and the subject's relationship with others receive more attention than the subject's relation to the world. The effect of such theorizing about the self on the notion of self-esteem is another investigation. Problematic as the self is, we know enough about what we are referring to in talking about the self, however troubled we are in theorizing about it. I will move on to what is involved in our estimation of our self and focus my consideration on self-esteem, without trying to further specify what the self is.

Self-esteem

Any old esteem of any old self is not what's wanted. One of the major problems about self-esteem is a tendency for it to slip into emptiness when it is taken as just a feeling state. Although this corresponds to the standard dictionary definition (for example, OED gives "self-esteem" as "favourable appreciation or opinion of oneself"), it is not enough. This problem is posed by Guin (1992). The danger is evident from considering the results of taking self-esteem as feeling good about oneself. Against all our intuitions, this would equate the self-esteem of a drug pusher, a do-gooder, and a dimwit, who all feel equally good about themselves.

The cultivation of self-esteem as a mere feeling state is of dubious value. To have the development of self-esteem, in this sense, as an educational goal is highly questionable. Not only is it an empty notion of self-esteem, but it is likely to have undesirable consequences.

We might be encouraging the self-esteem of bullies, which is surely not desirable, where it is a matter of encouraging their self-esteem qua bullies. Should bullies be encouraged to feel good about themselves in the name of self-esteem if this means that their bullying habits are being endorsed as a matter of prowess?

There may be some cases where it would be desirable to encourage the self-esteem of someone who is a bully because their very low self-esteem is a factor in their being a bully. The point here is that it is not desirable to increase the self-esteem of bullies qua bullies. There may be another, different, social point, however, to the practice of encouraging someone to take pride in an otherwise unrewarding, unpleasant or dirty job, such as being a soldier or a garbage collector.

Nor is it desirable to endorse naughtiness in the name of self-esteem. Consider a child who takes pride in being the naughtiest child in the class. The fostering of self-esteem, if it is bringing kids to feel good about themselves for what they are "good" at, could result in *very* naughty behavior being promoted on the grounds that it is the one and only thing they are good at. This is like the way that a well-meaning application of encouragement by making clear that "everyone is good at something" can be trivialized into merit cards for "smiling a lot." It may be a start, but it is seriously limited as a long-term strategy. It is perverse if self-esteem can be feeling good about yourself without regard to whether what you feel good about, is good or not. To be worthwhile, especially in the educational context, self-esteem cannot just be feeling good about oneself.

Worthwhile Self-esteem

Self-esteem has to involve a value dimension: what is esteemed must be of value. Nor is it even just a matter of a subject's estimation of their own worth, it needs to be an estimation which will be upheld amongst their peers and within their community. The question of what makes a self valuable is not addressed here directly, although some issues are touched on later. The problem of just what we do mean by the self affects what is included in our valuation, and how various factors are to be weighted. The main point is that in regarding self-esteem as a desirable educational goal, its value dimension and its social dimension are crucial.

Someone's self-estimation might be misplaced; cases will not only be those which we might think of as pathological or self-deceptive, for example the drug dealer, or someone suffering delusion; they might also be due to mistake or misjudgment, or lack of feedback. For one's own estimation of self-worth to be appropriate and useful, it has to be justified and in general it needs the social reinforcement of others.

Self-esteem might be largely generated from a subject's own estimation. If someone estimates him or herself to have a certain worth without any justification, such a person would be valuing what has no value, and would appear to be quite unrealistic about him or herself. In such a case the subject's confidence may be strong as a result of their self-esteem, but it will be misplaced and their estimation of their self will be mistaken.

Someone might hold him or herself in high esteem and this estimation may not correspond to anyone else's valuing of the person in question. It might happen in exceptional cases that everyone else misjudges. But usually self-esteem is not independent of the social worth of a person and if others do not regard someone to be of high value, then a high self-esteem is inappropriate. In this way self-esteem is a social concept. It is partly a matter of a person's recognition of their socially acknowledged worth. That is why low self-esteem is particularly sad when it is unwarranted in terms of a person's otherwise acknowledged value.

So far in investigating self-esteem as an educationally desirable goal, it has been claimed that both a value dimension, and a social dimension of self-esteem have to be recognized if it is not to be an empty notion. This means that the value attributed to the self needs to be appropriate and socially reliable.

The issues considered are (i) that the cultivation of self-esteem as just feeling good about oneself, is not only inadequate but dangerous in the educational context because it fails to consider the value dimension; (ii) that the value dimension is not only self-generated but needs to reflect the social context. Self-esteem is both a value concept and a social concept. Its usefulness to the individual depends on a realization of both dimensions, as does its desirability as an educational and social goal.

This brings me to examine what is involved in practice in developing self-esteem. Esteem, to be genuine, requires knowing, understanding, and valuing what is esteemed. This means that we have to know, understand, and value our self if we are to esteem it. The way in which the community of inquiry provides an ideal setting for knowing and understanding one's self is well known (Glaser, 1991).

According to Glaser the development of self is one of the important functions of the community of inquiry. In her terms, the person is the "I" of reflective consciousness, what makes me me, both as a first person subject and from my own 'third person' sense of myself as a spatio-temporal being. In this account, participation in a community of inquiry brings us to understand our self in various ways (Glaser, 1991, p. 21). One is that by reflection on our activities in the community of inquiry, we understand what we and others are as persons, both in general terms, and in our own particularity. Secondly, by the encounters we have in the community of inquiry, we understand how we function in our relations with each other. Glaser also claims that through developing self-esteem we come to realize our own power to effect change in ourselves, and more widely.

As I see it, understanding the self is exemplified in the way that, in the process of sharing ideas in the community of inquiry, we appreciate the similarities and the differences between ourself and others. We learn that our own point of view is one amongst others. We exchange views and listen to and tolerate the views of others.

The further issue I want to explore is how the philosophy classroom helps towards the question of *valuing* the self. And particularly, given the points already raised, to explore this issue with the realization that it must be both worthwhile and socially reliable self-esteem.

The Role of Philosophy in Self-esteem

How does the philosophy classroom help towards the development of self-esteem with regard to valuing the self? I have shown that to esteem something requires that it be known, understood, and valued. To further explore the value dimension of self-esteem, I want to shift the emphasis from the mechanisms of the community of inquiry, which are essential in the philosophy classroom, and which have been emphasized in explaining how we can come to know and understand the self, to the philosophizing itself in the community of inquiry. Of course the social and cooperative nature of the community of inquiry is also essential to that, but I will take that for granted.

How does the philosophical community of inquiry – the philosophy classroom at school – help to develop self-esteem? In broad terms, I want to suggest a model for developing self-esteem in respect of coming to value the self, or of raising low self-esteem, analogous to the model for the judgment of ideas which is fostered in the philosophy classroom. This contributes to an analysis of how the philosophy classroom helps to develop self-esteem.

The development of judgment in the philosophy classroom

In the usual practice of the community of inquiry, the students set the agenda of questions, so it is their inquiry. They cooperate in pursuing the inquiry by sharing their ideas to follow through an issue. Here they are philosophizing. In this process they put forward ideas or views, analyze them, examine them, criticize them, and try to arrive individually or together at a tentative solution, or at least to come up with a range of reasoned positions not as yet finally settled. This is a simplification and a community of inquiry is subject to many variations, such as changing the direction of the inquiry, substituting a different question, and so on, but it suffices for the present purpose.

The ground rules of the community of inquiry crucial to this process are the establishment of trust, the function of respect, and the expectation of tolerance, which guarantee the community of inquiry as a safe environment in which to venture forth your ideas. In this philosophizing process, judgment is developing. Ideas are constantly being judged, either critically or creatively. When a question is being analyzed, judgments are made. When alternative views are being examined, judgments are made.

There are many kinds of judgment involved. Lipman (1991, Ch. 9) gives an account of the strengthening of judgment in education. He sees inquiry and judgment to be related as are process and product. Judgment can be developed, either through attention to principles or to practice. It can be either top down or bottom up.

We can characterize the kinds of judgments and their interactions by considering how they operate. Judgment developed through principles operates with the universal, while judgment developed through practice operates with the particular. We can come to judgments from the direction of the concrete instance and move towards abstract principles, or from the direction of an abstract principle and move towards the concrete instances. Most importantly, there is an interplay between the two, in both directions.

Lipman (1991) emphasized the importance of both critical and creative judgment. He characterizes the critical and creative in this context as follows:

> ...the critical thinker looks for answers in the form of questions that will point the way to the elimination of inquiry. The creative thinker looks for questions in the form of answers that will lead to the perpetuation of inquiry. (Lipman, p. 162)

So that for example, in the course of an inquiry, someone might raise a question which exposes a misplaced assumption, and draw the inquiry to a halt; this would be an example of critical judgment. Or someone might answer a question by asking a further question; this would be an example of creative judgment.

Before we reach the level of judgment that we tend to think of most readily, such as making value judgments in ethics or aesthetics – what Lipman calls culminating judgments – there are many other sorts of judgements that we make, for example, of identity or of difference, of analogy, of relevance, and so forth, which can be categorized into three orders: generic, mediating, and culminating. Lipman illustrates this with the image of a wheel, with the rim, spokes, and hub. Whilst the hub represents culminating judgments, in the educational context particularly, attention to the development of other sorts of judgments which contribute to the process is important and valuable. As will be obvious from the earlier account, philosophizing in the community of inquiry requires and deals explicitly in all these different sorts of judgments. It provides the ideal environment for the practice and development of judgment right down to a very basic level.

Lipman (1991) makes the additional point, about the expressive character of judgments, which is particularly significant for the question of self-esteem, that:

> Judgments, unlike skills, are minuscule versions of the persons who perform them. This is so in the sense that each and every judgment expresses the person who makes the judgment and at the same time appraises the situation or world about which the judgment is made. We are our judgments and they are us. This is why the strengthening of my judgment results in the growth and strengthening of myself as a person. (p. 171)

Valuing the self

Lipman has shown, in his account of the strengthening of judgment by doing philosophy in a community of inquiry, how we develop our ability to make value judgments and how this applies to the making of value judgments about our self and about others. Further, I want to suggest that in testing our ideas out in the community of inquiry, we are thereby testing ourselves out. In this way we are better placed to estimate our own value. It is this analogy that I want to explore further.

The question of what one's worth is to be judged from is contentious here. Guin (1991) implies that self-esteem is a matter of the worth of one's deeds, but I would argue that this is too restrictive. The sense in which our judgments form part of what we are is relevant to this. And our ideas are part of what we are in a sense, just as our judgments are. Deeds and ideas are equally important in the value we give our self. We are not just our deeds, our outwardly manifested actions already performed, but our thoughts, and our plans as well.

Self-esteem is about what we can achieve as well as what we have achieved. Our deeds are always in the past, but our self also refers to what we will, or would like to, become. This is why Rawls' account of self-esteem includes our life plan (Rawls, 1992). This recognition of our self as having a future is evident from Lipman's view on good judgment:

> ... it is likely that, in the long run, what makes good judgments good is their role in the shaping of future experiences: They are judgments we can live with, the kind that enrich the lives we have yet to live. (Lipman, 1991, p. 171)

The analogy to valuing the self

When a kid puts forward an idea in a philosophy discussion in the community of inquiry, it will be tossed around as it were, played about with, examined, analyzed, amended, criticized. It will both be recognized as belonging to the kid who thought of it, and contributed it, but it will also in a way be distanced from that kid, because it is an idea towards a cooperative inquiry, it is there to be shared and used. It may be absorbed in the general enterprise, modified, or kicked out. This process of the testing of ideas is familiar from the notion of hypothesizing in science. An idea is generated, subject to criticism, adopted, modified or rejected, or subjected to further testing. The value of the idea from the point of view of its contributor will become clear, and the way in which the idea is valued by other members of the community will also be evident. It is by trying out ideas that we find out what they are worth, both to us and to others. Insofar as we put ourselves forward when we offer ideas in the arena of philosophical discussion, we find out our value and how others value us also.

Because each idea is taken seriously and constructively developed, feedback is readily available on whatever someone puts forward. Those whose self-esteem has been low because they have lacked feedback on how others regard them, or because they have not absorbed the available feedback, cannot but be aware of the reception of their ideas when it is explicit in the community of inquiry. Given the circumstances, this is a non-threatening process. What's more, for those who may have traditionally been low in self-esteem, for example, girls or ethnic minorities, this process is particularly useful. They may be strengthened to discover that there are different kinds of value within their community and society, or that what peers value is different from their parents, and so on.

On the other hand, those who have had an inflated idea of their own worth, cannot but recognize that it lacks justification in the eyes of others. It will still be self-estimation, but tested against the estimation of others of this self, or the response of others to our own self-estimation.

What the analogy suggests is that philosophizing in the community of inquiry develops self-esteem in the social and value dimensions by analogy with the way it tests our ideas. This involves the putting forward of our ideas in a safe environment, the examination of alternative positions and points of view, and critical reflection of and judgment on the ideas presented.

Conclusion

The value in self-esteem as an educational goal lies in its benefits to the individual and to society. The reliability of our self-estimation with respect to the regard in which others hold us is an important test of our judgment. The regard in which others hold us is significant as a measure of confirmation of our self-estimation. We know in practice that the philosophy classroom helps develop self-esteem. I have been exploring the theoretical analysis of this. Self-esteem involves the knowing, understanding, and valuing of the self. The value and social dimensions of self-esteem are crucial.

The role of the philosophy classroom in developing self-esteem, and especially for those with low self-esteem, is both in the functioning of the community of inquiry and in the philosophizing process itself. Not only is judgment strengthened so that our judgment of ourselves becomes more reliable, but we have the opportunity to test our ideas in a trusting environment and testing our ideas is analogous to testing ourselves.

References

Descartes, R. (1969). *Discourse on method* and *Meditations*. In *The philosophical works of Descartes*, Vol. 1. E.S. Haldane & G.R.T. Ross (Trans.). Cambridge: Cambridge University Press.

Foucault, M. (1985). *The use of pleasure*. New York: Random House.

Foucault, M. (1988). *The care of the self*. New York: Random House.

Gatens, M. (1983). A critique of the sex/gender distinction. In J. Allen and P. Patton (Eds.), *Beyond Marxism? Interventions after Marx* (pp. 143-163). Sydney: Intervention Publications.

Gilligan, C. (1988). Remapping the moral domain: New images of self in relationship. In C. Gilligan et al. (Eds.), *Mapping the moral domain* (pp. 3-19). Cambridge: Centre for Study of Gender, Education, and Human Development, Harvard University.

Glaser, J. (1991). Reflections on personhood. *Thinking, 10* (1), 19-21.

Gross, E. (1986). Philosophy, subjectivity and the body: Kristeva and Irigaray. In C. Pateman and E. Gross (Eds.), *Feminist challenges: Social and political theory* (pp. 125-143). Sydney: Allen and Unwin.

Guin, P. (1992). Philosophy for children should address the slippery idea of self-esteem. Paper read at ICPIC.

Lipman, M. (1991). *Thinking in education*. Cambridge: Cambridge University Press.

Lloyd, G. (1980). Woman as other: Sex, gender and subjectivity. *Australian Feminist Studies, 10*, 13-22.

Lloyd, G. (1989). *The man of reason*. London: Methuen.

Locke, J. (1960). *Two treatises of government*. New York, NY: Cambridge University Press.

Locke, J. (1961). *An essay concerning human understanding*. New York, NY: Dent.

Rawls, J. (1972). *Theory of justice*. Oxford: Clarendon.

Rousseau, J.J. (1950). *The social contract*. G.D.H. Cole (Trans.). New York, NY: E.P. Dutton.

Sasseville, M. (1992). Self-esteem, logical skills and philosophy for children. Paper read at ICPIC.

Smith, P. (1988). *Discerning the subject*. Minneapolis: University of Minnesota Press.

Taylor, C. (1989). *Sources of the self: The making of the modern identity*. Cambridge: Cambridge University Press.

CHAPTER 3

Text-Characters and Lump-Characters

Ronald Reed

In a recent article, Richard Rorty (1991) distinguishes between "texts" and "lumps":

> Think of a paradigmatic text as something puzzling which was said or written by a member of a primitive tribe, or by Aristotle, or by Blake. Nonlinguistic artifacts, such as pots, are borderline cases of texts. Think of a lump as something which you would bring for analysis to a natural scientist rather than to somebody in the humanities or social sciences–something which might turn out to be, say, a piece of gold or the fossilized stomach of a stegosaurus. A wadded-up plastic bag is a borderline case of a lump. (pp. 84-85)

As Deweyian, as pragmatist, Rorty (1991) tries to dissolve the dualism, and suggests that it is momentary "...convenient blocking-out of regions along a spectrum, rather than a recognition of an ontological, or metaphysical or epistemological divide" (p. 84).

In this essay, I propose to adopt a parallel line of inquiry – but here the focus will be on the difference between "text-characters" and "lump-characters." In the manner of Rorty, I will attempt to point the way to a partial dissolution of the dualism suggesting that, in many ways, it is more of a convenient blocking out rather than an indication of significant epistemological (or metaphysical) divides. In particular, I will focus on borderline cases – specifically those cases where lump-characters function as text-characters – and will examine the political and/or religious ramifications of that cross-over. Finally, I will attempt to relate the preceding to one part of the Philosophy for Children corpus, that is, the Brian-giraffe episode in *Pixie* (Lipman, 1981) and to one of the more significant political goals of Philosophy for Children – giving a "voice to" people who were previously silent.

The current Vice-President of the United States, Margaret Thatcher, and the person sitting next to you in this room – assuming that you are not alone and that your companion is living – are examples of lump-characters. Raskolnikov, Romeo, and Emma Bovary are examples of text-characters. Borderline cases are Imelda Marcos' next husband, Edgar

Allen Poe's Lenore, all of the characters in *Remembrance of Things Past*, my maternal grandfather, and your infant daughter.

An obvious difference, besides the perhaps more obvious spatial and temporal ones, and the main difference I will concern myself with in this paper, is that of narrative construction. Lump-characters can and frequently do construct narratives by means of which they "situate" themselves, explain themselves to others (and themselves), and understand themselves and their environments. Thus, "I am a staple of numerous comedians' monologs and the immediate successor, should death or impeachment or other impairment occur, to the current president of the United States," explains Vice-President Quayle. In contradistinction, text-characters exist in narratives which are not of their own construction. Even in a first-person narrative, the construction of the narrative is a function of the author, say J. D. Salinger, and not the narrator, Holden Caulfield. The text-character acts out the narrative. She/he acts in the narrative. But she/he does not make the narrative. The text-character is discovered in the narrative, but the lump-character, even though she/he may be discovered in narratives of her/his own construction or of someone else's – rumors about the scandalous behavior of the Duchess of York – has the ability to "spin," to create her/his own narratives.

Once one sets up the distinction, however, it quickly becomes apparent that the bifurcation is porous. Narrative construction for lump-characters is transactional in the sense that it involves the relating of specific narratives to pre-existing narratives. The lump-characters, if they are to make sense, must be cognizant of pre-existing narratives and must relate the new narrative to pre-existing ones, that is, Margaret Thatcher *could* begin her story with "As the first female Prime Minister of Great Britain …" but Dan Quayle could not. Lump characters, again if they are to make sense, do not and cannot create *ex nihilo*. In effect, their (lump-characters) narratives are sorts of literary analogs of the work of normal scientists.[1] Although it may make sense to say they tell their own stories, it may make even more sense, it may be more accurate, to say that their stories are told through them. That in effect, it is the *situation* that is telling the story, it is the situation that is playing itself out, "using" the lump character in ways analogous to those used by the creator of the text character.

The distinction is porous precisely because what might be called a "narrative determinism" affects equally both lump-characters and text-characters. Once the situation begins, once it *is* a situation (as opposed to a series of discrete or random happenings), it has its own dynamics, its own gestalt, and the situation determines what is possible, what stories can still be told, and what stories are silenced forever. Neither the child born in Paraguay in 1952, nor any of the street hustlers in Nelson Algren's fictional *Chicago*, have any chance of being French Enlightenment figures. Pre-exiting lump narratives and text narratives preclude that. The argument, so far, has been to show that there is a certain similarity between text-characters and lump-characters. Lump-characters are bound by the same sorts of what might be called "rules of the context" which determine the behavior of text-characters. There is, however, one obvious difference between text and lump: while both text characters and lump characters exist *within* a situation, texts are human artifacts and lumps are not. The novelist (and here one speaks of "novelist," but one could as easily speak of "painter" or "poet" or "composer" or "dramatist") is not compelled to pick Prague and not Dublin, Praetoria and not Belfast. The protagonist need be neither male nor female, Anglo nor Hispanic, Catholic nor Protestant. There are no rules that the novelist has to consult when deciding which situation to create. The novelist has the freedom that is denied to both lump-characters and text-characters. The novelist is freed from the demands of the context. She/he is god-like. Prior to the first pen stroke, the first keyboard tap, there is no context and, hence, no demands of the context. A terrifying, exhilarating moment of freedom, but then the novelist begins and like other lump-characters and all text-characters, she/he becomes bound by the situation she/he has created.

Now consider the writer who chooses to incorporate historical figures into her/his fiction. American fiction has a long and interesting history of such inclusion – Franco and Stalin and James Dean in the work of John Dos Passos, Joan Crawford in Jack Kerouac's work, Ho Chi Minh in Robert Olen Butler's short stories, Joan Vollmer Burroughs in the work of William S. Burroughs, and most recently, Mary Jo Kopechne in Joyce Carol Oates' *Black Waters*. At first glance, one might argue that the inclusion of the historical figure (or the fictionalization of the historical figure) would introduce constraints on the novelists' art. In the next section of this paper, I will attempt to show that although the introduction of the historical figure may introduce constraints, it also creates a situation that does, of course, transform the original text situation and may transform the original lump situation.

Two Case Studies:

(1) Mary Jo Kopechne accepted a ride with Senator Ted Kennedy in 1969. There was a car accident and Senator Kennedy escaped with his

life but Ms. Kopechne drowned. Since Senator Kennedy was married at the time to someone other than Ms. Kopechne, and since alcohol was involved, and since the Kennedy name is well-known, and since Senator Kennedy left the scene of the accident and waited hours before seeking help, the accident generated a number of stories ranging from various "official" ones – those told by the Kennedy family, those told by the Kennedy family in consort with the Kopechne family, those told by the District Attorney's office – and less official ones – those told in the tabloids, those hinted at and alluded to, and so on. The story that was not told and could not be told was that of the victim.

(2) One of the more famous literary deaths (the ambiguity is intended) occurred in Mexico City in 1951. There, William S. Burroughs and his wife Joan Vollmer played a fatal game. Both Burroughs were drug addicts, dabblers in hallucinogens and, on the night in question, were drinking. Bill leaned over to Joan and, for reasons not clear, whispered to her that it was time to "go into their William Tell act" (Morgan, 1988, p. 194). With that, Joan Vollmer rose, walked across the room, and put a highball glass on her head. William Burroughs took out his pistol, aimed, and accidentally shot his wife to death. Again, there were a series of official versions – the Mexico City police ruled it an accidental homicide (and, not accidentally, asked Burroughs to leave the country). Burroughs himself has suggested that most of his writing, from *Naked Lunch*, *Nova Express*, and *The Soft Machine* through *The Place of Dead Roads* and *Cities of the Night*, is illuminated by that single event and, in effect, are his attempts to tell the story of that tragedy. In addition to the official versions, there have been numerous other versions of the event. What there has not been, of course, is Joan Vollmer's version. Using the language of this paper, a necessary condition for narrative construction by lump-characters is that they be alive. Dead persons neither wear plaid nor tell stories.

But what if one takes seriously the claim made earlier in this paper – the claim that it may be more accurate to say "that their stories are told through them. That, in effect, it is the situation that is telling the story, it is the situation that is playing itself out, "using" the lump-characters in ways analogous to those used by the creator of the text character." If one does take that claim seriously and if one can, in a sense, get "inside" the situation and discover its gestalt, one can allow the situation to tell itself through a character who is no longer alive. That, *precisely*, is what Joyce Carol Oates does in her moving novel, *Black Waters*. The American author, in effect, goes along as passenger and when the Senator frees himself from the submerged vehicle, Oates stays behind and listens and records as the car is filled by black water and by Ms. Kopechne's fears and memories and hopes.

That, *precisely*, is what William S. Burroughs has done in *Deconstruction of the Countdown*.[2] There, over the course of eleven short acts, Burroughs plays the shooting scene over and over again, finding different threads in the narrative each time he returns. Where Oates finds a single narrative, Burroughs find a series of narratives jostling each other, cutting into each other, and frequently contradicting each other. In each, Joan is present but she is always silent. Her silence, however, is not without meaning. In the most explicit of the scenes, the Burroughs' character mounts a bizarre Zeno-line argument where, comparing the speed of sound and light, he "proves" that it is impossible for the bullet to ever reach his wife. He does this while preparing to shoot her. While this is going on, Joan stands at the far end of the stage, powerless to stop what must occur, but silently "mouthing" an argument against it. Her silent argument is as eloquent as it is inefficacious.

The point, here, is something more than a simple literary one: that a good novelist can use historical figures and persons to good effect when telling a story. That point, given innumerable examples, is fairly straightforward. The more interesting point, it seems to me, says something about lumps and lump-characters, about the "real" world, and about life and death.

What the novelist does when she/he uses the historical character, especially in cases where characters have been silenced, is to recreate or reconstruct the situation so that which did not occur can now occur. The novelist, assuming that the novelist *succeeds* in her/his art, allows the situation to tell the story (stories) which is (are) implicit in itself through a character who, previously, had been silenced. Another interpretation of the situation is made explicit and the interpretation, since it is one story (a new story) among the set that constitutes the lump narrative, changes the nature of that narrative. When, in effect, Joan Vollmer and Mary Jo Kopechne are "allowed" to speak, their voices become part of the chorus that allows us to make sense of historical situations. What Joyce Carol Oates and William S. Burroughs do, in many ways, is analogous to what coroners and district attorneys do. All start from the facts of the case – a wrong turn was made on a darkened highway, a shot was fired – but where the district attorney and the coroner attempt to create a story to explain the facts, Oates and Burroughs have attempted to create (or recreate) a storyteller who in turn will create a story to explain the facts. Conceptually, we might block off the field and distinguish between fact and fiction, but there seems little ground for suggesting an epistemological or metaphysical divide. All of the questions that can be asked of the novelist – did it really happen this way, is this a "correct" slant on things, how do you know it happened this way and not some other – are the same sorts of questions that can be and frequently are asked of coroners and district attorneys. Unless one is committed to a modernist view of reality that yields a God's eye perspective to which all other perceptions must conform, the district attorney and the coroner and the novelist all tend to answer the questions in similar ways: this interpretation has explanatory force, this interpretation enables us to construct a narrative which explains more, which makes more sense than previous narratives did, this interpretation fits with, or adds something of significance which previous interpretations did not, and so forth.

The distinction, once again, between lump and text, proves porous. The narratives that the novelist constructs can be and sometimes are constitutive of the lump situation. The novelist's task can be and sometimes is religious in precisely the sense William James (1961) alludes to at the conclusion of *The Varieties of Religious Experience.*

> ... *Religion, in her fullest exercise of function, is not a mere illumination of facts already elsewhere given, not a mere passion, like love, which views things in a rosier light. It is indeed that, as we have seen abundantly. But it is something more, namely, a postulator of new facts as well. The world interpreted religiously is not the materialistic world all over again, with an altered expression; it must have, over and above the altered expression a natural constitution different at some point from that which a materialistic world would have. It must be such that different events can be expected in it, different conducts must be required. (pp. 400-401)*

When one says that all novelists "play at" being God, the claim may be inaccurate not because it says too much but because it says too little. When the novelist is successful in allowing the (lump) situation to tell its story, she/he does, as James suggests, change the nature of reality, create new facts and confer a kind of immortality on characters after resurrecting them. *Pace* Joyce Carol Oates, Mary Jo Kopechne is no longer silent. *Pace* William S. Burroughs, Joan Vollmer Burroughs will forever mount a silent argument until her execution.

To recapitulate, the novelist can, through the literary event, reconstruct situations so that the situations themselves have been changed. By creating a place in which my maternal grandfather, dead these sixty years, or your infant daughter, less than three weeks old, can speak, the novelist has created a world in which the previously inarticulate, those who were precluded from narrative construction, those who were unable to be conduits for the situation telling its stories, can now speak. That *is* a transformation that does change the world. That is religious, in James' sense.

Note, too, that what is being changed, what is being reconstructed, is not just our understanding of the past. What is being changed, what is being reconstructed, *literally* is the past. The past *is* the situation and the situation is as reconstructed, it is the past itself which undergoes change. Thus when the great Irish poet Patrick Kavanaugh (1972) eulogizes his mother, he is doing something more than merely recalling her to mind; he is having a sort of argument with the present in which he brings his mother back to life:

> I do not think of you lying in the wet clay
> Of a Monaghan graveyard: I see
> You walking down a lane among the poplars
> On your way to the station, or happily
>
> Going to second Mass on a summer Sunday –
> You see me and you say:
> 'Don't forget about the cattle – '
> Among your earthiest words the angels stray
>
> And I think of you waking along a headland
> Of green oats in June,
> So full of repose, so rich with life –
> And I see us meeting at the end of town
>
> On a fair day by accident, after
> The bargains are all made and we can walk
> Together through the shops and stalls and markets
> Free in the oriental streets of thought.
>
> O you are not lying in the wet clay,
> For it is the harvest evening now and we
> Are piling up the ricks against the moonlight
> And you smile up at us – eternally

Great poets perhaps, most obviously great Irish poets like Kavanaugh and W.B. Yeats, can change the course of events; they can, obviously, change the future. One thinks of the poet articulating an ideal for which the farm boy, the farm girl, willingly gives a life. But perhaps of more significance is their reformation and, sometimes, revolution of the past.

Now, one of the traditional claims made about Matthew Lipman's Philosophy for Children novels is that they model a community of inquiry. Real children can see fictional children inquiring together and can, in turn, imitate that behavior. That is a neat, clean description but, in many significant ways, it flattens the novelist's art; it turns it into a simple pedagogical tool. It assumes, using the language of this paper, a hard and fast distinction between lumps and texts, where, in effect, the text-character teaches and the lump-character learns. It assumes that the distinction between lump and text is non-porous.

Such a flattening may indeed be necessary for pedagogical reasons, but when we look at some of the more powerful, the more literary sequences, in the traditional Philosophy for Children corpus – most notably the exchange in *Pixie* (Lipman, 1981) between Brian and the Giraffe which culminates in the claim "you-are-so-beautiful" – one finds a clear reconstruction of lump-like situations where children (and animals) communicate well but their communication does *not* culminate in a linguistic utterance and is thought, therefore, to be dumb, to be unintelligent. What Lipman may be construed as doing is, on one level, delving into the lump-situation and making explicit what is already there: that the situation is fraught with meaning, that children are communicating (and inquiring and problem-solving, and so on) *already*, prior to formal schooling and prior to Philosophy for Children. "You-are-so-beautiful" is a significant addition. The linguistic utterance does add something of importance to the situation, but at the same time it is also a validation of what is already taking place.

In a similar fashion, Philosophy for Children may be said to be a significant addition to the educative process but it is based in a set of pre-existing conditions – lump-like situations in which children inquire well and reason well but, for historical and political and social reasons, are not allowed linguistic reconstruction. Historically, children *qua* children, have been silenced as much as Mary Jo Kopechne and Joan Vollmer Burroughs. Just as Oates and Burroughs, through their literature, have transformed the lump-world (the "real world") by giving silent characters a voice, it may be argued that Philosophy for Children, in addition to its pedagogical mission, has this transforming function. It is not just for the generation of children to come. It is, just as much, for the generation of children who have been. And this may, in the long run, be the key to educational reform. Just as feminists in philosophy and art and education have unearthed whole schools, whole traditions within disciplines which have been ignored and which now give contemporary feminists traditions of their own on which to build, so too may Philosophy for Children be said to be in the process of "unearthing" traditions of child scholarship on which contemporary children might build.

Notes

1. The reference, of course, is to Thomas Kuhn's *The Structure of Scientific Revolution*.

2. *Deconstruction of the Countdown* is a dramatization of the works of William S. Burroughs performed at The Caravan of Dreams Performing Arts Center, Fort Worth, Texas, April 30, May 1-2 and May 7-9, 1992.

References

Burroughs, W. (1992). *Nova express*. New York, NY: Grove Attic.

Burroughs, W. (1992). *The soft machine*. New York, NY: Grove Attic.

Burroughs, W. (1987). *The place of dead roads*. New York, NY: Holt and Co.

Burroughs, W. (1982). *Cities of the night*. New York, NY: Holt and Co.

James, W. (1961). *The varieties of religious experience*. New York: Collier Books.

Kavanaugh, P. (1972). *The collected poems*. London: Martin Brian & O'Keefe.

Kuhn, T. (1970). *The structure of scientific revolution*. Chicago, IL: University of Chicago Press.

Lipman, M. (1981). *Pixie*. Montclair, NJ: I.A.P.C.

Morgan, T. (1988). *Literary outlaw: The life and times of William S. Burroughs*. New York: Henry Holt and Co.

Oates, J.C. (1993). *Black water*. New York, NY: New American Library/Dutton.

Rorty, R. (1991). *Objectivity, relativism, and truth*. New York: Cambridge University Press.

CHAPTER 4

Thoughts after Piaget

Gareth B. Matthews

Piaget had a very special kind of genius. He was able to think up experiments with these three crucial characteristics:

(1) They have *arresting* results. They show children reacting to experimental situations in ways that surprise us because they are so very different from the ways in which *we* would react. [Two balls of clays that, as the child agrees, contain the same amount of clay are flattened – the one drastically, the other minimally. "Are they still the same?" asks the experimenter, cagily. "No," says the child, obligingly. Then, pointing to the thicker one, the child adds, "That one is heavier." (Piaget & Inhelder, 1974, p. 5)]

We are startled by such results. We become intrigued.

(2) The experiments are *replicable*. Piaget's most famous experiments, such as the conservation experiments, are, in fact, fairly easy to replicate. You don't need fancy equipment. You don't need to choose "the right children;" most any children will do. You *do* need to ask the children exactly what Piaget asked – or at least you do need to come as close as your own language will allow. But you don't need complicated scoring manuals to record the results, let alone special training sessions to be able to observe what is going on.

(3) The experiments reveal an *age-related sequence*. It matters how old the children are, and, in general, if you bring back the same children a couple of years later – almost regardless of what has happened in the meantime, so long as Mother Time has ticked away for a couple of years – the children will react differently. With only the slightest encouragement from Piaget, we can see from the experiments that the children are now *at a different stage*.

Only a first-rate genius could think of lots of experiments that all, or almost all, have these three features.

These three features, just by themselves, go a very long way toward selling us on Piaget's theory. Perhaps better: these very general features of Piaget's experiments are pretty much enough to sell most people on the *general idea of a Piagetian theory of cognitive development*, with really very little regard for what the detailed content of that theory turns out to be. Note how this is so.

(1) The fact that the experiments produce *arresting* results easily convinces us that, knowing our children so well, we don't in fact know them at all. It convinces us that our children are, in important ways, strangers to us. It's not enough, we quickly conclude, to be with our children all day long to get to know them. We need a *theory* about them. The expert, the theoretician, needs to tell us parents and teachers what our children are really like. Piaget's arresting experiments bring home that message.

I remember being caught up short by having a fourth-grade teacher ask me, "What's the thought of fourth-graders like?" *He* spent his whole day with fourth-graders. Certainly I didn't. Yet he wanted *me* to tell him what these creatures he spent his whole day with were like, or anyway what their thought was like. He had been influenced by Piaget's arresting experiments. He was open to being told by some supposed expert that the thought processes of the very children he saw every day were really very different from anything his massive exposure to them would lead him to expect.

(2) The fact that these experiments are *replicable* makes it quite plausible to think there lurks a science in this vicinity. There must be, it seems, a scientific theory that these experiments confirm, a theory quite on a par with the theories that get confirmed by similarly replicable experiments in physics and chemistry that our colleagues in the natural sciences run every day.

(3) The fact that these experiments display an *age-related sequence* of results makes it virtually impossible to resist the conclusion that cognitive development is a *maturational* process, in fact, a maturational process quite analogous to familiar processes of biological maturation. We know it is no good trying to teach a new-born infant to walk. The bones, muscles and nervous system of the infant need to mature first. Similarly, it is overwhelmingly natural to conclude from Piaget's experiments that it's no good trying to teach kids anything except what is "age-appropriate." Mental bones and psychological muscles need to mature, too.

Without going into any detail at all concerning Piaget's experiments, and without considering the specific content of the theories Piaget takes them to support, I want now to make some comments on what one might suppose all this has to do with these two questions:

Question 1: Do some children *naturally* do philosophy, that is, make philosophical comments, raise philosophical questions, and even engage in philosophical reasoning?

Question 2: Is it worthwhile *encouraging* children to do philosophy?

Consider first the *maturation* point, that is, the point that seems to be brought out by the age-related sequences of interestingly different responses to Piaget's questions. This point naturally prompts one to ask whether doing philosophy is a cognitively *mature* activity, or, instead, a cognitively immature activity. If it is a mature activity, then we shouldn't expect anyone to engage in it naturally who isn't her or himself cognitively mature. More particularly, one shouldn't expect to find that doing philosophy is a natural activity of childhood. Evidence, or apparent evidence, to the contrary would be highly suspect. *Prima facie* evidence to the contrary would have to be chalked up to either (i) overinterpreting the data, that is, reading philosophy into the words of young children, or else, (ii) having an insufficient grasp of what real philosophy is, and hence mistaking only apparently philosophical comments and questions for the real thing.

As for the second question – "Is it worthwhile encouraging children to do philosophy?" – if philosophy is a cognitively mature activity, then the answer would seem to be "No." To encourage children to do philosophy would be as pointless, perhaps even as damaging to the child, as trying to get newborn infants to walk. Doing philosophy would not be an "age-appropriate activity" for children, certainly not age-appropriate for young ones.

These are responses to my two questions on the assumption that doing philosophy is a cognitively mature activity. Alternatively one might try supposing that philosophy is a cognitively immature activity. In that case one would certainly expect to find children naturally engaged in doing philosophy all right, but then there would be no point in *encouraging* children in this, for it would be something the normal ones, anyway, could be expected to grow out of. (Professional philosophers like me would be children, who, in an important respect, simply never grew up.)

Now none of this fits either what we know about children or what we know about philosophy. Suppose philosophy is taken to be a cognitively mature activity, hence, presumably not something either naturally found in children or appropriately to be encouraged in them. I have myself presented evidence in my book, *Philosophy and the Young Child* (1980), that some young children do quite naturally make comments, ask questions, and even engage in reasoning that professional philosophers can recognize as philosophical. When in that book Ian, aged 6, lodges a protest with his mother over the fact that the three unpleasant children of his parents' visiting friends have taken over the TV set and kept him from watching his favorite program, he asks, provocatively, "Why is it better for three people to be selfish than for one?" deftly he turns on its head the utilitarian justification for that particular case of aggrandizement, namely, "Three people are being made *happy*, rather than just one." Ian's question, even if motivated by rage and frustration, is philosophically acute. It is not proto-philosophical, or semi-philosophical; it is the real thing, the very same kind of probing and questioning that takes place among professional philosophers in their seminars, conferences, and informal discussions with each other (perhaps also, in some cases motivated by rage or frustration, or the need to get a job, rather than the pure love of wisdom).

I have also presented evidence in my book, *Dialogues with Children* (1984), that even after children have been, as I should say, socialized out of doing philosophy naturally, say, between the ages of 8 and 12, they respond beautifully to the opportunity to engage in philosophy when it is presented to them with some imagination. Of course, the remarkable success of the Philosophy for Children Program developed by Matt Lipman and his colleagues provides much more substantial testimony to the same effect.

As for supposing that philosophy is a cognitively immature activity, that simply doesn't fit the reality. It is, of course, true that there is something characteristically naïve about philosophy; but it is a profound naïveté, not a cognitively immature sort. Consider these examples (both taken from Matthews, 1980, pp. 58-9):

Kristin was four years old. She was teaching herself to use watercolors. As she painted, she began to think about the colors themselves. Sitting on her bed, talking to her father, she announced, "Dad, the world is all made of colors."

Kristin's father reacted positively. Yet, recognizing a difficulty, he asked, "What about glass?"

Kristin thought for a moment. Then she announced firmly, "Colors <u>and</u> glass."

And here is a second anecdote about Kristin. She was five this time, and learning to read. She was learning to recognize syllables and to sound them out so as to be able to recognize words. She was quite proud of her success.

Again, sitting on her bed talking to her father, she commented, "I'm sure glad we have letters."

Kristin's father was somewhat surprised at that particular expression of gratitude. "Why?" he asked.

"'Cause if there was no letters, there would be no sounds," said Kristin. "If there was no sounds," she went on, "there would be no words . . . If there was no words, we couldn't think. . ."

If that's *im*maturity, what's so great about maturity?

One way out of this awkward dilemma posed by asking whether doing philosophy is a cognitively mature, or cognitively immature, activity, is to say that sometimes it is one and sometimes the other. Piaget himself often suggested that children, in their cognitive development, recapitulate the history of Western philosophy. According to this suggestion, they begin by being little pre-Socratics. They go on to become, successively, Platonists, Aristotelians, Scholastics, Cartesians, and then, perhaps, British empiricists. Now I myself don't think the evidence supports any such claim of general development. But suppose it did. The problem about maturity would not be solved, unless one supposed that the history of philosophy itself exhibits a maturational process. And surely there is inadequate reason to suppose that. It would, I think, be quite easy to argue that on any reasonable scale of maturity, Plato was as mature a thinker as Quine, or Kripke, or Habermas, or Derrida.

To consider the Kristin anecdotes again, it is natural to see at least some limited affinity between Kristin's idea that the world is made of colors and familiar ideas that the pre-Socratic Milesians – Thales, Anaximander, and Anaximines – put forward about "world stuff." Then perhaps we could liken Kristin's breath-taking reasoning about how without letters there would be no world to the later pre-Socratic philosopher, Parmenides. After all, Parmenides said something like, "The same thing can be thought as can be." (Compare Kristin's "If we couldn't think, there would be no world.")

Yet even if we suppose Parmenides to have been a more mature thinker than the Milesians, there is an obvious way in which you simply don't get any more *mature* philosophically than someone who can say, "Without words there would be no thought and without thought there would be no world." That is remarkably close to absolute idealism; it's also close to modern deconstructionism. Kristin at 12 or 20 or 48 may well *reject* that line of reasoning, or, more likely, forget it or become interested in something else instead; but if she does any of those things the explanation will not be that she has become a more *mature* thinker.

Frustrated with this problem about how to fit child philosophy into a story about cognitive development suggested by Piaget's arresting experiments, one might try saying that philosophy hasn't anything much to do with cognitive development at all. Perhaps the interest in doing philosophy and the ability to do it well is something that occurs in childhood quite independently of the capacities cognitive psychologists are interested in.

Of course we can make "cognitive development" a technical term for whatever is revealed by Piaget's arresting experiments. And then it will be true, I think, that philosophy has very little to do with cognitive development – whatever cognitive development, so understood, turns out to be, that is, whatever the best account of those arresting experiments should turn out to be. (It might turn out, say, that those differential responses are largely a matter of progressive socialization. But I needn't take any stand on that question here.)

This last move invites the obvious question, should we as parents and teachers be interested in philosophical thinking in young children, rather than just cognitive development – where cognitive development is now taken to be simply the Piagetian stuff? I myself think the answer is clearly "Yes." But whether or not I am right, we get no help from the now trivialized truth that philosophy has little to do with cognitive development.

Let's return, though, to the fourth-grade teacher, who took me aback with his question, "What's the thought of fourth-graders like?" I think he assumed I could tell him something interesting and worthwhile about the *stage* of cognitive development characteristic of fourth-graders, maybe that I could recount some arresting experimental results in the fashion of Piaget and give him a little theory to help him make those arresting results intelligible to himself.

I may have left the impression earlier that I, as a philosopher, could certainly do no such thing. But in fact I think there is a service philosophers can render to nonphilosophical parents and teachers that is at least partially analogous to what the fourth-grade teacher wanted me to do for him.

Philosophers, in devoting their lives to the study of the profoundly naïve questions of philosophy, can help nonphilosophical parents and teachers to recognize and appreciate some of the naïvely profound questions of childhood. It isn't that a philosopher can say, "At age five you can expect your daughter, if she is normal, to be concerned with the problem of the external world." Or: "At age seven you can expect your son, if he is developmentally on track, to be preoccupied with the problem of induction."

What a professional philosopher can do is to collect examples of philosophical thinking in young children and then, by linking those childish thoughts to our philosophical tradition, help parents and teachers to recognize philosophy in their children, respect it when it appears, and even participate in it and encourage it on occasion.

Consider this anecdote from Christa Wolf's recent novel, *Storfall*. Hans-Ludwig Freese (1989) begins his wonderful book, *Kinder sind Philosophen*, with this wonderful passage. The narrator is having a telephone conversation with her daughter about the daughter's son, a boy of presumably six to eight years of age. The boy's mother talks first, then the grandmother, that is, the book's narrator.

> *"He roars around outside the whole day on his bicycle . . . Otherwise he occupies himself with the basic questions of existence. Today, for example, sitting on the potty he asked his father through the door, 'How does the big bathroom door get through my small eye?'"*

> *"For heaven's sake," I said; "and what happened then?"*

> *"Naturally his father produced a precise drawing for him: the bathroom door, the eye, in which the rays of light cross, the route through the optic nerve to the visual centre in the brain, and that it is the business of the brain to enlarge the tiny image in the consciousness of the observer to the normal size of a bathroom door."*

> *"Well? Did that satisfy him?"*

> *"You know him. Do you know what he said? – 'And how can I be certain that my brain really makes the bathroom door the right size?'"*

> *"Well," I said after a pause; "what do you think? How can we be certain?"*

> *"Stop it!" said my daughter; "not you, too!"*

Although this incident appears in a novel, it is almost surely based on a real-life event. Let's call the child, who is given no name in the story, "Karl."

Karl's worry about how the bathroom door, which is big, can get through his eye, which is small, is a little like a worry my own son once had, a worry I report on in the following passage from *Philosophy and the Young Child*.

> I am tucking my eight-year-old son, John, in bed. He looks up at me and asks, quite without warning, "Daddy, why don't I see you double, because I have two eyes and I can see you with each one by itself?"
>
> What do I say?
>
> First, I try to make sure that I understand what is puzzling him.
>
> "You have two ears," I point out. "Are you surprised you don't hear double?"
>
> John grins. "What is hearing double?"
>
> "Well, maybe my-my voi-voice wo-would s-sound li-like thi-this," I say.
>
> He reflects. "But your ears both go to the same place."
>
> "And couldn't it be that your eyes both go to the same place?" I suggest.
>
> He gets serious, thinks, then grins again. "You're just giving me another problem," he protests. "I want to think about the one I already have."
>
> Fair enough. "Maybe," I suggest, "it's because the picture you get with your left eye comes together with the picture you get with your right eye. When they come together they make one picture."
>
> We experiment with two fingers, one closer to our eyes, the other farther away. We try focusing now on one, now on the other. The aim is to see how, by focusing on the nearer finger, we can see the farther one double and vice versa. The moral is supposed to be that the two pictures don't always come together to make one, though they usually do.
>
> My son is not satisfied. It turns out that he has constructed for himself, elaborating in various ways on what he has learned at school about vision and the retinal image, a complex theory of vision according to which one image comes through each eye, is reversed, rereversed, and then projected in front of the subject. No wonder he is worried about why we don't see double!
>
> I suggest several ways of simplifying his theory, but he won't accept simplifications.
>
> "I'll have to think about is some more," he says. "I'll talk to you again after I get it worked out." (Matthews, 1980, pp. 8-9)

John's schoolteacher, like Karl's father, seems to have thought that the fact that we have retinal images explains how we can see. But, as philosophers from Descartes and Leibniz right down to the present day have pointed out, the fact that we have retinal images brings with it problems of its own. We have two retinal images, yet normally we don't see double: why? (John) Or: Okay, so projecting an image onto the retina, in fact a *very small* image onto the retina, is how a big object like the bathroom door gets into something as small as an eye. But how can the brain use a tiny image to figure out what size things really are? Does it in fact generally figure out what size things really are? (Karl)

I don't think there is any age, such that it is natural for children of that age to ask why it is that we don't generally see double. Nor do I think that there is any standard age for them to ask how the large objects one sees can get through the small opening in one's eye, or how we can be certain that one's brain makes the bathroom door seem the right size. Yet many young children do puzzle over vision, and many puzzle over it in a genuinely philosophical way.

In any case, Karl's questions, like John's, are an invitation to do philosophy. A parent or teacher who doesn't hear the questions, or doesn't understand that they are more than, and different from, a mere request for information, misses a chance to do philosophy. That parent or teacher also misses out on something interesting and important about Karl, and other children like him. It is something Piaget's remarkable experiments will not help us to appreciate. If anything, they stand in the way.

If I am right about all of this, or even some of it, then it is imperative that we not let the results of Piaget's genuinely remarkable experiments set our educational agenda or define for us the capacity for thought and reflection in our young children.

References

Freese, H.-L. (1989). *Kinder sind philosophen*. Berlin: Quadriga Verlag.

Matthews, G. B. (1988). Philosophy as a rational reconstruction of childhood. *Canadian Children 13*, 56-69.

Matthews, G. B. (1984). *Dialogues with children*. Cambridge: Harvard University Press.

Matthews, G. B. (1980). *Philosophy and the young child*. Cambridge: Harvard University Press.

Piaget, J. and Inhelder, B. (1974). *The child's construction of quantities*. London: Routledge & Kegan Paul.

CHAPTER 5

Whole Language and Philosophy for Children

A Dialog of Hope

John P. Portelli and Susan Church

The dialog that we present here is an edited version of the one that emerged as a result of several conversations in which we identified common issues and concerns we have encountered in our practices as teacher educators. We have both worked closely with and in support of teachers' attempts to offer a more meaningful and challenging education. Susan has worked with teachers interested in whole language; John has worked with teachers interested in developing philosophical discussions in schools. Teaching critically is never easy; we are almost constantly being faced by the habitual, routine activities in which we find ourselves submerged. So while the dialog is critical of myths and misinterpretations that we have encountered, our aim is not to denigrate the work of teachers. The aim of the dialog is to offer a background and to identify and clarify theoretical and practical issues about "whole language" and "doing philosophy with children." It also aims to explore the relationship between whole language and doing philosophy with children and to raise some of the concerns we have encountered in relation to both "movements."

We agree that these two "movements" share several common beliefs and practices and hence we view them as being complementary. Unfortunately, there are commonly-held beliefs and practices associated with both "movements" — beliefs and practices which have created myths or misinterpretations that have hindered a critical development in the theory and practice of both "movements." Such myths have created an alienation from critical teaching and a reification of narrow, technocratic, traditional teaching. Both situations are problematic for us. The former discourages us from dealing with serious and difficult problems in teaching; the latter reduces teaching to a blind habit.

We hope that this dialog offers at least a first step at eliminating some of the myths and misinterpretations that hinder the development of critical teaching. We purposely offer our ideas and reflections in the form of a dialog. This format, in contrast to parliamentarian debates, offered us the possibility to begin to genuinely and honestly inquire into issues that matter to us and that, we believe, are also of concern to teachers. This dialog is not complete: while it offers clarifications and our views on the issues discussed, it also offers questions and the invitation for further discussion.

We would like to acknowledge the questions, dilemmas, and challenges that teachers have offered us in our work. This dialog would have never taken place were it not for such responses. We also acknowledge the support of some of our colleagues who have read and commented on earlier versions of this dialog. In particular, we are extremely grateful to Ann Vibert for her encouragement and her prompt, detailed, critical, and yet always supportive comments.

Part One

Susan : The term whole language is frequently attributed to Ken Goodman (1992), but he makes a strong point of saying, "I didn't found whole language. Whole language found me." He wants it made clear that it emerged about twenty years ago both as a movement and as a name among North American teachers. Although it is frequently referred to as a method for teaching reading and writing, whole language is really a philosophical stance, a theoretical framework for how humans learn. The idea of "whole" language came in response to the very strong skills-model of literacy instruction, based on a behaviorist learning theory, that dominated in North America for many years. In that model, literacy development is seen as mastering the parts (letters, sounds, words, sentences) first and then building meaning from them. In a whole language model, meaning comes first. Children read and write for real purposes from the very beginning and, through this meaningful use of language, gradually learn about the parts. The wholeness also comes from the belief that all aspects of language (reading, writing, speaking, listening, viewing, representing) are mutually supportive and integrated. At one time we used to have a separate "creative writing" time that had no connection with what children were reading. Of course, there is a great deal more to it than that, which we'll get to later I'm sure, but that is my understanding of why the term came into use.

John : Whole language, then, started in the 1970s in reaction to a certain learning theory with regard to language. And in contrast to the behaviorist learning theory, whole language proponents formulated a counter theory of learning for language. Is this theory also applied to areas other than language learning? Does it have implications for things other than language arts? I realize this can be an awkward question because it may be seen that I am assuming that everything has to be neatly carved into little niches here and there called subjects. I do not have a problem with distinguishing different perspectives or subjects, as long as one does not close any connections or relations between these perspectives or subjects. The question still arises: How will a whole-language teacher do science, math, social studies, or whatever?

S : I suppose to be more precise we should talk about whole *learning* because the underlying learning theory certainly does apply to all subject areas. As I look at current thinking in mathematics, science, or social studies education, it seems to me there are more and more commonalities among the disciplines in terms of philosophy and practice. Many teachers who work from a whole language perspective make an effort to integrate the curriculum so that learners can make connections among all they are learning. Some of the most effective classrooms I've seen are ones in which interesting topics in social studies or science become a major focus and all forms of language are used as tools for exploring these content areas. Here, surely, philosophy ought to contribute, as we help children to think, talk, and write critically about important issues.

J : Yes, especially if philosophy is seen as an activity as in for example "*doing* philosophy with children."

S : So there is a difference between "philosophy for children" and "*doing* philosophy with children?"

J : The phrase "philosophy for children" has different meanings. It refers to the program developed by Matthew Lipman and his associates at the Institute for the Advancement of Philosophy for Children (I.A.P.C.) in the 1970s and early 1980s. But it also refers to the very idea and practice of doing philosophy with children. Lipman's program is only one way of introducing philosophy to children or one way of doing philosophy with children. Ronald Reed (1987) has noted that twenty years after Lipman's original idea, "philosophy for children is, in many ways a movement of more-or-less like-minded individuals" (p. 82). The notion of a "movement" indicates progress such as an increased interest on the part of educationists, philosophers, and philosophers of education, and the undertaking of serious empirical and theoretical research in the field. But the notion of a movement also indicates change and variation. Thus, some within the movement, while acknowledging Lipman's seminal work and sympathetic to the original aims and ideal, have been reviewing the work done in the last two decades, identifying some problems, dealing with other contemporary movements, such as whole language, feminist pedagogy, critical pedagogy, and postmodernism, and suggesting alternatives.

S : But are there some common or basic assumptions underlying the movement, as you call it?

J : Notwithstanding the differences and variations within the movement, there are some commonly held assumptions. These assumptions are not meant to be seen as a doctrine. First of all is the view that philosophy is seen as an activity and not as a dead body of knowledge which people have to learn by heart and reproduce in exams. Neither is philosophy, contrary to popular conceptions, seen as a general belief system or a set of principles arising from a general perspective about the world and from which, it is purported, follow specific guidelines or strategies for solving practical dilemmas. Philosophy is seen primarily as an activity which involves the critical inquiry and discussion of concepts, beliefs, assumptions, and practices. And the purpose of this activity is not a matter of winning or losing an argument, as is sometimes perceived.

S : I should think a real difficulty in interesting teachers in doing philosophy in the classroom would be their preconceived notions about it.

J : Yes. It happens so frequently that you get used to it. Mind you, this is not a notion that only teachers hold.

S : Many of us, me included, remember philosophy as a class we took early in our undergraduate careers in which we read many dense and difficult texts by long-dead philosophers and tried to make sense of the various schools of philosophy in order to come up with the right answers on exams. Until quite recently, I know philosophy was not something I thought *I* would find very relevant to my life, much less to the lives of children I might teach. But, the way you describe it and the way I have seen some teachers use it in their classrooms, it seems to me it has great relevance. But, I interrupted you, what are some other assumptions?

J : That's quite all right. It is these very "interruptions" that form the core of doing philosophy and make it exciting. But I'll continue with another assumption. Children are seen in a positive light. It is held that children are capable of engaging in philosophical inquiry if some conditions are met: they are provided with a rich philosophical environment; they are encouraged to raise and engage in philosophical questions which are of interest to them; ordinary language is used in the discussions. This view of children challenges both the conservative and romantic liberal views. While it is not being argued that children are "full-fledged philosophers," the traditional view that children are totally immature persons capable only of receiving factual information is rejected. And so is the romantic liberal stance that since children are essentially good, they will develop their natural qualities positively if they are not hindered by adult intervention. From the philosophy-for-children perspective children are seen as being capable of doing certain things (including philosophical inquiry) but they need nurturing. This is neither meant as a mediocre stance nor a *via media* to sort of appease both conservatives and liberals. It is meant as a realistic position or as Michael Pritchard calls it, a "hopist" stance which avoids the pitfalls of both extremes. (See chapter 1 by Michael Pritchard in this collection).

S : In my work with teachers in relationship to whole language, I have found this problem of polar extremes very difficult to deal with. The debate over whole language vs. skills-based instruction is based on the notion that we can only take one of two stances. The reasoning seems to go: whole language advocates believe direct teacher intervention is harmful, so if some of us associated with whole language begin to talk and write about how teachers might intervene to support children's development of language skills, it means whole language is dead. The famous pendulum has taken another swing. We seem destined to couch all these complex issues in polarities. I find it very frustrating, especially when certain beliefs are attributed to me simply because someone has heard I belong to the "whole language camp." From what I've seen of the "communities of inquiry" created by teachers doing philosophy with children, that's the very sort of either/or thinking they try to avoid.

J : This problem of polarities is rather unfortunate, especially when we realize that it is not a new problem at all. Dewey (1938), for example, spoke quite frequently and fervently about the problems of the "either/or" mentality. This issue gets me to the third assumption, the belief of the importance of the idea and practice of a community of inquiry in developing philosophical inquiry. Philosophy as an activity can be done in private or in a public forum. The emphasis here is on philosophical discussions with others who are willing and able to discuss issues of common concern. The community of inquiry is meant to provide the support and testing ground

needed in developing one's ideas. Such a community is characterized by: open-mindedness; willingness and ability to express one's
views honestly but in a non-threatening manner; acceptance of
criticism with no hurt; sincerity; genuine support to each other, even
if members disagree; trust; genuine curiosity and eagerness to
inquire; willingness to look for assumptions and provide reasons in
support of one's position; and willingness to change one's view if
"evidence" shows otherwise. This is different from either striving
to achieve consensus or promoting an anything-goes attitude. All
of this, it is argued, is central to the development, sustenance and
reconstruction of a democracy. How can we have a democracy if
people are not prepared to question, discuss, if necessary, challenge,
and attempt to change things?

S : But that's what's so scary about philosophy and about whole
language for many individual teachers and certainly for school
systems. How will our authoritarian, bureaucratic institutions – or
our orderly, teacher-directed classrooms – run if everyone starts
asking questions, and even worse, challenges and tries to change
things? In the current restructuring movement we have a great deal
of rhetoric about empowerment and school-based decision making,
but not much concrete evidence of power shifts. And, to be realistic,
many teachers have been acculturated to the way things have been
done for years, and find the idea of empowerment threatening – it
certainly means taking more responsibility as well as having more
say. We just don't have a tradition for that in the institution.

J : Yes, and not much of this really happens in schools. Unfortunately
schools are still set up and administered as though the aims and
context of schooling are still exactly the same as when compulsory
schooling was introduced about a century ago! My point is that if
we are serious about democracy, then philosophy has to be taken
seriously as well. Doing philosophy and developing democratic
attitudes and dispositions are intertwined, and both require practice
or doing. This does not exclude the need for direction and modelling
from an adult who is aware of the philosophical dimension. Neither
is it assumed that everything has to be learnt by doing or is best
learnt by doing. But with philosophy, given that it is an activity, that
very activity is best learnt by actually being engaged in that kind of
activity. And this holds not just for children but also for adults. This
actually leads me to another assumption, which is really an extension of the third one, namely that teachers will best learn to do, and

to help others to do, philosophy if they themselves have had preparation which involved doing it.

S : How are those assumptions translated into classroom practice? Can you give some examples of what it means when a teacher "does" philosophy for children?

J : A very direct reply is: by attempting to do philosophy as described above. Of course, to be able to do philosophy one would be better off if one is aware of the philosophical dimensions and the nature of philosophical inquiry. (The same can be said for any subject or area of study/inquiry.) We have to start somewhere. A reasonable starting point would be for the teacher to create an environment or provide "materials" that are rich with philosophical issues.

A typical session would consist of a short reading of a selection or viewing of a film or any other "material" rich in philosophical issues that interest the children, followed by a reaction of the students to the materials. The teacher keeps track of the leading issues or ideas that result from their reaction, and these ideas or issues will form the agenda for analysis and discussion (not the same as an exposition of the teacher's interpretation of these issues). In the initial phases, the teacher, as the leader of the discussions, will have to "model" for the students by keeping track of the points made, intervening by asking questions that move the discussion forward, making occasional comments in order to help clarify the difference between a philosophical perspective from other perspectives with regard to the issue at hand, encouraging them to compare differing points of views, carefully demanding clarifications and reasons when these are lacking, and so on. Of course, an insightful teacher will learn to balance his or her interventions while allowing and encouraging the students to express their views, question one another's ideas and those of the teacher. This is a very crucial point, especially if students are not used to engaging in any form of discussion. Eventually students will get used to this approach and they will ask to lead discussions themselves. In those instances, the teacher, as a participant or member of the community of inquiry, will still have the responsibility to guide the discussion as necessary, but never to a predetermined or fixed point. The direction of the inquiry ought to be determined by the nature of the questions asked or the problem posed and by the kind of replies and further questions that arise in the inquiry.

S : That requires some sophistication on the part of the teacher and of the students, doesn't it?

J : Of course. And I would add patience and stamina.

S : I am reminded of the beginnings of process writing. When we first started holding conferences with children about their writing, many of us struggled with what to ask when we ran out of the series of questions we had seen in books and articles about process writing. We found the questions really did not take us very far when we sat down with a student to talk about the writing. What we had to do is get beyond the stock questions to authentic responses to the writer and to the piece: How do I react to this piece as a reader? Did it grab my attention? Where did the writer lose me? What is this writer trying to do? These sorts of questions lead to a genuine discussion, as both writer and teacher contribute to solving whatever problems the piece might be posing. In the end, to be an effective teacher of writing, I had to write myself and participate in conferences as a writer. Through that, I learned what kinds of questions and responses were helpful.

J : In philosophy, too, if a predetermined or pre-established path channels the direction of the discourse, in the sense that the teacher will only allow or expect one kind of reply, the one he or she really wants to hear, then of course, no discussion has really taken place. This approach owes a lot to the Socratic Method, that is the method of discussion, inquiry, "teaching" employed by Socrates as captured primarily in the early Platonic dialogs (Portelli, 1990); the Socrates who says to Critias in the *Charmides*: "you come to me as though I professed to know about the questions which I ask . . . Whereas the fact is that I am inquiring with you into the truth of that which is advanced from time to time, just because I do not know; and when I have inquired, I will say whether I agree with you or not. Please then allow me time to reflect."

S : This notion of philosophy as an activity and the practices that flow from it surely connect with the whole learning perspective that emphasizes the importance of encouraging and helping children to think, talk, and write critically.

J : I find your reference to whole learning important. It reminds me of practitioners claiming that there are different interpretations of whole language. Are there any common or basic elements?

S : The biggest problem in explaining whole language is that it isn't simply a method or approach; it is a theoretical framework, a set of beliefs. Perhaps, at the risk of over-simplifying something that gets more complex the more you know about it, I will give you a list of assumptions that Judith Newman and I used in an article we wrote a few years ago (Newman and Church, 1990):

Learning

is social;

requires risk-taking and experimentation;

involves constructing meaning and relating new information to prior knowledge;

occurs when learners are actively involved, when they have real purposes, when they make choices and share in decision-making;

uses language, mathematics, art, music, drama, and other communication systems as vehicles for exploration. (pp. 23-24)

I see the beliefs about learning as fundamental; the most important aspects of whole language.

J : Is it being assumed that there is only one learning theory applicable to all learning situations and which is best for all children? As I raise this question, I am immediately reminded of Jane Roland Martin talking about how she learned to serve in tennis. Let me read a bit of that:

Consider this example. Tennis instructors are fond of saying: 'Watch my racket as I serve the ball.' I, for one, can watch till doomsday without its having any apparent effect on my serve, while my more visually oriented colleagues proceed to hit aces. No doubt some of these fast learners have more aptitude for the game than I. But not all. When finally the instructor analyzes the serving motion verbally, introduces a meaningful metaphor, tells me to listen to the sound the ball makes, or takes hold of my arm and puts it through the correct motions, my serve will equal my colleagues'. Where education is concerned, natural talent is only part of the story. People with similar talents often learn in different ways. . . . To the extent that people learn differently, they require different educational treatment to attain the same ends. (1985, p. 19)

S : I think if there are aspects of a learning theory that don't apply, perhaps the learning theory has not been articulated fully or that it is being interpreted too narrowly. I think there is a great deal we don't know about human learning, so we have to be open to changing our theories based upon new information. Margaret Meek

Spencer (1993), one of our most generative thinkers in the area of literacy learning and teaching, frequently warns about the danger of final answers. She suggests the most important question is, "What if it's otherwise?" It seems to me that question causes us to examine what we believe and what we do continually, rather than expecting that some day we will arrive at "the truth" forevermore. But some whole language proponents certainly do present their views as "final truths."

J : Yes, unfortunately I have encountered that. Here it would be helpful to distinguish between having *an* answer in contrast to having *the* answer, in the sense that nothing will make one change the answer even if evidence shows otherwise. It is the latter which exemplifies dogmatism and disregards differences in contexts. Inquiring with the aim of trying to make sense, of arriving at some kind of a resolution or answer, in itself, is not problematic to me. This stance, which is captured by the notion of "tentative conclusions" and "reasonableness" in philosophy for children, contrasts with either extreme subjectivism (which leads to contradictions and an "anything goes" mentality) or dogmatism of the traditional kind.

S : I like your notion of resolution.

J : Of course, I mean a resolution for the moment.

S : But it provides you something to hook on to, so to speak.

J : Yes, and some sense of direction or vision. Even if at times the vision gets muddied or blurred. We can talk more about this if you wish, but I am curious about some things you said about the qualities about learning you mentioned earlier.

S : Fine. Go ahead.

J : I realize that the qualities about learning you listed cannot all be elaborated here. I do not really disagree with any of those qualities. And I think none of the philosophy-with-children proponents would really argue against these qualities. My question is: Are these necessary conditions for learning to take place? For example, if one is not in a social context (say I am reading alone in my office) does that mean that one cannot learn? Or am I misunderstanding the meaning of "learning is social?" Is there no other kind of learning other than social learning?

S : To me, social learning does not necessarily imply that I am always learning with someone else. In fact, I think that has become one of the "myths" of whole language – that children must always be learning in groups. It does mean, however, that knowledge is socially constructed – that our understanding of the world is shaped by the social community. The meaning we bring to our experiences is mediated by our social context. So, while I might be learning by reading a book alone in a room or by exploring some ideas in writing, that is still social learning in the sense that I can never not be part of the social context within which I live and learn. And, whole language theory certainly suggests my learning will be enhanced if, after I generate some ideas through reading and writing by myself, I seek out some other people to talk with about what I am thinking. So, one of the important instructional implications of whole language is that children should have many opportunities for interaction with each other and with adults. In some ways, of course, I am never really reading or writing alone; I am always in conversation with the author, even when that author is me.

J : Your point about having opportunities reminds me of your earlier point that learning involves choices. Does this mean that no learning takes place at all when one makes no choices?

S : The issue of choice, too, cannot be interpreted too narrowly. It's another aspect that has resulted in the myth that children should always be able to choose what they do in the classroom; the teacher should never impose. It seems to me in every learning situation the learner does choose: to engage or not engage, to attend to certain aspects and to ignore others, to solve a problem one way and not another. In a whole language environment, the teacher might, in fact, ask children to try a certain kind of writing or to think about a particular set of questions in response to a text, but he or she would invite the children's active involvement in exploring how best to carry out either task, encouraging them to think about the choices they make along the way and to reflect upon the consequences of making different kinds of choices either in writing or reading.

J : This seems very similar to the role of the teacher in developing philosophical discussions. While allowing for teacher intervention when necessary, the power relation in the class changes: the power relation between teacher and students and students themselves ought to be more cooperative, open, and less threatening than the one found in traditional classrooms. Now the teacher is no longer viewed as the purveyor of all the truth who mechanically implements a totally pre-planned curriculum irrespective of the context. Mere teacher didactic talk will give way to the give and take of open yet constructive discussions. While the teacher retains the ultimate responsibility, the students are realistically and prudently invited to share in this responsibility.

S : As I reflect on that list of qualities of learning, I think I would revise it now to convey a stronger political stance. Increasingly, for me, a whole language agenda is becoming a political agenda. When teachers begin creating classroom contexts based upon the principles above, it changes the power relationships within the classrooms. The teacher no longer dominates; instead teachers and children share control. A major goal in a whole language classroom is to help children to assume responsibility, to make decisions, to work as part of a learning community, and to reflect upon both what and how they are learning. The political agenda extends beyond the classroom, however. It suggests a change in power relationships in the institution, one that vests much greater decision making in the classroom, where, to my mind, it belongs. But, it challenges a great deal of the way we do business in our hierarchical, authoritarian school systems.

J : Your point about the change of power relations in class reminds me of an incident which I will never forget. This incident happened at the one-month summer institute I attended at I.A.P.C. in 1983. We were about seventeen people in all (including Ann Margaret Sharp and Matthew Lipman) from eight different countries – an excellent, unforgettable, community-building experience. At any rate, the incident is about one of the participants in the institute who was quite conservative at first about pedagogical issues, but very sharp philosophically and very open about his views. We became very good friends and still correspond. I will never forget the look on his face, when after a week working together as a group, one evening we chatted for three hours exactly on the changes of the power relations needed if we are going to take philosophical discussions with children (or any one for that matter) seriously. He was really getting into the methodology (not just the methods or procedures). He was used to lecturing to big numbers of students taking philosophy at the university level. At the end of the conversation, he sort of grabbed his hair and gently banged his head on the table while exclaiming: "Incredible! All of that excitement of talking to big numbers of students! All of that has to change!"

S : Surely that was also a powerful example of how the social context shapes our thinking!

J : Your point about reflecting on the social context reminds me of the fact that Matthew Lipman really came up with the idea of philosophy for children when, as a full professor of philosophy at Columbia University in New York, he reflected on the student unrest of the late 1960s as well as the kind of teaching that existed both in universities and schools. His conclusion was that we need to take philosophical thinking seriously at an early stage. And he pondered how to do that without replicating the traditional methods that were not working. It is exactly his reflection on his social context that made him arrive at the theoretical and practical stances about philosophical discussions with children via a community of inquiry.

S : Yes, that is also another example of what I have been saying. You mentioned the institute at the I.A.P.C. Was that your first encounter with Philosophy for Children?

J : No, it wasn't.

S : When did you first hear about it and what has been your relationship with Philosophy for Children?

J : The first time I heard about Philosophy for Children was in 1979. There was a reference in *Educational Theory* to Lipman's work and the results in schools. I had never made any connections between philosophy and children and simply discounted it. My attitude was a rather closed-minded one until in 1983, I was invited by Judy Kyle to her grade 6 class in a public school in Montreal. Judy Kyle had written a M.A. thesis (1976) in philosophy of education which dealt with the possibilities of doing philosophy with children via language arts. This was entirely the result of a teacher who had a background in philosophy and applied that background to her own classroom – an excellent example of teacher as researcher and intellectual. In this class, 27 grade 6 students, who were seated in a square formation, read a selection from *Harry* by Lipman (1982), identified issues or questions they wanted to discuss, and then actually discussed some of them. And this went on for about an hour. I will never forget this session. It is a landmark for me. It really brought about a turning point in my thinking about (i) the nature of teaching and (ii) the relationship between children and philosophy. I was struck by several things. The children were discussing an issue which they selected themselves, a philosophical issue which they themselves phrased as "What is mind?" They offered differing positions, some support for their positions, and even challenged each other's ideas. It was very obvious that the children were interested and engaged in the lively discussion. They were putting forth "classical" philosophical positions about the nature of mind. And no philosophical jargon; just ordinary language. And no references to any of the philosophical figures. Moreover, the children were the ones who did most of the talking, which was quite rigorous and organized. I learnt later that they were following their own procedures for the discussion – obviously procedures guided by the nature of philosophical inquiry. In short, then, the children were able to raise and engage in philosophical questions and discussion, they were interested and enjoyed what they were doing. Needless to say, I continued to go to Judy's class. And by May 1983, we had done some video tapes of these sessions.

S :   Judy's experience certainly puts in a different perspective some of the criticisms of philosophy that I have heard from a few Nova Scotia teachers. Some have described the practice as highly teacher-directed, with no opportunity for student input. It appears in this situation Judy created opportunities for the children to become highly self-directed; she helped them gain the skills they needed to carry on productive discussions on their own. To my way of thinking, this is not much different from teaching children anything else: to swim, ride a bike, play hockey, or read and write. I wonder how we got in such a muddle with whole language and child-centred learning. I find it hard to fathom that some teachers really believed these stances implied children would learn everything they needed or wanted to without the teacher's intervention. But, that myth certainly dies hard, especially among parents. After working with Judy, what did you do next?

J :   In July 1983, I spent almost a month at the I.A.P.C., which had organized an institute for people who had a background in philosophy and were interested in teacher preparation in this area. Between the fall 1983 and 1985, Judy and I organized several workshops. Given the context in Quebec, namely the required classes in moral education (for those students who either did not have religious education or who wanted a combination of both), there were lots of possibilities for philosophy for children to flourish in the schools.

In August 1985, I came to Halifax. The context here was very different from Montreal. Very little interest in moral/values education. The buzz word was "whole language." Since I started teaching at Mount Saint Vincent University, I have conducted several workshops for teachers on the topic and a graduate seminar for teachers on the topic almost every year. And I have worked with two teachers who have written a M.A. thesis on philosophy for children. As a result of this, 3 years ago we formed a support group for teachers interested in philosophical discussions. The nature and membership of the group changes as usually happens with support groups. The approach to teaching taken by philosophy for children requires lots of follow-ups and supportive work among teachers. I wish I had more time to work *with* teachers, not to dictate to them!

S : You came to Halifax when we were in the honeymoon stage of whole language. As I look back, it was a very exciting time. We were challenging a great many of the firmly held assumptions about how to teach reading and writing. We were opening up our classrooms to a whole wealth of children's literature. Our children were writing and publishing their own books. Some of us began to write ourselves and to have our first pieces published in books and journals. I can see how you, as an outsider to the community, would feel there wasn't much place for what you were doing. It is only as whole language has evolved and a number of us have come to understand it as much more than a theory for literacy learning, that we have seen the connections. Not everyone who espouses whole language, of course, has moved in that direction, but those of us who have read the critical theorists (Freire and Macedo, 1987; Giroux, 1987; Mitchell and Weiler, 1991; Simon, 1987) and become interested in feminist pedagogy (Brookes, 1992; Gilligan, 1982; Gilligan et al., 1990; Smith, 1987; Weiler, 1988) have broadened our perspectives considerably – as have many of the teachers who have taken your courses and participated in workshops. And it seems that there has been considerable interest in philosophy for children among teachers in Nova Scotia. How *are* people using philosophy for children in their classrooms?

J : I am not sure how widespread either the interest or the practice is. Perhaps you are in a position to have a better idea of that since you meet more teachers than I do. Since 1986 just over 100 teachers have taken the graduate class on philosophy for children. As far as I know, most teachers start doing philosophy at a separate time and then eventually incorporate it into the rest of the curriculum. Some still have some separate time for "philosophical discussions" while allowing it to happen in all other areas. Some teachers have also made connections between doing philosophy and "critical/feminist pedagogy." I would like to see more of this in practice. But I know that it is hard especially with (i) the popular misinterpretations about whole language and sometimes even the cult of whole language and (ii) the conservative critique of schools.

S : It's not only that, John. I find it is becoming more and more difficult to engage teachers in considering innovative practices of any sort. They are under pressure to have their children do well on standardized tests, they have an increasingly challenging group of students to deal with, the families of their children and they themselves are feeling the stresses of this protracted recession, and they seem to be garnering criticism from every quarter these days. Ironically, of course, it is the very sort of curriculum that you envision that would help students and teachers grapple with the complex issues that face them – that would, perhaps, help them to feel less powerless.

J : I agree and that is why I would also like to see more formal recognition from, for example, the Department of Education of the need and value to have these kind of discussions and explicit attention to dealing with value issues in teaching. It is hard to encourage something (in whatever form) when it does not have the formal recognition that other subjects or movements have. It can be very disheartening both for me and the teachers when what you do is continuously treated as a frill. It is a continuous struggle. But then, that has been the history of philosophy in relation to schools/educational institutions especially in North America (I think the situation is quite different in Europe). The irony, of course, is that the continent that proclaims and boasts to be the backbone of democracy ought to have been more accepting of the spirit of philosophical discussion central to the sustenance of democracy itself! And this should be reflected in schools as well. But the massive technocratic influence on education, which, for example, in our context has been revived via the resurgence of the narrow, standardized testing, militates against this vision of teaching. And, of course, this philosophical perspective toward teaching arises from a certain vision of the good life.

S :   Some of the problems and dilemmas you encountered are similar to ones I have encountered as I continue to work with and support teacher's work in relation to issues of whole language.

J :   Before we move to these problems and dilemmas, I should ask you what has been your relationship with whole language.

S :   I first encountered these ideas in the mid 1970s when I began reading the work of Ken Goodman (1967, 1973), Frank Smith (1971, 1978), and others (Cambourne, 1977; Ryan and Semmel, 1969). The ideas had appeal to me because I was very frustrated with my experiences in trying to teach children with learning problems in my role as a reading/resource support teacher. I knew that systematic skills instruction wasn't working for them and I was looking for another way. Not long after I moved to Halifax in 1979, I did a summer workshop with Judith Newman and became intrigued by what she was saying about how children learn to read. I began taking courses from her and then joined a study group. Over the years, I changed both my beliefs and practices profoundly. I began to write about what I was doing and thinking and have continued to publish articles in books and journals. As I mentioned above, however, things are less clear than when I began. I have more questions than answers, the more I think about the implications of the belief system for the classroom and for the institution, especially the shift in power relationships.

J :   It is not unusual for educators in Canada to refer to Nova Scotia as a province that has welcomed whole language. How did this come about? How were teachers prepared?

S :   Whole language began with individual teachers, like me, questioning what we were doing. Our inquiry was well supported by teacher educators like Judith Newman, then at Mount Saint Vincent University, David Doake, then at Acadia University, and Andrew Manning of Mount Saint Vincent University, early in the 1980s and later by others in the universities. We also had strong leadership from the provincial Department of Education. The late Patricia Barnes, the language arts consultant, understood how to build teacher networks and how to support the change process. Professional organizations, such as the local and provincial International Reading Association groups, brought in many resource people to present at conferences and workshops. In 1986 the Department published a curriculum guideline (Nova Scotia Department of Education, 1986) that mandated a holistic language arts program.

J : How was the program received? What changes did it bring about to teacher development?

S : With that directive came the usual problems of large-scale, top-down implementation. District school boards, many of which did not have the resources to provide sufficient leadership for the change, varied in their approaches to implementation. Most provided their teachers some in-service training, many purchased new literature-based language arts materials, and some made a commitment to long-term staff development. Many teachers engaged in their own professional development through university courses, conferences, study groups, and individual reading. Now, a number of years down the road, we have many teachers who have the necessary theoretical understandings to develop practice based upon whole language principles. We also have many teachers who have incorporated a number of whole language practices, but do not have a strong theory base.

J : I wonder whether this last point together with a top-down implementation have contributed to some of the issues (concerns, problems) that have arisen as whole language became popularized. What are some of these issues?

S : Right now we are experiencing a wide-spread backlash against whole language from parents. Their primary concerns are about a perceived lack of attention to phonics, spelling, and grammar. I think we do have some problems in this area, mainly because of the weaknesses in our approaches to implementation. We really did not help teachers to understand enough about how children learn language and thus many are confused about how to help children develop the necessary skills like spelling and grammar within a whole language context. There also has been confusion about the role of the teacher; I think for a time, many teachers were reluctant to intervene when children needed support because they thought that kind of instruction wasn't part of whole language.

J : This seems like the same kind of problem I have encountered in philosophy for children seminars when teachers claim that teacher intervention is not natural.

S : We also have done a poor job of helping parents understand what we are trying to do. There are still many parents who have no idea why it is important to let children experiment with language, for example to use functional spelling as they get their ideas down. They see these attempts as misspellings that will become bad habits to be unlearned later. We need to find ways of truly including parents as partners in their children's learning and to foster three-way communication among teachers, parents, and children.

One of my biggest concerns, however, is that, in many classrooms, we haven't moved beyond the surface trappings of whole language. We have some different kinds of activities going on and children are doing more reading and writing, but the agenda is still tightly controlled by the teacher. We haven't created communities of learners who are engaged in purposeful inquiries. Most of the questions are still teacher questions, often ones to which the teacher already knows the answer. To promote those kinds of changes, we need to provide a different kind of professional development for teachers, experiences that give them opportunities to participate in those kinds of learning environments themselves, and to reflect philosophically on them.

J : Given that philosophy is a critical inquiry that attempts to clarify issues, unearth assumptions, and seek reasons or justifications for our beliefs, views, and actions, yes, I agree the philosophical dimension would help. What I hear you saying is that the philosophical element is missing. Am I correct? And I do not say this because I believe that philosophy is a panacea to all the educational ills. That would be a scary position. I simply hold that philosophy helps.

S : Yes, I think the philosophical element is missing. But, unfortunately, I think philosophy, like research, is seen as Philosophy with a capital "P" by many people, something that men with grey beards do! Recently, there has been a strong "teacher as researcher" movement in which teachers, themselves, inquire into questions about their own practice, often not in a formal way, but as part of being teachers. Reflective teaching is a form of research. In the same way, it seems to me, philosophy is a way of thinking that is accessible to all of us, not just people who have studied philosophy in a formal sense. Like research, however, philosophy has tools we can learn to use to help us be more effective. And, the kinds of questions posed through philosophical discussions are important ones that help both teachers and children to become better thinkers. And, it seems to me engaging in philosophical discussions does hold promise of creating the kinds of communities of inquiry envisioned by many of us who espouse a whole language philosophy.

J : But if the teacher does not ask these kind of questions, and/or the students are not allowed or given the freedom to wonder philosophically – and that may be for various reasons – then, we may never actually create communities of learners.

S : You seem to be talking now about problems arising from common misperceptions of philosophy. We've experienced the development of myths and misconceptions surrounding whole language. Do you see similar difficulties with philosophy for children?

J : Yes, I am talking about some misperceptions about philosophy, which surely do not help people see the worthwhileness of the philosophical dimension. But some do understand the dimension and yet still disregard it. And the reasons for this may be varied. For example, it may be seen as a waste of time, or it may be deemed too alienating for children because they, it is argued, are not really capable of handling philosophical questions. Some may even see it as not being "natural" and hence restrictive.

S : The philosophical dimension doesn't fit very well with reductionist, mechanistic beliefs about learning that still underlie much of what happens in schools, despite our efforts to develop a constructivist theoretical framework for instruction. What about myths that arise from the practice itself?

J : First of all one has to keep in mind that in the province, the idea and practice of doing philosophy with children is not as widespread as whole language. Moreover, philosophy, contrary to the case of whole language, has not been mandated or compelled by the government. I mention this because these two differences have contributed to the development of myths and misconceptions about whole language. So, in this respect, philosophy has an advantage. However, interestingly enough, the myths and misconceptions about whole language have unfortunately contributed to some resistances to and myths about doing philosophy with children. The following are some examples of the myths I have encountered:

(i) Any kind of talk is equivalent to a philosophical discussion. As long as the students are expressing their opinions, then that is fine. We are doing philosophy.

(ii) One can do philosophy with no awareness and knowledge of the philosophical dimension.

(iii) Identifying "materials" for the use of doing philosophy is pre-scriptive and contrived.

(iv) In philosophical discussions with children, the teacher just stands back and never really intervenes in the discussion lest she or he will influence the students' interests and ideas. Intervention is equivalent to indoctrination and not natural.

(v) A community of inquiry is the same as a *philosophical* community of inquiry.

(vi) Philosophical discussions will have to happen accidentally or else they will not be natural. To identify or distinguish philosophical discussions as such is elitist.

(vii) Doing philosophy is equivalent to implementing Lipman's program.

Unfortunately, these myths have contributed to the misperception that philosophy for children and whole language are not compatible. I do not think that is the case. I still think that there are lots of similarities about how they view children, the role of the teacher, the importance of learning by doing, the need to take students' interests seriously, and the importance of the development of democratic attitudes and dispositions in the classroom. Conceptually there are lots of similarities. In practice, however, there are differences. In my view, these differences emerge from a certain element of dogmatism as well as misperceptions about whole language.

S : You're certainly right about the misperceptions about whole language! In the article that Judith Newman and I (1990) wrote that I mentioned earlier, we attempted to challenge a whole series of "myths of whole language." The response to that article, from all areas of North America, certainly confirmed our belief that the problems we identified were not limited to Nova Scotia. It's interesting, too, to note the many parallels with your list. Without repeating everything we wrote in the article, let me just summarize what I see to be the major issues.

*Assuming that the whole language belief in active, learner-directed curriculum means a laissez-faire approach to teaching in which the teacher must keep hands-off: no teaching of skills, no intervention, no expectations, "soft" evaluation, unlimited student choice, and so forth.

*Seeing whole language as a method: all you need is a whole language commercial program; using practices such as small groups, children's literature, or journals makes you a whole language teacher; there is one right way to teach whole language – a recipe.

In the four years since we wrote that article, I can't say that I have seen much change, except, perhaps, to see the confusions and the criticisms increase. It's not surprising, however, since we are not addressing the fundamental changes that need to take place. In our conclusion to the piece, Judith and I tried to capture the enormity of the shift. Here's a bit of what we said:

Whole language isn't an add-on. It's not a frill. We can't just do a little bit of whole language and leave everything else untouched. It's a radically different way of perceiving the relationships between knowledge and the knower, between compliance and responsibility, between learner and teacher, between teacher and administrator, between home and school. Taking a whole language stance makes for a very different classroom – a classroom in which both teachers and students have a voice. (p. 26)

Part Two

After transcribing, editing, and reflecting on Part One, we discussed several issues dealt with in our dialog. As we conversed about these issues, it gradually became clear to us that several of the specific issues following our reactions to Part One are related to a number of major myths we have encountered in our work. These myths arise from misunderstandings about two broader concerns identified both in the literature and practices: the issue of "prescription" and the issue of "the natural/contrived" dichotomy. The dialog in Part Two focuses on these two issues.

S : For many teachers, whole language had appeal because it was such a radical departure from the basal reading programs, worksheets, and other artifacts of skills-based instruction that de-skilled them as teachers. Given the difficulties with basal programs (Goodman et al., 1988), I can understand why some advocates of whole language took very extreme stances in regard to any published materials. I don't disagree with their criticisms of these reading schemes that tell teachers what and how to teach, using materials written specifically to introduce certain words or language patterns rather than to tell a story or present information – to say nothing of gender and cultural bias. And I also see a problem with using meaningless practice exercises to teach skills outside the context of reading and writing and with the teacher tightly controlling what happens in the classroom. Unfortunately, however, this critique seems to have led to a belief that any kind of framework or structure is not consistent with whole language because it is too prescriptive.

From my perspective, this is a serious misreading of whole language.

J : I've seen evidence of that in my classes. Given my understanding of prescription, I used to be quite baffled when I encountered teachers, proponents of whole language, who said, ironically quite prescriptively, that prescription is bad, or prescriptive teaching is bad teaching. The first thing that comes to my mind when I hear the word "prescription" is the order or strong recommendation from a doctor to take a certain medicine given a certain illness. It implies a rather definite direction.

S : But that isn't the only sense of prescription.

J : No, there are other meanings. And that is part of the confusion, I think. The word "prescriptive" is used quite frequently in philosophy to refer to issues or concerns that refer to values or norms. Hence we refer to a "prescriptive stance" in contrast to one that is primarily factual. A prescriptive or normative stance refers to a value or set of values, that is things or beliefs that one considers to be worthwhile. I want to argue that since we do not live in a void, that is, there are no completely neutral contexts, we cannot avoid, directly or indirectly, making or referring to or having a prescriptive stance. To put it bluntly, given that we are human beings who exist in this kind of world, we are continuously involved in value issues. We cannot escape this.

S : And the same can be said with regard to political or power relations in the sense that we cannot help but have political implications for what we do.

J : I agree, and that is why one would end up in a rather contradictory situation if one holds that by rejecting "prescriptive teaching" then all is fine because we are not prescribing. The assumption here, of course, is that we can do away with all elements of prescription and that all prescriptions are of the same kind. I think now I understand more what they meant to say. These teachers were reacting to the fact that in the past they were constantly being told in a step-by-step fashion how to teach or how they are expected to teach. They were reacting to programs or manuals based on a heavily reductionist dosage (it fits with prescriptions doesn't it?), constructed by "experts" who dictated to teachers what they were to do if they expected a certain specific outcome. So teaching was divided into minute slices and for each slice a set of directives were heavily prescribed.

And if you were not following, or deviating from, these prescriptions, then you were not considered to be doing your normal job. Quite a strong dose of normalizing people and making people become paranoid! I sincerely sympathize with teachers who were made to go through this process. I disagree with this. But I also disagree with the view that holds that since this view is not appropriate (for good moral reasons), then any sense of direction, planning, agenda setting, clarifying what we are doing, or even analyzing what follows for practice from our beliefs, and intervening when appropriate – is prescriptive and therefore unacceptable. The problem arises if the direction, planning, and so on are not seen as possibilities, that is if they are seen as monolithic or unilateral directives or commands. But to immediately associate any form of direction, planning, and so forth as being dogmatic or restrictive, is itself an example of dogmatism!

S : What is an example of something teachers thought was prescriptive?

J : Some teachers who espouse whole language yet resist philosophy for children have claimed there is too much focus on discussions. What we need is simply conversations. Discussions are too prescriptive. In your view, are inquiry, conversation, dialog, discussion the same?

S : Some people have begun using the term conversation, I think, to distinguish it from the kinds of teacher-led pseudo-discussions we often see in classrooms – the ones in which the teacher tightly controls the talk and poses many questions to which he or she already knows the "right" answer. My sense of philosophical discussion is that, although procedures are used, the teacher does not control the talk, in the sense of directing the children's ideas and, in fact, he or she tries not to interject his or her arguments too early so that the children, themselves, take control of the talk. The teacher's role is to lead or guide children to think about issues in ways they might not have thought of themselves and to help them to make different kinds of connections. Is that getting close?

J : Yes. The very concept of a discussion (not debate or chit-chat, that is) involves an open quest or inquiry into different perspectives of the issues at hand. Or else, there is no discussion at all. I am not saying that the only valuable talk is discussion. But not any form of talk amounts to a discussion.

S : But, in fact, conversations also have procedures and rules, ones that differ among cultures and certainly between genders (Tannen, 1990). So, conversations really are not free from constraints; they may not be explicit or conscious, but they certainly exist. I see inquiry as a much broader process of pursuing possible answers to questions that intrigue us – a process within which there is embedded a great deal of exploratory talk (by this I mean talking to generate thought rather than primarily to communicate) that might be termed discussion, conversation, or dialog. In the classroom it seems to me a more important question than "What should we call the talk?" is "What is the quality of the talk?"

J : This gets us back to the issue of what do you do if someone is not aware of a philosophical inquiry? There is no doubt that there are different *kinds* of inquiry: literary, mathematical, scientific, historical, political, spiritual, and so on. Philosophical inquiry has not traditionally been explicitly included in what we do in schools. As a result very little of it has really happened. My experience has shown that most teachers are not aware of the nature of a philosophical inquiry. (And there are reasons for this which both you and I alluded to earlier in Part One.)

S : That may actually happen as well in other areas.

J : A colleague of mine makes a similar point about scientific inquiry. In practice we encounter quite a bit of pseudo-science, and hence very little genuine scientific *inquiry* happens in schools. One way this can be remedied is by clarifying what is involved in doing science. I argue that the same holds for doing philosophy. When I conduct the graduate seminar on philosophy for children, my aim and role is to help teachers become aware of the nature of a philosophical inquiry/discussion and the diverse possible ways it may be encouraged and developed. So, while we actually discuss philosophical issues, we attempt to clarify what is involved in this kind of inquiry. We explore by clarifying meanings, analyzing concepts and positions, uncovering assumptions, investigating the implications of our ideas, views, or beliefs, attempting to give reasons for our views (by offering examples, evidence, counter-examples, considering criticisms), comparing differing views, attempting some kind of resolution or conclusion which may be tentative and hopefully leads to some kind of action. Teachers, especially those who are not used to this kind of inquiry, protest that this is prescriptive and hence unnatural.

S : Well, that seems to go right back to the point I raised earlier. Any sort of structure is seen as prescriptive. I am reminded here of the work of Aidan Chambers (1985). To frame children's talk about books, he has developed a whole series of possible questions that lead children to think more critically about what they are reading. It's not a prescription that closes down possibilities and narrows the learning, but a framework that really opens up new ways of thinking. His questions or prompts begin with "Tell Me..." One prompt he suggests teachers use to open up discussion is very similar to ones used in philosophy with children: "Tell me about anything that particularly caught your attention." The framework includes two types of questions: those that lead the reader to report what happened during and since the reading, that is, thoughts, feelings, observations, and so on; and those that are structural and focus on form, for example, "Who was telling the story? Do we know?" Chambers believes that these two types of questions lead naturally to discussion of the content of the text. I've participated in sessions led by Chambers and have never failed to see insightful, critical discussions evolve. In these discussions there is a great deal of attention to the text itself, that is, supporting your opinions with evidence, going back to the text frequently, considering different ways the text might be interpreted, and so on. So, children learn to become more perceptive, questioning readers through this kind of experience.

J : Exactly. My purpose and, I have no doubt, the purpose of the whole movement of doing philosophy with children, is to reach the level where the children would start asking and taking into account those kinds of questions. You see, there is a missing element, and this is not with regard to whole language, this is with regard to the whole educational process – if what happens in schools is educational. There are many missing dimensions, but surely one of them is the philosophical dimension, the sense of philosophical wonder.

S : Chambers would probably agree with you. He believes children are capable of critical thought, but that it does not happen without the teacher being actively involved in fostering it. So, is that prescriptive? Or not consistent with whole language? I don't see any contradictions with whole language philosophy in the procedures he has developed. And they don't seem very different in kind from the kinds of procedures involved in philosophy for children.

J : From what you have described, they seem to be identical.

S : I haven't had extensive experience in using Chambers' framework with children or with teachers, but in the few instances I have tried it, the questions have seemed awkward and somewhat formulaic because they are not yet a part of my repertoire. I suspect as I gain experience, I'll use them much more flexibly.

Let me ask you a question here. One of the criticisms of philosophical discussions I've heard is related to this whole issue of prescription, I think. Teachers have told me that the discussions are too teacher-directed because they are always in a large group. Small group learning is an important part of whole language. Let's be clear, I'm not saying you have to always be working in small groups to be consistent with whole language! But I wonder if you envision children eventually being able to carry on their own philosophical discussions in small groups once they gain experience?

J : I have seen children leading their own discussions in big groups. Not that much in small groups – this is not to say it could not happen in small groups. A number of the teachers I've worked with at one time or another have had the children working in small groups. I don't know exactly what happened in all of the small groups. That is the problem with small group discussion; you can only be in one group at a time. Certainly I believe, and I imagine there are other people within philosophy for children who would agree with this, that eventually the aim ought to be that the discussion would be led by one of the children themselves. If we are really going to have a full-fledged community of inquiry, that is where people ought to be aiming. It does take time though for the students to reach the level to be able to lead a discussion well.

S : That's true of literature discussion groups and other small group learning experiences, as well. Some teachers have become frustrated, I think, because the discussions haven't been productive. They haven't realized how much support children need as they learn how to handle the discussion themselves.

J : Judy Kyle (1984) developed the idea that the students themselves identified, so to speak, rules or procedures that they developed as a group and that they would change if the need arose. These were procedures for the leader and for the participants, general moves that may be of help to "spice up the salad" as one of the students used to say, to move the discussion forward, I guess. And these were in the class on charts. You could see that these were procedures that belonged to the students and they were extremely cautious that they would be faithful to them. It took a year and a half for the children to get to that point. So it is possible, and in terms of an aim, it is definitely a worthwhile aim, if one takes the notion of community of inquiry seriously. Conceptually, I don't see any contradiction or problem with small groups, although the dynamics are different from a big group.

S : One of the reasons I asked this is because as we have been exploring the use of small literature discussion groups, we have found one of the advantages is that people get more opportunity to talk. Many students who might be reluctant to speak out in a large group, might be willing to speak in a small group. Also the groups can be formed on the basis of children's interests and questions. The issue you raised about the amount of time it takes for children to learn to do this is an important one. There is a real problem of inconsistency. One year a group of students might have extensive experiences with discussion of literature; the next year the teacher does nothing. So the children don't have an opportunity to develop sophistication. We haven't really tested this out to see what the potential might be and how far we might take children in discussions of literature, philosophy, or anything else.

J : The other thing with small groups is that unless the members of the group are aware of whatever kind of discussion they are having, for example, an historical discussion, a scientific discussion, or a philosophical discussion, there may not be anyone in the group who is able to move the children to different kinds of thinking. Then the children may never actually do that. They may talk, talk, talk but never get to focused historical, scientific, or philosophical talk.

S : Or in discussions of literature the questions may never get beyond surface meaning or personal connections, which of course can be a starting point, to more critical or interpretive kinds of questions. That's why the teacher needs to be actively involved in showing children how to talk critically about what they are reading, as Chambers suggests through his framework. But some seem to think that the teacher taking an active role is imposing on the children, rather than the way I see it which is extending the children's understanding and helping them think about things in different ways.

J : I return to my earlier point. If we are not aware of a certain kind of inquiry and the nature of that inquiry, then will we ever, whether in a small group or a large group, be able to inquire well within that form of inquiry? Several teachers who have taken the seminar on philosophy for children remark at the end: "It is incredible. I have read most of the stories we discussed in the seminar before, but never saw the things I saw this time, since we focused on the philosophical dimension which I was not taking into account before." And I said earlier, the same could apply to other areas. The most visible thing we have from the formal curriculum is science. Why is it the case that we don't have much scientific inquiry in schools? My suspicion is because teachers are not aware of the nature of scientific inquiry. I've heard people say in relation to elementary education: "Well this is just an elementary program, it is enough for teachers to be barely aware of knowledge or inquiry in a subject area because this is just elementary."

S : That's a major issue of teacher education isn't it? I worry that, because of the very issue you raise, we don't build upon what children know when they come to school. I think children ask philosophical questions without knowing they are philosophical. Three-year-olds ask scientific questions and historical questions. But do we in school help them to raise those questions to a higher level by leading them into a thought process through an extension of those questions?

J : Actually children ask all kinds of questions – mathematical, scientific, philosophical, historical, and literary questions and so on – which take us by surprise. They ask questions which we may not be aware of ourselves, so we completely disregard them. And this is why I keep on saying the more we, as adults, are aware of the various kinds of inquiry, then I think the better the possibilities for actually recognizing the questions when children ask them and taking them seriously. But the critique coming from some of the teachers is that this is prescriptive and not natural. That is a stumbling block!

S : Yes. I see it in literacy classrooms where there are a lot of activities going on in the name of literacy instruction but the children themselves may not understand how that relates to them as readers and writers. Children, then, don't become skilled, critical, effective readers and writers because they can't make that connection. I think we need a great deal more reflection: What's going on here? How does what we are doing relate to reading and writing? How can we use what we have learned? The whole idea of looking carefully at texts: How did you respond to this character? How did the writer accomplish that? How could you do that in your own writing? Those kinds of conversations are not taking place in many classrooms. And I think some whole language proponents would find them too prescriptive.

J :   Which relates back to my question about what is prescription. There may actually be a confusion here between (i) becoming aware of something new, clarifying or defining it and even being open to extend one's understanding and knowledge, and (ii) prescribing a rigid, detailed, specific method. To achieve (i), one needs to identify some of the very qualities that make up that very thing (whatever that may happen to be). The point I feel I need to emphasize here is that philosophy is not just one monolithic thing. There are different philosophical activities and it can be done in degrees and in different ways.

With regard to prescribing a rigid, detailed, specific method, I add that this *kind* of prescription goes against the very nature of philosophy. However, a rejection of this kind of prescription does not imply that we should never focus on a specific dimension. As human beings we can't do everything at the same time! We can't help focusing. There are different kinds of inquiries. The fact that some or perhaps many are related to each other, does not mean that there are no differences between these inquiries. A literary inquiry is not the same as a scientific inquiry which in turn is not the same as a philosophical inquiry. To, therefore, assume that the literary inquiry (or any other inquiry) encompasses all and therefore we do not need to explicitly focus on the other dimensions, is quite imperialistic in nature. The question becomes: which focus? in whose interest? why is a certain inquiry or focus more privileged?

S :   My notion of prescription would be the kinds of things we used to find in basal reader lessons that told the teacher what to ask and what answers to expect. And to keep on going until she or he got the answer the textbook author expected. It's back to the pseudo-discussion I mentioned earlier. Those kinds of practices, to me, are prescriptive and contrived. Which gets us to the whole issue of texts, which I know have been a bone of contention with some teachers in your classes.

J : Yes, indeed, the issue of "texts" is another example of where I have encountered some resistance which, in my view, is partly based on the broader issue of prescription.

Let me start by saying that I do not agree with the view that discussions ought to simply happen by accident. I am not saying that, therefore, the teacher should set up the classroom in a certain way so that the students would raise a certain issue and say certain or specific things about that issue which the teacher happens to think is the correct view. That would be a classic example of manipulation. Neither am I saying that we should not deal with issues that arise unexpectedly as teaching develops – to let the discussion develop by its own dynamics, means exactly that. None of my views expressed here support the view that teaching happens in a void. Teaching, of whatever kind, always happens within a certain context. That is an inevitable human condition whether we like it or not! The question that arises then is: where do we start from? This is where "texts" come in. And I am using the word "text" in a wide sense. Texts are part of what provide the opportunity for discussion. What texts should one use? I believe that there are a variety of texts that are worthwhile. It is not appropriate to stipulate a text to be applied universally to all teaching contexts. And expect it to be worthwhile for all those different contexts. As I see it that is the problem with basal readers.

S : Now that so many more teachers are using children's literature rather than basal readers, concerns are being raised about how the literature is used. There have been critiques of the basalizing of literature, where teachers, and many publishers, develop comprehension questions just like the ones in the old basal readers, for children to answer after they read trade books. If the literature is simply used to teach children to read, what happens to literature as an art form? What's the difference when texts like children's picture books or young adult novels are read at home as part of daily living and when they are read in school as part of the reading curriculum? These are important questions about context.

J : I find this quote from Patrick Shannon (1991) helpful:

> *Although most textbooks attempt to standardize curricula among users, basal readers also determine the method by which that content is transmitted from teacher's guidebook, to teacher, and then to students. Publishers promise to supply a complete system that will teach all children to read if the materials are implemented according to the detailed guideline*

that accompany each series. In sum, basal readers eliminate the guesswork
for teachers in the classroom. . . . [B]asal readers give the illusion that they
alone are the tools through which school districts, schools, and teachers
can legitimize their reading programs in the eyes of the taxpaying public
by raising students' test scores. (p. 217)

Given such a characterization of basal readers, the problems include: there is only one way to achieve x, y, z, and that is by following the directions in the basal readers programs; what is appropriate for one context is appropriate for all contexts; there is one fixed answer to questions raised and that is provided in the program and the teachers have to transmit that answer to the students who are simply to accept that answer. The restrictive element is scary especially if teaching is seen as an art rather than a blind mechanical implementation of rigid directives (Van Manen, 1991).

S : Yes. And I find it particularly problematic when the principles underlying basal programs – those restrictive elements – are applied in literature-based programs. That's the basalizing of literature I mentioned before.

J : The problems I have encountered arose from the view – a narrow one in my view – that any text, simply because it is a text, suffers from the problems identified in basal readers. So, for example, any of the "novels-qua-texts" written by Lipman, or even a teacher selecting a story like *The True Story of the 3 Little Pigs! By A. Wolf* (Scieska, 1989) is seen as problematic. I think, in this instance, some teachers have fallen into the other extreme so characteristic of "soft liberalism" (Portelli, 1994).

When Lipman came up with the idea of relating philosophy to teaching, including teaching at the elementary level, he was, like any teacher, faced with the question of where to start from. He started writing "texts," "novels-qua-texts" as some call them, not as the usual literary texts, but as something which provides the context in which people, mostly children, are talking about issues of a philosophical nature. He *never* intended these to be used as a traditional text nor as a basal reader. You know that I have problems with those who say that the only way to do philosophy is to use these texts. Yet, to be fair, some people have – and I am not sure what their intentions are – completely misrepresented the purpose of anything that Lipman has written.

S : I want to offer my response to the two texts (Lipman, 1981 and 1982) you gave me to look at. I haven't had the opportunity to work with them in the classroom, but I did get a sense for how they are written. I have some problems with calling them novels because they were written for a very different purpose than a novel. It seems clear that the characters and story were created for the purpose of demonstrating philosophical thinking and talk and of generating philosophical discussion in the classroom. In that sense, the texts are contrived. There is little character development or plot elaboration and I found the conversations stilted. I can understand why some whole language teachers find them problematic, especially if they are presented as being of the same nature as a novel written as literature. As well, I can understand the concern about these texts in light of their perceived similarity to basal readers, which were books written for the sole purpose of teaching children to read. On the other hand, I can see that these texts might, in fact, serve a purpose in a classroom, if they help teachers and children understand more about what it means to do philosophy. They wouldn't be used as examples of good literature or as a focus for discussion about characterization, theme, or setting, as you might do in responding to literature. And, you certainly wouldn't want doing philosophy to be only reading and discussing those texts. As you have said, however, they can be springboards for discussion.

J : I completely agree with the gist of what you said. But with regard to Lipman's texts being "contrived," I have to ask: What is a non-contrived text? Are not all texts constructed and therefore, in a sense, contrived? This leads to the whole issue of contrived/natural. I mean, is a frog talking to a toad as if they were human beings natural?

S : No, but if the Lipman texts are called novels, I assume I should apply the criteria I would to any other literary text. From that perspective, it seems to me the story-line, characters, and the dialog are contrived, notwithstanding that the texts may serve a purpose as a springboard for philosophical discussions.

J : I agree that if whatever is going to be called "novels" then one would expect what one normally finds in novels. This, of course, raises the issues of what is good literature and what to expect in a novel, which is yet another construct. Things do not appear in the world with a label on them "I am a novel." Something may not conform to the regular expectations of a novel and yet still be worthwhile. And I know that you agree with this latter point. The issue here, however, is broader than the problem with Lipman's texts, as for some teachers the very selection of books by a teacher or bringing a book to the attention of students is not appropriate since that is deemed to be contrived. Some would even go to the extreme of saying that the very identification of a book as being philosophical, scientific, or whatever, is contrived. The assumption here is that we can always neatly distinguish between "what is natural" and "what is contrived;" and more dangerously, that what is deemed to be natural for a group of children is natural for all children. I always encounter surprises about what children in different classes, and yet with very similar qualities and backgrounds, find interesting and intriguing.

S : Early on one of the major shifts in whole language classrooms was from the use of basal readers to the use of children's books, written not to teach reading but as literature, both fiction and non-fiction. There was a great deal written about the importance of using authentic texts with natural language. While I'm not arguing against the use of children's books, I think we have to be careful about the use of such words as "authentic" and "natural." We need to ask, "What counts as literature?" In the canon of great literature, it's mostly what has been written by white males. Is what we think of as "natural" language in North American culture, "natural" elsewhere in the world? Is the direct sequential writing style of English more "natural" and "authentic" than the circular, poetic, and indirect construction of Asian languages (Poplin, 1989)? In our schools is it enough to have literature or do we have to ask: Whose stories are we allowing to be heard? Whose perspective is being presented as truth in a non-fiction text?

J : These are the kinds of things I had in mind when I criticized the "soft liberal" position. What your examples clearly highlight are the inevitable political implications of these decisions. And it is this very inevitability that scares some teachers. For example, a very sincere teacher who participated in my seminar this summer commented in relation to an article by the African-American, Lisa Delpit (1988), and Philosophy for Children: "Lisa Delpit describes a very special kind of listening – it requires not only open eyes and ears, but also open hearts and minds as well as through our beliefs. Full engagements in listening and hearing is blocked by fear that one's position may be undermined, that one's grip of certainty in one's beliefs may be lost. I believe that the resistance to allow children access to philosophical discussion reflects this fear." Not focusing explicitly on philosophical issues and discussions is limiting, and has dangerous political implications for the nature of a democracy. I am not saying that children should, therefore, be compelled to discuss philosophical issues. All I am saying is that unless we include the philosophical dimension, via whatever text (including children's own lives!) that raises philosophical issues, then the children who want or need to discuss such issues are being hindered from doing that. The notion of voluntariness is crucial here. But the voluntary choice does not exist if the different options or dimensions are not offered or included!

S :   From my perspective, what is natural is all children's capacity to learn. We don't have to create elaborate skills sequences and reward schemes to entice them to engage. So if there is anything "natural" about whole language, it is this trust in children. But to help every child to make the very best of this natural capacity, the teacher has to have an agenda. Of course the children's interests come into play. If we are talking about literature, certainly they have to have opportunities to choose what they will read. Equally, they need to have choices in what they will write about. But as teachers, we also have a responsibility to broaden their perspectives. If a student is choosing a steady diet of books on a particular topic or perhaps reading material that is not in the least challenging, I would intervene. I might invite the student to be part of a small group that is reading a book that will offer a bit more of a challenge. I might choose a book to read aloud that I think will engage him or her. I might establish a framework for the whole class that sets out some expectations for attempting different kinds of reading and writing. And in terms of the entire class, I would ensure that I included in my classroom library a wide range of genres, both fictional and expository, reflecting many different cultures and a variety of perspectives. I would see it as my responsibility to challenge racist or sexist attitudes and beliefs. So, I would actively intervene in a number of ways. I don't see that as at all inconsistent with whole language.

J :   And neither do I. And the same holds for philosophy with children. If we are going to do philosophy then we have to have an environment that invites the participants to that kind of inquiry. Providing that kind of environment may not seem "natural" to a teacher who is not aware or not used to the philosophical dimension. And this is why even we, as adults, need to be positively challenged to entertain new dimensions. I cannot see how one can consistently take openness to the curriculum seriously and then not be able or willing to entertain new possibilities other than what already exists within the current or dominant curriculum which is really a traditional one. Unless we entertain new possibilities, then, as Jane R. Martin (1982) has pointed out, we would be trapped in the dogmas that curriculum is God-given and that it is unchangeable by nature. Intentionally planning new possibilities does not amount to imposing; neither is it restricting the students' interests. The confusion arises only when people think that there can be a completely neutral, non-influencing, non-communicative, non-transmitting exchanges. Everything influences, communicates, or transmits something. The crucial question becomes the manner in which this is done and its intention. And this leads to the role of the teacher.

S : There are some very clear differences between the kind of teacher role I described above and one in which the teacher imposes a curricular agenda on children. I have always liked Garth Boomer's (1982) notion of the "negotiated curriculum." In this environment, teachers and children share decision-making power and responsibility. Yet, that doesn't just happen. There is nothing "natural" about this kind of classroom. In fact, it stands in direct contradiction to much of what most adults experienced in schools and what is still the norm in most situations. A teacher who decides to work in this way has to consciously structure the environment and, in reality, "impose" an agenda on students – one in which they are expected to play an active role in their own learning and in the classroom community. It's a social agenda that fosters the development of independent, self-directed learners who then can actively contribute to shaping the curricular agenda.

J : And this reminds me of Dewey's view of teaching as a cooperative enterprise rather than either a dictation or a mere accident. In Dewey's own words:

The teacher's suggestion is not a mold for a cast-iron result but is a starting point to be developed into a plan through contributions from the experience of all engaged in the learning process. The development occurs through reciprocal give-and-take, the teacher taking but not being afraid also to give. The essential point is that the purposes grow and take shape through the process of social intelligence. (Dewey, 1938, p. 72)

Part Three

Through our dialog, we have identified many issues of common concern. We also share a strong sense of possibility regarding the potential for positive change if we can move beyond the myths, misperceptions, and orthodoxies that seem to plague both philosophy for children and whole language. In this final section, we offer some closing comments on four broad areas of commonality: beliefs about teaching; community of inquiry; "What if it's otherwise?"; and the political agenda: philosophy and whole language for what?

Beliefs about teaching

S : Through the dialog, we both have articulated a view of teaching that avoids the two extremes; I certainly see teaching as neither child-centred nor teacher-dominated. Creating a supportive teaching/learning environment requires complex orchestration on the part of the teacher. The teacher, after all, has much experience, knowledge, and skill to bring to the situation. Surely, our responsibility as adults is to share with children what we know, and, at the same time to value, respect, and build upon what the children themselves bring to the process. Of course, this is very easy to say, but in my experience very challenging to do. The most important thing is for all of us who teach to be aware of the pitfalls of either turning too much control over to the children or maintaining too much control in the hands of the teacher. In reality, the balance constantly shifts in that ongoing process of negotiation that Boomer (1982) describes.

P : The view of teaching we have articulated involves a lot of give-and-take from all involved in the teaching-learning encounters. This vision of teaching does not support the extreme either/or dichotomies that have plagued contemporary educational practices. The balance you refer to, however, is not meant as a calculable half-way between both extremes; it goes beyond the extremes, namely, technicism or reductionism, on one hand, and *laissez-faire* attitude, on the other. This vision of teaching has been referred to as "interpretive" or "constructivist" (Rowland, 1987).

Community of Inquiry

S : My greatest interest in this topic comes from the perspective of my role as a curriculum leader in my district. If we want teachers to understand what it means to work within a community of inquiry, they themselves have to experience that in their own lives as contributing members of an organization, whether it be the school or the school district as a whole. That means a profound change in the way we do things in all areas: professional development, decision making, planning, curriculum development and implementation, staff meetings, and day-to-day communications.

I hope that the restructuring movement currently underway in many school districts will result in greater decision making and control at the school level. But that shift will really make no difference if administrators and teachers don't have the understanding and skills to build communities of inquiry among the professionals in the schools. There will need to be a great deal of leadership for the change at the district level, but the problem is there are so few people in leadership roles at that level who themselves understand how to create these sorts of communities. They have no more experience than the teachers.

It seems we do have a window of opportunity, however, to make fundamental changes if we have the will and commitment to carry it through. Perhaps philosophical discussions have something to offer us. One of the books I have been reading and thinking about lately, Peter Senge's *The Fifth Discipline*, offers that perspective. Senge (1990) writes about the need for dialog among professionals who function on teams within an organization. He describes most of the usual interaction as discussion (he is obviously using discussion differently than you have been) in which the aim of each participant is to win others over to his or her point of view. While there is a place for discussion, he sees a need for a complementary focus on dialog:

In dialogue, a group explores complex difficult issues from many points of view. Individuals suspend their assumptions but they communicate their assumptions freely. The result is a free exploration that brings to the surface the full depth of people's experience and thought, and yet can move beyond their individual views. (p. 241)

This sounds to me like what you have been calling a philosophical discussion. In the school system, as in many other organizations, we might benefit from some practise in philosophical discussion ourselves!

J : Indeed! And to do that we have to change the negative attitude toward philosophy, an attitude which rests partially on a misinterpretation. At present, as Willam Hare (1985) has put it, philosophy is seen as a vocational handicap. But if philosophy is seen and practised as a sincere, open, critical inquiry and discussion, we might start changing that attitude. Of course, this outlook toward life can be scary for some, especially those who are used to having everything boxed into neat, separate compartments. But this is exactly where the notion of inquiring philosophically within a supportive community plays a crucial role. And needless to say, the kind of discussion or dialog in such a community would be quite different from the kind of debates, for example, that we encounter in the parliaments of western democracies! The contrast between the Socratic attitude and the sophistic attitude is still relevant to us today. Our challenge is not to have education based on sophistry but truthfulness (Russell, 1972).

"What if it's Otherwise?"

S : Margaret Meek Spencer's wonderful and challenging question needs to be kept at the fore in classrooms and among teachers as we consider what we believe and what we do. To ask it means to take the stance that there are no easy right answers, especially in something as complex as teaching and learning. Your notion of resolution is useful, I think. We can agree upon some answers for today, but we need to be open to considering other possibilities in the future. We need to be looking for evidence that supports our temporary answer, but just as actively be seeking evidence that seems to contradict it. In supporting children's literacy development within a whole language environment, that means we should avoid the "shoulds" and the "nevers." For example, one of the statements I have heard frequently is: "Never tell a child how to spell a word." While I believe it enhances children's fluency in writing if we encourage them to use functional spelling in early drafts, I also have been in situations when the right decision was to help the child arrive at the correct spelling. When the child truly wants to know how to spell a word these can be valuable "teachable moments." To say "never tell a child how to spell a word" is one of those final answers that does not serve children, or teachers, well. It seems to me "What if it's otherwise?" is a fundamental philosophical question that could help us all keep teaching dynamic and responsive to the learners.

J : This is definitely a basic philosophical question. Without it there can be no genuine philosophical inquiry. Once again, this question reminds me of Socrates' response to Critias, in the dialog

Charmides, which I mentioned earlier. This stance does not imply that we never know anything at all or that everything is continuously suspended up in the air. It simply calls for the ability and willingness to re-open our investigations when evidence shows us otherwise. And to do that requires both humility and courage (Hare, 1993). There is no doubt that this stance can be risky. This is why teachers need to form support groups. But also, those who head school boards and other educational bodies need to understand and adopt this kind of stance or attitude. The quick-fix approach and extreme technocratic attitude adopted by many educational administrators is contrary to the philosophical stance; that approach leaves very little room for "what if it's otherwise?"

Political Dimension: Philosophy and Whole Language for What?

S : Both whole language and philosophy for children, as we have envisioned them in our dialog, are, by their very nature, political. Asking "what if it's otherwise?" is to take a political stance. If children and teachers take this question seriously, what might be the outcome? Within the classroom, they might begin to question the version of history they read in their approved texts. They might begin to question why certain cultural groups are privileged in our society. They might wonder why they themselves have no voice in the decisions made within and outside the school that affect their lives in the classroom. Teachers might ask why their views of reality, grounded in classroom experiences, are so seldom reflected in the official discourse about schooling. Some teachers, principals, and others in roles like mine are asking these kinds of questions, but to date, it seems to me most of those involved in whole language have not made the political agenda explicit. If we are to survive, in the face of growing attacks from ultra-conservative groups who would have us adopt a "back-to-basics" curriculum and of the rising pressure from business and government who blame progressive movements like whole language for our economic malaise, we must become much more political. We, and our students, need to use our skills of literacy and thinking, developed through curricula like whole language and philosophy for children, to make a difference in the world.

J : The philosophical stance as captured in "what if it's otherwise?" is central to the sustenance and reconstruction of the democratic ideal.

This political ideal, as you very clearly explained, has some direct implications for education. Unfortunately, we have been somehow trained not to make explicit such a political connection. Even in philosophy for children this connection has not been made as explicit as it should have been. If we are serious about the philosophical stance then we have to not just inquire academically about issues, but also explore the political implications and act accordingly. Surely, not just Socrates, but also recent philosophers, such as Dewey, Russell, and Hannah Arendt, and the contemporary, Paulo Freire and Maxine Greene, provide us with admirable examples!

References

Boomer, G. (Ed.). (1982). *Negotiating the curriculum.* Sydney: Ashton Scholastic.

Brookes, A. (1992). *Feminist pedagogy: An autobiographical approach.* Halifax: Fernwood Books.

Cambourne, B. (1977). Getting to Goodman: An analysis of the Goodman model of reading with some suggestions for evaluation. *Reading Research Quarterly, 12* (4), 605-636.

Chambers, A. (1985). *Booktalk.* London: The Bodley Head.

Church, S. (1985a). Blossoming in the writing community. *Language Arts 62*(2), 175-179.

Church, S. (1985b). The war of the words. In J.M. Newman (Ed.), *Whole language: Theory in use* (pp. 153-162). Portsmouth, NH: Heinemann.

Church, S. (1985c). Inservice education: Becoming our own experts. *Reading Canada Lecture 3*, 182-186.

Church, S. (1987). Fostering change from within. *Reading Canada Lecture 5*, 158-160.

Church, S. (1988). It's almost like there aren't any walls. *Language Arts 65* (5), 448-54.

Church, S. (1990). Helping children to 'read the world.' *Reading Today 8* (3), 25.

Church, S. (1992). Rethinking whole language: The politics of educational change. In P. Shannon (Ed.), *Becoming political* (pp. 238-249). Portsmouth, NH: Heinemann.

Church, S. (1993). Is whole language really warm and fuzzy? *The Reading Teacher, 47* (5): 362-370.

Delpit, L. (1988). The silenced dialogue: Power and pedagogy in educating other people's children. *Harvard Educational Review, 58* (3), 281-298.

Dewey, J. (1938). *Experience and education.* New York: Collier Books.

Freire, P. and Macedo, D. (1987). *Literacy – Reading the word and reading the world.* New York: Bergin and Garvey.

Gilligan, C. (1982). *In a different voice.* Cambridge, MA: Harvard Educational Books.

Gilligan, C., Lyons, N. P. & Hanmer, T. J. (Eds.). (1990). *Making connections – The relational worlds of adolescent girls at Emma Willard School.* Cambridge, MA: Harvard University Press.

Giroux, H. A. (1987). Critical literacy and student experience: Donald Graves' approach to literacy. *Language Arts, 64* (2), 175-181.

Goodman, K. (1967). Reading: A psycholinguistic guessing game. *Journal of the Reading Specialist, 6,* 126-135.

Goodman, K. (1973). The 13th easy way to make learning to read difficult. *Reading Research Quarterly, 8* (4), 484-493.

Goodman, K. S., Shannon, P., Freeman, Y. S. and Murphy, S. (1988). *Report card on basal readers.* Katonah, NY: Richard C. Owen.

Goodman, K. S. (1992). I didn't found whole language. *The Reading Teacher, 46,* 88-199

Hare, W. (1985). Philosophy as a vocational handicap. In W. Hare, *Controversies in teaching* (pp. 99-105). London, Ont.: Althouse Press.

Hare, W. (1993). *What makes a good teacher.* London, Ont.: Althouse Press.

Kyle, J. (1976). *Philosophy for children.* Unpublished MA thesis, McGill University, Montreal.

Kyle, J. (1984). Managing philosophical discussions. *Thinking, 5* (2), 19-22.

Language arts in the elementary school. (1986). Halifax: Nova Scotia Department of Education.

Lipman, M. (1981). *Pixie.* Montclair, NJ: First Mountain Foundation.

Lipman, M. (1982). *Harry.* Montclair, NJ: First Mountain Foundation.

Martin, J. R. (1982). Two dogmas of the curriculum. *Synthese, 51,* 5-20.

Martin, J. R. (1985). *Reclaiming a conversation: The ideal of the educated women.* New Haven: Yale University Press.

Mitchell, C. & Weiler, K. (Eds.). (1991). *Rewriting literacy: Culture and the discourse of the other.* Toronto: OISE Press.

Newman, J. M. and Church, S. M. (1990). Myths of whole language. *The Reading Teacher, 44,* 20-26.

Plato. (1970). *Charmides.* In *The dialogues of Plato vol. 2: The symposium and other dialogues* (B. Jowett, Trans.) (p. 53). London: Sphere Books Ltd.

Poplin, M. (1989). Education: The revitalization of America. Address to The President's Forum, Claremont Graduate School.

Portelli, J. P. (1990). The socratic method and philosophy for children. *Metaphilosophy, 21* (1&2), 141-161.

Portelli, J. P. (1994). The challenge of teaching for critical thinking. *McGill Journal of Education, 29* (2), 137-152.

Pritchard, M. (1995). Reasonable children. In J.P. Portelli and R. Reed (Eds.), *Children, philosophy, and democracy* (pp. 17-46). Calgary, AB: Detselig Enterprises Ltd.

Reed, R. (1987). Philosophy for children: Some problems. *Analytic Teaching, 8* (1), 82-86.

Rowland, S. (1987). Child in control: Towards an interpretive model of teaching and learning. In A. Pollard (Ed.), *Children and their primary schools* (pp. 121-132). London: Falmer Press.

Ryan, E. B. and Semmel, M. I. (1969). Reading as a constructive language process. *Reading Research Quarterly, 5*, 59-83.

Russell, B. (1972). Freedom versus authority in education. In J.L. Nelson et al. (Eds.), *Radical ideas and the schools* (pp. 321-333). New York: Holt, Rinehart, and Winston.

Scieszka, J. (1989). *The true story of the 3 little pigs! By A. Wolf.* New York: Viking.

Senge, P. (1990). *Fifth discipline.* New York: Doubleday.

Shannon, P. (1991). Basal readers and the illusion of legitimacy. In M. Apple (Ed.), *Textbooks in American society* (pp. 217-236). Albany, NY: State University of New York Press.

Simon, R. I. (1987). Empowerment as a pedagogy of possibility. *Language Arts, 64* (4), 370-382.

Smith, D. E. (1987). *The everyday world as problematic – A feminist sociology.* Toronto: University of Toronto Press.

Smith, F. (1971). *Understanding reading* (1st ed.). New York: Holt, Rinehart, and Winston.

Smith, F. (1978). *Reading without nonsense.* New York: Teachers College Press.

Spencer, M. M. (1993). Memorial Lecture for Patricia S. Barnes, Mount Saint Vincent University, Halifax, NS (March 27).

Tannen, D. (1990). *You just don't understand.* New York: Ballantine Books.

Van Manen, M. (1991). *The tact of teaching: The meaning of pedagogical thoughtfulness.* London, ON: Althouse Press.

Weiler, K. (1988). *Women teaching for change: Gender, class and power.* South Hadley, MA: Bergin and Garvey.

Section II

*The Community of Inquiry as an Expression
of Democratic Values*

CHAPTER 6

Educating for Violence Reduction and Peace Development

The Philosophical Community of Inquiry Approach

Matthew Lipman

Education, Not Indoctrination

What I shall not do in this paper is extol the virtues of peace and deplore the viciousness of violence. To do so would be to fall into the trap in which so many attempts to educate for peace and against violence have been swallowed up. To be sure, the face of peace is most attractive and that of violence is most unattractive. However, when it comes to education with regard to these values, it is not enough to cultivate immediate emotional responses, or to reiterate how good peace is and how bad violence is. Instead, we have to help children *both understand and practise* what is involved in violence-reduction and peace-development. They have to learn to think for themselves about these matters, not just provide knee-jerk responses when we present the proper stimuli.

It follows, on the one hand, that students must become much more conversant than they presently are with the *meaning* of such concepts as peace, freedom, equity, reciprocity, democracy, personhood, rights, and justice, even though this may bring to the surface profound disagreements about such meanings. On the other hand, it follows that students must become much more practiced in the procedures of rational deliberation, of stereotype exposure, and of prejudice and conflict reduction.

These two requirements lead to the same culmination: the conversion of ordinary classrooms into *communities of inquiry*, in which students can generate and exchange ideas, clarify concepts, develop hypotheses, weigh possible consequences, and in general deliberate reasonably together while learning to enjoy their intellectual interdependence. Like juries, which they in many ways resemble, these classroom communities develop skills in inquiry, reasoning, and concept-formation, skills that enable them to isolate subsidiary problems for manageable discussion and resolution, even when the settlement of the larger issues is elusive.

If people are ever to learn to use improved methods of conflict-resolution in their daily lives, it will have to be by first having learned to question together, to reason together, and to make judgments together. Valuable as debate and argument may be in some contexts, such as the courthouse, it must be admitted that students can benefit far more from acquiring foundational skills in thinking critically and creatively, in engaging in exploratory dialog, and in learning to take into account the other sides to each issue. Valuable, moreover, as research assignments can be, and helpful as books and libraries can be, it must be acknowledged that working together for peace is inherently a social, communal matter, developing skills in analyzing evidence and reasons together, in working out compromises, and in reaching consensus about such matters as can be decided by consensus.

Students can acquire significant practice in mediating with one another and in arriving at settlements only if they are first confronted with problems that speak to them directly and are genuinely unsettling. It is here that the discipline of philosophy, suitably reconstructed so as to be accessible to even the youngest school children, can be of enormous service. Philosophy provides ideas for people to chew on – ideas that don't get used up because they are perennially contestable.

As good friends cherish friendship and strong communities value community, peaceful societies recognize the value of understanding what peace means and what conditions must be in place if peace is to be maintained. Societies that make little effort to understand how peace is to be achieved and preserved are unlikely to have it or enjoy it.

Sermons and lectures denouncing violence and extolling peace are all too often exercises in stereotypical thinking. They frequently take it for granted that those who listen to them should be *for* peace and *against* violence without qualification – without consideration of the context or the circumstances, without wondering whether the violence in question was of a justifiable or an unjustifiable variety. What this leads to is a kind of one-dimensional moral thinking that feeds upon stereotypes. "She's passive; she must be good." "She's meek and mild; she must be virtuous." "He's dashing; he can't be a violator of other people's rights." In other words, we are taught to pay lip service to the stereotypes, but in practice to indulge actions which represent clearly unjustifiable inferences or appraisals. Under such circumstances, it is hardly surprising that rape is often treated indulgently as a male prerogative and child abuse is treated indulgently as a parental prerogative. It is not simply that the protests of the victims are disallowed; they are not even heard. After a time, those who have been violated cease to protest because they see that it is hopeless to do so, and their failure to protest is taken as a sure sign of their having been permissive, or of their having deserved the treatment they got.

Educating for violence-reduction and educating for peace-making are therefore two different sides of the same coin. It is the coin as a whole that has purchasing power, not just one side or the other.

We are all familiar with the fact that those who educate for violence-reduction frequently do so by portraying violence and then condemning it, a strategy that seldom works, because their audiences revel in the depiction and ignore the condemnation. The same is often true of peace-advocacy, which paints peace in such dull colors as to make people want to avoid it like the plague. After all, was this not what happened in the case of the tympana of Romanesque and Gothic cathedrals – with worshippers coming to enjoy the lively depictions of torture in Hell, rather than the bland serenity of Heaven?

Thanks to the obsessive curiosity many people now have about violence, it is no problem for the mass-media to play upon that weakness and exacerbate it still further. The books, movies, TV, and newspapers of the contemporary world play up every aspect of every violent incident because they know that it sells. Violence is associated with high-intensity experience, with thrills – which is similar to the reasoning of many who turn to drugs, because drugs yield experiential "highs." Violence is highly marketable.

The passive television watcher finds satisfaction in the depiction of violence because it provides an experiential texture he or she can appreciate. Since it is a vicarious experience, it has none of the responsibilities of a real-life happening, while preserving much of its excitement.

What does this obsession with violence tell us? On the one hand, it suggests that this is the desperate recourse people have when their lives are indescribably dreary, and when they long for a richly textured life-experience, far more intense and enjoyable than the one they presently endure. On the other hand, it suggests that people who feel that their powers are alienated, their hopes betrayed, their energies wasted are likely to be people who fantasize violence as a way of siphoning off their own repressed bitterness and resentment.

People struggle to find meaning in their lives, and when they cannot find it there, they struggle to make it. But their well-intentioned efforts frequently run aground, because they are incapable of distinguishing the meretricious thrills to be derived from surrounding oneself with images of violence from the excitement of living a life that is rich in meanings, intense in quality, and overflowing with constructive human relationships.

So that is, all too often, how we are: incapable of distinguishing the fools-gold from the real gold. The education we must talk about has to help avoid making egregious mistakes of this kind.

To What Criteria Can We Appeal?

In educating for violence-reduction and peace-development, to what criteria can we appeal? This is a preliminary question of great importance.

(a) We can cite our own experience, and endeavor to show that this makes us authorities on the matter.

(b) We can appeal to the child's own experience.

(c) We can attempt to persuade the child through argument and rhetoric.

(d) We can make use of reason – both the child's and our own.

(e) All of the above.

(a) *We can cite our own experience.* Agreed. As adults, we can claim that our experience has taught us that peace is commendable and violence is deplorable. Children can learn from our experience. But can we simply assume that our experience is an adequate substitute for the child's? And is this, after all, the goal of education, that only *our* experience be utilized, in order that the children's views ultimately should coincide with ours? Isn't it important that they form their own independent judgments, rather than just make carbon-copies of ours?

When we adults speak of "our experience," we do not mean only yours and mine. We mean the experience of humankind, as embodied in history. But is this what we are going to do, draw unequivocal lessons from history, to the effect that, in the long run, violence achieves its goals less often than non-violence? Does the history of the human past really provide clear moral standards for the human future? If we are inclined to think so, we could do worse than read Freud's "Thoughts for the Times on War and Death," (1915) in which he notes how people perk up in wartime: their lives have suddenly become more meaningful, and they can take pleasure in the sufferings of their enemies. The tangled skeins of history provide us with little that is unequivocal or unproblematic. Santayana was being glib when he said that those who had forgotten the past were condemned to repeat it, for he was as aware as anyone that, in some sense, what happens to us will always be like something that happened in the past, and in another sense, our lives and experience are always unprecedented and fresh. The only way history can be of use to the child is if the child is capable of careful reasoning and sound judgment.

The same is true with regard to the child's use of our adult experience. Unless the child is able to think critically, we can fill his or her mind at will with our most outrageous notions. Not only must children be taught to think better, but they must be taught to think for themselves.

(b) *We can appeal to the child's own experience.* Obviously, for any particular child, experience is in short supply, although children probably do make up in quality what they lack in quantity. Moreover, the experience the child has had may be more different from our own than we realize. And even if it is the same, the chances are that we have forgotten so much of our own childhood experience that we do not know what to appeal to in the child's.

On the other hand, a different picture appears when we take into account the children's experiences that are marshalled in a community of inquiry setting. Here children collaborate in citing experiences to back up each other's opinions, and can even combine their touchingly fragmentary observations into a massive whole. And so we definitely should not leave out the criterion of the *children's* own experience.

(c) *We can attempt to persuade the child through argument and rhetoric.* Of course we can. But should we? Argument is a reasonable thing to employ, insofar as the child is capable of constructing a counter-argument. Besides, presenting the adult point of view in the form of an argument provides the child with a model of the kind of response that the parent would deem reasonable. Small children can construct small arguments – minimal arguments such as a conclusion supported by a reason. But if we attempt to employ *force majeure*, such as an enthymeme or a chain of syllogisms, the child will see that he or she is outmatched and will withdraw into a resentful silence.

Likewise, with our rhetorical stratagems. Recourse to irony or sarcasm is generally counter-productive, since children can rarely fight back with these same weapons. Besides, if our only goal is persuasion, and we are willing to employ any rhetorical means to attain that goal, we are no longer in the realm of education. We are approaching manipulation: getting children to do what we want them to do while making them think it is what they want to do. And isn't manipulation a form of violence against the mind of the child?

Using argument with children who can reply in kind is not unreasonable, but it is not the only reasonable alternative open to us.

(d) *We can make use of reason – both the child's and our own.* An alternative form of reasonableness is to engage the child in discussion, in which conflicts of opinions regarding facts or values quickly come to the surface and can be deliberated upon and reflected upon. In other words, we can engage the child in dialog, with neither party knowing quite how the inquiry will come out, but willing to follow the investigation wherever it leads.[1]

(e) *All of the above.* In a community of inquiry, there is a pooling of experience in which each is as ready and willing to learn from each other's experience as from his or her own. There is also a commitment to reasonableness, that is, to rationality tempered by critical and creative judgment. One can even condone efforts at persuasion in such a context, where it is evident that mutual trust prevails, and that the effort to persuade is well-intentioned.

In a community of inquiry, students and teachers are co-inquirers engaged in deliberating together about the issues or problems at hand. Such dialog is a form of reasoning together. It is not an attempt to substitute reasoning for science, but an effort to complement scientific inquiry. The information derived from science – its theories and data and procedures – are not in dispute. What reasoning helps do is: (a) *extend* knowledge through logical inference; (b) *defend* knowledge through reasons and arguments; and (c) *coordinate* knowledge through critical analysis.

When we underscore the word "inquiry" in "community of inquiry," we emphasize the investigative role of such communities. This is the role that leads them to deliberate with regard to concepts, evidence, jurisdictions, reasons, definitions, and other matters directly involved in or complementary to the experimental aspect of scientific inquiry. The dialog in a community of inquiry is aimed at practical results, such as settlements, determinations, decisions, or conclusions. All of these are *judgments.*

When we underscore the word "community" in "community of inquiry," we stress the social, affective, and creative aspects of the process. *Social*, because the community's members recognize their interdependency, and at the same time acknowledge each other's distinctive points of view and perspectives. *Affective*, because participants in such communities exhibit *care* for each other and for the procedures of inquiry. And *creative*, because such communities encourage participants to think for themselves — independently, imaginatively, and with originality.

Violence and Justification

It is not my purpose to inquire whether or not there is such a thing as just violence, in the sense that Michael Walzer (1977), in his book *Just And Unjust Wars*, explores the possibility that, under certain circumstances, war can be justified. Nor am I concerned to examine the various aspects of violence and to show that some aspects are neither moral nor non-moral, while other aspects (for example, violations) are necessarily immoral. These are matters that are beyond the reach of this essay, even if I cannot resist alluding to them from time to time.

What I am concerned about is that education for violence-reduction and for peace is likely to go the way of countless other initiatives, such as teaching about drugs, AIDS, sexual harassment, and environmental issues. The problem is based on the fact that these educational efforts to instil particular sets of values in the public at large take for granted pedagogical techniques which even in the schools are being phased out as obsolete. I am speaking of the "lectures by authorities" approach. The public is expected to accept these values simply on the grounds that they have been recommended by experts. This approach works well with the gullible and poorly with the sceptical. The sceptics, aware that every interest group has its experts, paid or unpaid, are inclined to distrust claims of any kind that are to be accepted simply on the basis of the authority of the claimant.

But there is another method of obtaining the public's consent, and that is by invoking value terms or value concepts that would seem to be established *a priori*. In this sense, there is really nothing to educate people about, since they already know, if they are at all familiar with the language, that certain words have approbation built into their very meaning, while other words or concepts carry with them, at all times, a built-in social disapprobation. Listen to David Hume:

> *It is indeed obvious that writers of all nations and all ages concur in applauding justice, humanity, magnanimity, prudence, veracity; and in*

blaming the opposite qualities . . . Some part of the seeming harmony in morals may be accounted for from the very nature of language. The word <u>virtue</u>, with its equivalent in every tongue, implies praise, as that of <u>vice</u> does blame; and no one, without the most obvious and grossest impropriety, could affix reproach to a term, which in general acceptation, is understood in a good sense; or bestow applause, where the idiom requires disapprobation. (1985, p. 228)

Thus, it would seem that moral education need merely alert students to the terminology of the vices and virtues, and the built-in disapprobation or approbation will automatically teach the students the difference between right and wrong. One does not have to puzzle over these things: generosity is always right and cruelty is always wrong. For any given culture, learning to speak and think in the indigenous language is sufficient to educate children and newcomers into the way the good and the right are viewed in that culture.

This conventional approach to ethics has the merit of conveying to students the importance of taking into account the hidden praise or blame with which the moral terms we use are infected. On the other hand, it is mischievously misleading, for it lulls us into thinking that ethical inquiry is superfluous. If cruelty is always wrong, then our only problems are empirical and logical. All cruelty being wrong, we need only ascertain if this particular act was indeed an act of cruelty, and we can deduce that it was wrong. The conventional approach claims to solve the problem of ethics by confining it to the formulation of minor premises.

One of the things ethical inquiry must do – and this applies to problems involving force and violence as to anything else – is examine precisely what is normally taken for granted in moral discourse. A community engaged in deliberative ethical inquiry might take up questions such as these:

Can a person be cruel and still be kind?

Are there circumstances under which it would not be right to be generous?

Can we love someone we don't like?

Can we be jealous of someone we don't love?

Is veracity sometimes inappropriate?

Are justice and freedom in principle incompatible?

Are all vices matters of self-deception?

Can there be violations where there are no rights?

Can there be rights where there are no remedies?

Can someone be both violent and benevolent?

Notice that questions such as these emphasize compatibility, coherency, and context. Thus, even if justice is always and everywhere good, there is the possibility that other goods, such as freedom, might delimit its practical applicability. Coherency is often the objective of conceptual analysis, as when we ask for the clarification of concepts, inferences, meanings, and so on. And, of course, even those concepts that we most frequently take for granted may turn out to be troublesome in special contexts, as in acts of omission, questions of avoidability of infliction of pain and suffering, and jurisdictional disputes.

It cannot be emphasized sufficiently that the reason value concepts are not fixed and stable is that our understanding of them is not fixed and stable. We are a long way from knowing what, say, freedom means, if indeed we will ever know such a thing completely, and the same is true for other moral notions (Hampshire, 1956). Thus we cannot be sure that what the 21st century will understand with regard to such notions as peace and violence will be the same as what the 19th or 20th centuries understood them to mean. This much, however, is clear enough; the more we bend our efforts towards peace-making and violence-reduction, the better our understanding of these concepts will be.

What I am emphasizing is that values education ignominiously collapses when it is based solely on the notion that the values in question are somehow inherent or intrinsic, so that all the educator need do is *reveal* these intrinsic values to the student. Values are only as good as their justifications. We can agree that peace is fine and beautiful and that violence is nasty and ugly, but these characteristics are weak and unconvincing unless they are woven into the justificational fabric. The time is past when we could tell students that it is simply self-evident that, say, courage is good, without having them engage in the hard conceptual labor of distinguishing it from look-alikes such as fool-hardiness, or of citing the reasons that would justify it in particular cases.

It may be objected that I am ignoring considerations of character and disposition, but I do not think that this is the case. First, I would maintain that the build-up of moral character is the result of the successive superimposition of layer upon layer of justified moral acts, performed under a variety of circumstances. A person who is characteristically disposed to be reasonable is one who early on recognized the importance of connecting acts and the reasons that justify them, and who expects such connectedness in one's future conduct. Second, I would argue that we have seriously underestimated the role the intellectual virtues play in the make-up of moral character. Respect for other points of view, patience with other deliberators, dedication to rationality, intellectual creativity in the formulation of new hypotheses – all of these and many more form an indispensable portion of anyone's moral character. And thirdly, there are ways of building character and developing moral dispositions which do not rely on authority, persuasion, exhortation, or various other approaches of dubious validity. I am thinking of the character-building consequences of participating in communities of inquiry. But I will turn to this consideration shortly.

Here I would like simply to reiterate the point made in this section, that education for violence-reduction and for peace-making cannot do without linguistic, logical, and conceptual analyses, so as to get students to think critically about the language, reasoning, and informational structuring that are typically involved in such educational initiatives. If one student in a classroom claims that another student has been violent, the opportunity is there for a reasonable dialog, not about the violent act itself, but about the context in which it occurred and the reasons that might be adduced for and against it.

It may be said that we substitute thereby one set of self-evident values for another. In place of courage and cowardice, or patriotism and lack of patriotism, or benevolence and malevolence, we substitute moderation, temperance, and reasonableness, independently of *their* justification. But this is not so: moderation, temperance, and reasonableness, are no less susceptible to being made, at any moment, the subject-matter of ethical inquiry, than are courage, generosity, and good will. What makes these and other virtues similar to them of special importance is that they happen also to be related to the *procedures* of ethical inquiry. The justification for the emphasis upon consistency, scrupulousness, reasonableness, considerateness, attentiveness, and so on, lies in the fact that inquiry relies on values such as these. Without them, inquiry cannot be effectively prosecuted.

Ethical inquiry, in turn, yields strengthened ethical judgment, and strengthened ethical judgment intervenes to bring about violence-reduction, prejudice-reduction, and the alleviation of other deplorable acts and attitudes. The problem, therefore, is to find a way of introducing ethical inquiry into the classroom, not so much to sit in judgment on previous acts of violence as to give *preventive* consideration to future acts of that character. The classroom devoted to ethical inquiry should not have the pressure-cooker atmosphere that prevails in the jury room: it should be free to proceed at a more leisurely pace, without having to make decisions prematurely – indeed, without necessarily having to make them at all.

The Strengthening of Judgment Through Cognitive Work

It is a commonplace that one can strengthen one's judgment by frequently exercising it. But this really tells us very little, since so much depends upon the kinds of situations in which such exercises are performed. One makes judgments in doing crossword puzzles, answering riddles, and reviewing grocery receipts, but such challenges are relatively trivial and provide satisfaction in return for mere cleverness.

Is it the case then that it takes no great wit to find the answer to a question, where that answer is already known to the person who asks the question? Of course not. Questions can be asked with regard to matters of specialized knowledge, and one would have to be brilliant to come up with the answers to many of them, even though those answers are already known.

Nevertheless, there is a world of difference between asking a child a question the answer to which is known and asking a question the answer to which is unknown, or a matter of considerable controversy. If the questioner already knows the answer, what the child generally proceeds to do is to try to find out what the questioner knows, rather than embark on an independent investigation of the problem. The child knows better than to try to re-invent the wheel if he or she is merely asked what a vehicle is.

On the other hand, if the question is a meaningful one and the questioner does not know the answer, the classroom discussion that follows will likely demand that each participant think more and more judiciously. Consideration will be given to the circumstances under which violence is to be forbidden, under which it is to be tolerated or condoned, and under which it might be greeted with bouquets and accolades. Distinction making will be invited, so that seemingly similar behaviors can be differentiated from one another. (This is often necessary in the case of alleged sexual violence.) And careful attention will be paid to the bearings which existing legal statutes may have on the cases in question.

The strengthening of judgment that is a prerequisite for success in violence reduction or peace making is difficult to bring about unless students are seriously engaged in cognitive *work*. In physics, work is understood to be the overcoming of resistance. In cognitive matters, its meaning – or one of its meanings, in any event – is quite the same. The resistances to be overcome are not things like friction and gravity, but things like prejudice, self-deception, conflicting emotions, illogicality, fallacies of reasoning, unwillingness to compromise where a matter is subject to mediation or arbitration, and lack of respect for the opinions of others. These are powerful resistances to be overcome; to do so requires patient, deliberative inquiry – in effect, cognitive work.

Ordinarily, however, the obstacles to the performance of cognitive work are latent rather than manifest. We are not aware, in practising to become more reasonable, that in the process we are overcoming some of the prejudices or intellectual vices that have normally blocked our path. Breaking down these obstacles, or smoothing them out so that one can glide over them, can indeed be a long and arduous job – indeed, a never-ending job, since no one is able to get rid of such obstacles once and for all.

Nevertheless, just as we do not have to address ourselves directly to the notion of peace in order to engage in education for peace making, so we do not have to address ourselves directly to our prejudices or super-stitions in order to develop in ourselves more reasonable ways of think-ing. In the earlier stages of cognitive work, at any rate, one need not target the remaking of the self, even it is going to have to come to that sooner or later. As Edwin Muir (1965) in "The Question" puts it:

Will you, sometime, have sought so long and seek

Still in the slowly darkening hunting ground,

Catch sight some ordinary month or week

Of that strange quarry you scarcely thought you sought –

Yourself, the gatherer gathered, the finder found,

The buyer, who would buy all, in bounty bought –

And perch in pride on the princely hand, at home,

And there, the long hunt over, rest and roam?

In these earlier stages, the open-ended question can be sufficient to launch those powerful searchings that overcome resistances with hardly any awareness that they were there at all. For example, let a single student or a group of students be set the task of making a comparison between two things so similar that they might easily be taken for one another. The work that ensues is to spell out the differences – what Josiah Royce calls the process of interpretation (Royce, 1968, p. 302). Royce provides us with a simple, homely illustration. Take two strips of paper and paste the ends of one together to form a ring. Do the same to the other, but only after having first given the strip a half-turn. This, of course, makes the second a Möbius strip. Now ask the students to identify the points of difference, and they will begin to articulate their observations, such as that the first strip has two sides while the second has only one, and the first strip has two edges, the second only one. As we see, the elaboration of the distinction requires careful observation of specific points of difference, and these in turn provide criteria for further distinction making in other cases. Needless to say, the activity teaches children not only how differences are constituted, but how some of them can be generated. After having performed cognitive work such as this, the distinction the children make, after performing the comparison, will have become a knowing one, and their judgment, to that extent, will have been strengthened. And not a few students will confess themselves perplexed by the mystery of the Möbius strip which they themselves brought into being.

Educating for Values and Meanings Through the Community of Inquiry

Many of us have learned, often through bitter experiences, that peace is not merely desired but is actually desir*able*. It is something we *may* approve of before reflection or inquiry, but that we *do* approve of after reflection or inquiry. Furthermore, we would like students to share these convictions of ours, not just because they are ours, but because we are convinced that the students would benefit from accepting them as their own. And so we are strongly tempted to proselytize young people with these opinions of ours, barely managing to restrain ourselves by repeating to ourselves that preaching is not teaching.

For that matter, instruction is not very good education either, when it is a matter of educating for values. After all, in cases like these, where we feel sure we have already identified what is valuable, what we would like is for students to arrive at our conclusions through the use of *their* own reasonings. And this can be done effectively, I believe, only through the use of the community of inquiry mechanism.

There is a tendency to confuse the community of inquiry with cooperative learning, but the one should not be mistaken for the other. The chief point of difference is that cooperative learning stresses non-competitive discussion while the community of inquiry stresses shared, collaborative inquiry. Inquiry, in turn, emphasizes moving forward to investigate a problem situation, and it also seeks to bring about a product. The product may be a settlement of disagreements, it may be a judgment, or it may be a judgment enacted in behavior, but in any case, it is more than a simple process.

In values education, the cognitive workload requires that consideration be given to:

(a) the value in question (in this case, violence or peace) as an *ideal-type,* requiring conceptual analysis;

(b) the *phenomenology* of the value in question;

(c) the concrete *conditions* or *powers* that seek to approximate or bring about the value as an ideal;

(d) the *relationships* between the ideal and the powers that seek to realize it;

(e) the *educational setting*, in which what takes place is not merely the study of the above factors, but the bringing about of the desirable values that are under investigation.

These constitute five tasks for the community of inquiry. We can consider them briefly in a bit more detail.

(a) One way to begin a session of *education for peace* or *education for violence-reduction* is to have the participants read a text in which a fictional community of inquiry is to be found attempting to define the key terms, peace and violence. It will be discovered that the classroom community will allow itself to be influenced and guided by the fictional community, which it consciously or unconsciously attempts to emulate.

It should not be thought that Task #1 must be completed before beginning Task #2, and so on. Work on all five tasks may be carried on concurrently.

Nevertheless, students find it useful to clarify what is to be understood by the terms peace and violence. The first task is therefore definitional in character, and has to do with the elucidation of meanings.

(b) Secondly, in order to flesh out the meanings with which the community is attempting to come to grips, it may be necessary to engage in narrative or descriptive projects that can provide a phenomenology of the values or disvalues under investigation. Hobbes does some of this: he vividly describes the state of nature as a state of war in which human life is "nasty, brutish and short," denies there is an intermediate condition which we nowadays might call "cold war," and concludes, without further ado, that "all other time is peace." Peace itself is seldom described. And yet the implication in Hobbes is clear enough: peace is a time of commerce and industry, a time of unimpeded communication, in which the arts and sciences flourish, in which people travel at will, and in which people live without fearing their neighbors.

(c) Thirdly, the community must find out the *means* which are to be utilized in the attainment of the sought-after values, or in the successful avoidance of the disvalues. Thus, democracy is often cited as a guarantor of peace while political authoritarianism is held to be a guarantor of violence, just as protein-rich foods are thought to be conducive to health, while the lack of such foods brings about the lack of health.

(d) Then there are the means-end relationships to be considered. Clearly, the means-end relationship between protein-rich foods and health is what we call *nutrition*, and the means-end relationship between authoritarianism and violence may be thought of as *repression*. But obviously there are many things that can play the role of means and have a causal relationship with violence, other than authoritarianism. Child abuse, for example, is generally cited as a way of assuring anti-social attitudes in the children so affected, and of assuring their anti-social behavior in adolescence and adulthood. Abused children turn into abusive adults. Adults who disturb others often turn out to have been disturbed by others when they were children. In short, the fourth task involves learning the causal relationships or etiologies that can account for the flourishing of positive values in certain cases and of negative values in other cases.

(e) Fifth and finally, there is the educational setting or environment that is indispensable for the fostering of peace-making behavior and for the inhibition of violence, either in disposition or in action.

There are two major sources of violence. One is the thoughtless impulsiveness of individuals. The other is the internal as well as external aggressiveness of institutions. These sources are often tapped at the very first sign of frustration. There is little patience with procedures that attempt to defuse the conflict so that the violence may be averted, even where such procedures are familiar to the parties involved. Yet it is only through the establishment of sound conflict-resolution procedures that the campaign for peace can be won.

What I shall conclude by discussing – the community of inquiry as a means of reducing violence and strengthening peace in a school setting – has already been alluded to in earlier portions of this essay. I have previously insisted that values like peace and the absence of violence cannot be effectively taught. They must be practised, embodied, and lived. Yet we cannot just take it for granted that to achieve peace, we must simply learn to practise peace. For peace is an end, and what we must practise are the means to that end. Even to call such practice "peace-making" is a distortion. To succeed, the process we are to employ must be one that students find satisfying for its own sake, while at the same time, one of its outcomes is the achievement of peaceful social relationships.

So there are really two aspects to the community of inquiry considered as a process. One is its *means-end* aspect, where peace is the long-range objective. The other is its *means-consequence* aspect, where the process is engaged in for its own immediate rewards, but where peace emerges as a spin-off or consequence nevertheless. Unless this second aspect is present, the first is likely to be weak and ineffectual.

The community of inquiry is a wholesome social organization which provides a positive sense of belonging to its participants. In it, the participants are able to realize the reasonableness they are seldom able to practise amidst the turmoil and turbulence of the rest of their lives. It is within the community of inquiry, then, that they can appreciate their own heightened powers, which, in turn, leads them to enhanced self-esteem.

In a community of inquiry, the contributions of all are welcomed, and not just the contributions of those who are quicker or more clever. As the participants learn to listen attentively to one another, they find their mutual respect being strengthened. And as they begin to recognize their dependency upon the community of inquiry procedures, they begin to care for and feel protective of those very procedures.

This is a community in which each participant can interpret any participant to any other participant, or can mediate between this one and that one. Each can offer hypotheses; each is free to build on or elaborate the hypotheses of others. Each can make claims; each can offer counter-examples or counter-claims. Each is free to question, to offer reasons or evidence, to express puzzlement, to portray ideals, to raise points of order.

Each community of inquiry in existence is likely to have been inspired by some ideal or fictional community of inquiry which it attempts to emulate. Furthermore, each participant is likely to be inspired by some other participant to do likewise. If I observe you questioning what all have hitherto taken for granted, I too am emboldened to question what is taken for granted. If I note the rigor you are able to introduce into your reasoning by your familiarity with elementary logical principles like the prohibition of self-contradiction, I will want to study the same things so as to have the same rigor.

The community of inquiry takes the problematic seriously. It recognizes that human institutions are imperfect, human experience is often only partial, and human knowledge limited. It therefore recognizes the need for speculation as well as for analysis. It acknowledges that across-the-board solutions are seldom feasible, and that often we must fall back on compromises that do not do violence to our principles. In short, it accepts the role of judgment – itself a coalition of the critical and the imaginative – in arriving at settlements where rules and precedents provide inadequate guidance.

The practice of deliberative dialog in a community of inquiry setting introduces students to alternatives to violence. It enables them to see that a peaceful society cannot be a passive one, for such dialog does not terminate with the achievement of peace. Rather, the continuation of dialog is the best way of assuring that the tranquil conditions once achieved will be maintained.

So it is that education for peace can take place in every classroom, whether or not peace is the ostensible subject matter of study. The spirit of fallibilism that prevails in a community of inquiry is an invitation on the part of all participants to have their errors pointed out to them, so that ways of correcting them might be sought. Such a spirit helps to defuse the contentiousness that absolutism and fanaticism inspire, and thereby undercuts the violence to which such contentiousness often leads. The resolution to confront the problematic and deal with it in a spirit of reasonableness is a world apart from the inflexible insistence that education means the acquisition of knowledge that is authoritative and absolute. And if reasonableness prevails in the classroom today, then tomorrow, when today's students are adults and beginning to have children of their own, it will also prevail in the home. In time, other institutions may be transformed in a similar fashion, but it must all begin in the schools.

Notes

1. This is different from either rhetoric or argument as defined above.

References

Freud, S. (1915). Thoughts for the times on war and death. In J. Strachey (Ed. and Trans.), *The standard edition of the complete works of Sigmund Freud*, 24 Vols. London: Hogarth Press, 1948-74.

Hampshire, S. (1956). In defense of radicalism. *Dissent*, Spring, 170-176.

Hobbes, T. (1991). *Leviathan*. R. Tuck (Ed.). New York, NY: Cambridge University Press (p. 89).

Hume, D. (1777/1985). Of the standard of taste. In *Essays: Moral, political and literary*, Rev. Ed. (pp. 226-249), E. F. Miller (Ed.). Indianapolis, IN: Liberty Classics.

Muir, E. (1965). *Collected poems*. Oxford: Oxford University Press.

Royce, J. (1968). *The problem of christianity*. Chicago: University of Chicago Press.

Walzer, M. (1977). *Just and unjust wars: A moral argument with historical illustrations*. New York: Basic Books.

CHAPTER 7

Peirce, Feminism, and Philosophy for Children

Ann Margaret Sharp

The overall purpose of this paper is to explore three related themes: (a) feminist philosophy and philosophy for children have much in common, including pedagogy, an inclusive orientation, and a fallibilist but critical epistemology; (b) both feminism and philosophy for children benefit from a close reading of Peirce, but only philosophy for children draws explicitly on Peirce; and (c) because of this common bond, feminist philosophy and philosophy for children provide place to stand against the postmodern retreat to texts.

Not long ago, Richard Rorty was speaking at Inter-Continental University in Mexico City and voiced the view that feminist philosophy would do well to look to the pragmatists for a theoretical underpinning of their own work. One thesis of this essay is that they would find much in the work of Charles Sanders Peirce (1839-1914) that would be helpful in working out a feminist theory of self, and an epistemological, ethical, and educational theory.

Both elementary school philosophy and feminist philosophy have much in common in terms of theory and practice. In many ways, they share a philosophical framework that can be viewed historically as a response to the tensions and contradictions of the 1960s. Today there is growing consensus among philosophers that much of the history of philosophy would look very different if certain suppressed voices, the voices of the poor, of ethnic minorities, and of women had been taken into account. In the last ten years, elementary school children have been doing philosophy in thousands of classrooms around the world. Twenty-five-thousand children in Brazil alone do philosophy as part of their regular school day, and close to half that number of children in Australia, Quebec, and Spain do the same. The existence of philosophy in the lower schools has now given rise to the view that perhaps the history of philosophy would also look very different if children's philosophical views had been taken into account. Study of the philosophical dialogs in classroom communities of inquiry, many of them published in *Thinking* and *Analytic Teaching,* attest to the fact that not only can children do philosophy well when guided by a teacher who knows what to do, but that they are most capable of creating original alternative theories that, in certain contexts, give a new dimension to philosophy itself.[1]

The past 22 years of practice in classrooms have shown that children are not only capable of mastering formal and informal logic and the various components of critical thinking, often faster than their teachers, but that they have an ingenious disposition for the creation of metaphysical, ethical, and aesthetic inquiry. The younger the children are, the more fresh and unique their views and the more successful they become in a relatively short time in philosophizing well together. One has only to look at the video tapes of Professor Thomas Jackson of the University of Hawaii working with first graders over the period of one year to see that children are quite capable of doing philosophy well.[2] Certain rules of procedure become routine and dispositions of tolerance, listening attentively, critical questioning and inquiry, as well as the generation of original alternative views, are fostered and reinforced with every experience of doing philosophy in the classroom.

A study of both movements – feminism and philosophy for children – reveal striking similarities with regard to philosophical assumptions. Both stress the discovery of meaning and the advantage of taking many perspectives into account in coming to know. Both pay particular attention not only to the content under discussion, but to the way we do philosophy – the ethical, political, and social implications of the process. Both reject Cartesianism with its stress on clear and distinct ideas divorced from human experience and its assumed dichotomies of body and mind, subject and object. Both tend to see the self as relational and social. Both use the narrative as a valuable tool in motivating philosophical inquiry. In children's philosophy, the classroom community of inquiry is the pedagogy. In feminist philosophy, a similar procedure prevails. Stress is on cooperative rather than competitive inquiry, perspectivism, respect for persons, communal reasoning as an arbitrator, evaluation of criteria, norms, and ideals against the backdrop of human experience. Both see all theories as value-laden creations that continually must be tested against the experience of children, women, and men, as well as the rest of nature.

In this time of postmodern theory, both stand for the efficacy of communal reasoning and its ability to improve the world. Both reject the notion that reason is impotent. The postmodern retreat to the text has a political dimension that is unacceptable to both women and children who are just beginning to discover their rights and their rightful place in the world of intellectual conversation and decision making. The abandonment of trust in the efficacy of reasonable inquiry can be accompanied by a loss of hope and a sense of resignation, a nihilist position that there is nothing to be done in making the world more reasonable because nothing can be done. At a time when the weight of reasonable inquiry sustains prescriptions for the granting of children's and women's rights – rights they have never enjoyed before – it is counterproductive to accept a view of philosophy that claims that communal reasoning is impotent. Women and children do not have to claim absolute, a-historical validity for their views – the products of their communal inquiry. Their reasoning can be justified on the grounds that it has the capacity to offer different perspectives, illuminate existing social and political relations, and show the deficiencies of solely male adult perspectives.

Rather than signalling the *end of philosophy* as many of the post-moderns claim, philosophy for children and feminism has the capacity for breathing new life into the discipline. The ideal of absolute intellectual purity and belief in the possibility of unmediated knowledge of the world are passing out of the discipline. Feminism and Philosophy for Children are offering coherent alternatives to the old ideals (Bordo, 1987; Friedman, 1989; Grimshaw, 1986; MacKinnon, 1987; McFall, 1989; Raymond, 1986; Spelman, 1988; and Young, 1990).

Peirce's Conception of the Self

A study of the collected works of Charles Sanders Peirce (1931-1935; 1958) sheds light on the community of inquiry, reason's role (induction, abduction, and deduction) in bringing about a more reasonable world, and the nature of the self-in-community – three fundamental ideas that underlie philosophy for children, its pedagogy, and its stress on the social nature of the self. One need only to study the seven novels of Philosophy for Children and the various manuals to see Peircean ideas in chapter after chapter: the nature and importance of inquiry, the importance of fallibilism, the role of logic, the importance of the cultivation of good habits as a means of self-control, the social construction of knowledge, the role of the aesthetic in ethical inquiry, and many more. Philosophy for Children assumes with Peirce that it is immersion into logical, ethical, and aesthetical inquiry that can provide children with the norms and ideals that they need to make wiser judgements about their own lives. For Peirce, it is this immersion that will help each child discover: "How feeling, conduct, and thought ought to be controlled, supposing them in a measure to be subject to self-control, exercised by self-criticism and the purposive formations of habits" (MS 6555-24).

In feminist writings, there is little consciousness of how the philosophy of Peirce is in accord with feminist views and could help resolve many of the inner contradictions that have emerged in feminist writings on epistemology, the community, and the self.[3] Some American feminists, for example, Evelyn Fox Keller (1990), Naomi Scheman (1987), and Jane Flax (1990), have been drawn more to the British *object-relations* school, which emphasizes the development of the self in relation to others. Often elaborating on the work of Nancy Chodorow (1978), they have developed a fertile theoretical framework for exploring gender differences in early infant development, and their implications for male-dominated culture. The central target of criticism here has been the overvaluing of autonomy in our Western models of reason. But it is Catherine Keller (1986) who stresses the relational aspect of the self from a philosophical framework, in her case a Whiteheadian framework.

For both Peirce and Whitehead, the self is a process of growth that only makes sense in relation to the others that influence it. Further, the self grows only as it increases its own capacity for self-control over one's own conduct. Unlike Amelie Rorty (1976, 1988), who thinks of the self as a possessor of properties, and persons as unified centres of actions, choice, and control – the unit of both legal and theological responsibility – Peirce ascribes the characteristics of Rorty's persons to selves. The ultimate criterion which guides one's self-control is reasonableness and this reasonableness develops within community. For Peirce, "to be a self is to be a possible member of some community" (5.402). To think of the self as independent of society doesn't make sense to Peirce. Each individual self is continually in the process of creating and defining identity through give-and-take with the natural world and other people. "No mind can take one step without the aid of other minds" (2.220). In this sense, all selves are inter-dependent.

Peirce thought of the self as a sign. This sign is in the process of continual growth by means of a dialog one conducts with oneself and others. Such dialogs are of such intimacy with what one calls the self that they can be compared, he thought, with personal beings:

> *Two things here are all important. The first is that a person is not absolutely an individual. His thoughts are what he is saying to himself, that is, is saying to that other self that is just coming into life in the flow of time. When one reasons, it is that critical self that one is trying to*

persuade . . .The second thing to remember is that man's circle of society (however widely or narrowly this phrase may be understood) is a sort of loosely compacted person, in some respects of a high[er] rank than the person of an individual organism. (5.421)

Thinking is a process of internal dialog for Peirce. When the self thinks, there are always two selves operating: the critical self and the innovative self. When the self thinks, it is the critical self that the innovative self is trying to persuade. The former represents the habits of a person, the latter a challenge to these habits. The claim that thought is a form of internal dialog and that dialog presupposes a community in which there are standards and norms for discourse is one of the fundamental insights of Peirce which is later built upon by George Herbert Mead, John Dewey, and Lev Vygotsky. Since the innovative self is always in dialog with the critical self, there is a real sense in which we are always a mystery to ourselves – it is as if we are never quite sure of who we will be tomorrow.

Peirce thought that the human self is not confined to the body. Since the self is a sign, it can be compared to a word. Like words, it is possible that minds can be in two places at one time. In his later thought, Peirce not only saw the self as an evolving sign but as a centre of purposes and power, the power of autonomous self-control. To be a self is to be a person who controls one's own behavior in accordance with one's own ideals. Peirce draws a distinction between power as self-control or autonomy and power as force, especially force over others.

Peirce thought that all human beings are capable of evolving into autonomous selves or agents given the right education directed toward the cultivation of three very distinct powers:

The first of these is composed of powers of feelings, or say, of consciousness, of being or becoming aware of anything. The second consists of powers of action, that is to say, of really modifying something . . . The third power consists of powers of taking habits which, by the meaning of the word includes getting rid of them, since, in my nomenclature a 'habit' is nothing but a state of 'would-be' realized in any sort of subject that is itself real. In other words, a person – a full person – must possess the capacities to feel, to act and to learn. (NIM 142)

An education that empowers the child to "feel, to act and to learn" is one that provides the tools needed to become a full person. A person's capacities to accomplish new – and undreamt of – wonderful things is limitless. In Peirce's view, most of us accomplish only a small fraction of what we are capable. Certain things are beyond our control – hurricanes, blizzards, some diseases – all of which can incapacitate us. But given a supportive environment and the ability to control our own behavior, most of us could accomplish much more than we do. To live in community is to increase our possibilities of accomplishing more. It is the community that helps us gain more and more self-control over ourselves as we grow. Richard Berstein (1965) points out that for Peirce, there are several degrees or levels of self-control, one of which is the ability to regulate one's self-control. This power comes into being when one undertakes to reflect with others upon and improve one's rules of conduct through communal inquiry. Each time a classroom community of inquiry engages in logical, ethical, or aesthetic inquiry, there is a possibility that a child may practise the power of controlling her or his control of self-control.[4]

To speak of the essential self, or the real self, only makes sense to Peirce if one thinks of it as an achievement rather than as a discovery of something already there. The self is something that comes into being as we consciously impose habits, control of these habits, and control of the control of these habits in our everyday conduct. This control is always guided by the norms, criteria, and ideals that we have come to accept for ourselves as worthwhile. To be educated is to be given the opportunity to inquire with others into the disciplines of logic, ethics, metaphysics, and aesthetics so as to discover for ourselves the norms, criteria, and ideals that we want to live by. It is in this sense that we can envision the self as growing in self-control and wisdom, and becoming critically aware of one's own imperfections. The wonderful thing about being human is our ability to self-correct.

For Peirce, the eternal forms of Plato are the intrinsically admirable ideals that we come to respect as we inquire with others into the domains of philosophy. Moreover, it is not a totally active process. Yes, we have to do our part. We have to learn how to think well, listen to others, generate alternative views, identify assumptions, read the works of others, and immerse ourselves in the various disciplines. Further, we have to internalize the process of inquiry so that when we are alone we can continue to inquire with ourselves. It is hard work. However, as the process goes on, the ideals themselves begin to exert a pull or an attraction upon us to which we either respond or don't respond. Peirce assumed that most of us cannot resist the pull. Further he subsumed all ideals under the growth of concrete reasonableness in the world. It is, he thought, by committing oneself to the ideal of reasonableness that the self becomes itself in its fullness. It is at this point that the human being can think of herself or himself as a conscious agent cooperating with all of nature to grow new ideas, new institutions, new mores, new values that will help the world become more humane, more reasonable, more beautiful.

If the self can only realize itself through its commitment to ideals and if the commitment to even higher ideals paradoxically requires more and more surrendering of the self (or ego), then it follows for Peirce that the coherent, integrated self can only emerge when the unreflective, selfish, grasping ego is overcome. In his view, the selfish, grasping self rests upon the most vulgar delusion of vanity. Its self-absorption ultimately leads to self-destruction. On the other hand, the self-that-has-been-overcome by means of self-control is an autonomous power capable of dedicating herself or himself to the creation of a more beautiful world.

Peirce holds a view of the self as an agent that is brought into being through struggle for self-control and self-correction. His view renders a vision of the self in community as an instrument through whom the ideal of reasonableness becomes concretely embodied in reasonable habits, reasonable goals, reasonable arrangements in society that serve the growth of all people. In our capacity as instruments, we are signs – means by which nature itself is evolving into something characterized by mind. In this sense, the purpose of the self is to serve. Concrete reasonableness, its embodiment in the world, is what we are all about. It is to be distinguished from rationality that can be rigid, merely deductive, ahistorical, and uncreative of new criteria, norms, and values. The postmodern loss of faith in communal reasoning would make little sense to Peirce, for whom selves were part of nature and nature itself is always evolving into something more reasonable.

Epistemology-in-Community

Peirce was a fallibilist. He thought that all human thought is limited and therefore all good thinkers are those who habitually look to correct themselves, to discover the limitations of their own views and theories. The method he advocated was one of continual communal inquiry.

Fallibilism means that persons must internalize the fact that their views are probably wrong – or at least very limited. This internalization gives rise to the disposition of open-mindedness and critical thinking together as a willingness to welcome new horizons, new conceptual frameworks in which to view reality. Knowing, for Peirce, presupposes involvement in a social process replete with rules of compliance, norms of assessment, and standards of excellence that are humanly created. Although humans aspire to unmediated knowledge of the world, they will never attain it.

Such direct access is not possible. The only mode of finding out that has any credibility is through theory-laden hypotheses that organize and structure our observation by according means to observed events and bestowing relevance and significance upon the phenomena. It is human perception combined with social convention that is involved in all strategies for problem solving and identifying methods by which to test the validity of proposed solutions. Knowledge, then, is a convention rooted in practical judgements of a community of fallible inquirers who struggle to resolve theory-dependent problems under specific historical conditions. No investigation, no matter how contextual or critical or self-conscious can escape the fundamental conditions of human inquiry. This is the basis for fallibilism itself.

However, this is not reason to despair. Science, social science, and the humanities can still make progress – progress that is always open to revision. Because our cognition is always theoretically mediated, the world captured in human inquiry and designated as factual is always something that one can question. A fact, for Peirce, is essentially contestable. If our view of the order of things were to change, it follows that what we consider factual would also change (Skagestad, 1981, chapters 1 and 5).

For Peirce, like modern feminists, there is no such entity as the objective knower, a self who experiences the world independent of the social community to which one belongs. What is involved in any knowing is always heavily dependent on what questions are asked, what kind of knowledge is sought, what assumptions are taken for granted, what perspectives are taken into account, and the context in which the inquiry is undertaken.

A Peircean view of cognition as human communal inquiry – human practice – has a great deal to offer feminist philosophy, as well as philosophy for children. It can provide an explanation of adult male bias within dominant thought, while at the same time examining the specific processes by which knowledge has been constituted within this tradition. It can explore the effects of the exclusion of women and children from the inquiry process itself. A whole slew of reconsiderations of traditional epistemological problems (such as relativism, perspectivism, the role of emotions and body in knowledge, the possibility of ultimate foundations, and so on) is opened up. This is not to say that detachment, clarity, and precision will cease to have any value in the process of understanding. But perhaps modern feminist philosophers are more than willing to agree with Kant that objectivity itself is the result of human communal structuring and the *vagueness* as well as specificity, the particular as well as the general, tentativeness and valuation are essential to good thinking.

Thus women and children are raising different questions, challenging dominant views, posing different issues while at the same time attending to the method of inquiry adequate for a consideration of these issues, and can contribute significantly to the development of a more comprehensive understanding of human experience, the world, and philosophical inquiry itself. Fallibilism assures the community of inquiry of children and/or women that they are themselves always working within a framework of references that could change, while, at the same time, are calling the dominant tradition into question. Since there is no absolute certainty, all proposed ideas must be tested against the changing experience of reality and the verdict must often be delayed. Although Peirce does posit truth at the end of all inquiry – he reminds us that it will only come at the end of infinite inquiry by an infinite number of inquirers working together in community.

Peirce's view of cognition has metaphysical implications. While ideas are fallible and emerge through communal, tentative probings, they also form themselves into habitual patterns. Peirce was always struck by the power of habit to mold and govern the process of inquiry itself. Underlying a belief in the habitual structure of ideas is his metaphysical view that nature itself is evolving into certain patterns that can also be described as habits. The so-called laws of nature are such habits that prevail at a given cosmic epoch. These habits are subject to change across long stretches of time and can reform themselves into novel patterns. The centrality of the concept of habit in cosmology, epistemology, and ethics provides Peirce with a justification for both fallibilism, continual inquiry, and hope in the efficacy of human reason.

The Community of Inquiry and Evolutionary Love

For Peirce, pragmatism is future-directed and always open to novelty. One assumes that reality can never be adequately known by an individual inquirer. Since knowledge is fallible and since nature itself is subject to novel variation (Peirce's doctrine of tychism), the individual must rely on others for some form of reliable knowledge. For Peirce, the community of inquiry is the most adequate horizon for the quest for knowledge. Peirce thought reality can only be determined by sign series – that is, it can only be discovered by a community as it works across long stretches of time.

The real, then, is that which sooner or later, information and reasoning would finally result in, and which therefore is dependent of the vagaries of me and you. Thus, the very origin of the conception of reality shows that this conception essentially involves the notion of a community — without definite limits and capable of a definite increase of knowledge. And so these series of cognition — the real and unreal — consists of those which, at a time sufficiently future, the community will always continue to reaffirm and of those which, under the same conditions, will ever after be denied. (Peirce quoted in Corrington, 1987, p. 13)

Philosophy for children defines a community of inquiry as a group of people who are willing to deliberate cooperatively and collaboratively in a self-reflective and critical manner about an issue of concern to all of them. It need not be a scientific concern. Such a community is characterized by dialog that is fashioned collaboratively out of the reasoned contribution of all the participants. In such a community, participants learn to object to weak reasoning, build on strong reasoning, care for each other as well as the procedures of inquiry, accept responsibility for making their contributions within the context of others, follow the inquiry where it leads and collaboratively engage in self-correction. Such individuals come to take pride in the accomplishments of the group, as well as of themselves.

When Peirce talked of the community of inquiry, he had in mind primarily an ideal group of dedicated persons pursuing a self-correcting method of scientific investigation. It is self-correcting in the sense that objectivity lies not with the individual member but in the activity and deliberation of the entire community. Such a community combines many insights and talents in order to arrive at some consensus, that itself is tested against experience and recognized as tentative. Although Peirce was primarily thinking of scientific inquiry, the concept of community of inquiry was always innovated for him because it implies commitment to self-correction and critical reasoning. In such a community, all knowledge claims become subject to further analysis and evaluation. The community learns to welcome counter-examples and new frames of reference that force the participants to rethink the addictive inferences of their general theories. Such a community can make progress toward objectivity, if what we mean by objectivity is a more comprehensive understanding. For Peirce, inquiry can make a qualitative difference in our lives in bringing us a fuller understanding, not only of the world, but of ourselves.

The progress that the community of inquiry makes is dependent upon the ability of the participants to look at the data afresh and so conceive new frameworks in which to theorize. Once the new framework is established, the inquirers cooperate in working out its implication and in testing its consequences or results in the world. What has been verified in old frameworks rarely disappear altogether (although it conceivably could happen). Often it has its counterpart in the new framework but is seen in an entirely different way. Peirce insisted that the method of communal inquiry was preferable to methods of authority, tenacity, or *a priori* reasoning as a way to come to know.

Knowledge, which itself is based on signs, can be won only when the individual participants identify with the life of the community. The community of inquiry renews itself by placing all inferences under the skeptical eye of the investigators, who are dedicated to the search for counter examples. The community has the drive toward that ideal future in which knowledge is secure and based on general metaphysical principles such as agapism. For Peirce, the search for truth and understanding in the spirit of humility is one of nature's most powerful means of making the truth appear because right reason requires respect for the facts of experience, and, at the same time, it itself is a fact of experience which must be taken into account. Experience and nature then become our final teachers and the correctors of all human theorizing.

Despite his rejection of Cartesianism and his belief in fallibilism, Peirce never lost hope in the ability of all human beings to impress reasonableness on the world. For him, it was this task that sets human beings off from the animal world. The process is slow and halting. The conclusions are always fallible, but ultimately he thought such inquiry would result in a more just, reasonable world. This optimism is characteristic of the pragmatic movement of the first half of the twentieth century and it is just this optimism that is questioned by modern philosophers today.

To be a participant in a community of inquiry is to voluntarily undertake communal reasoning with others. Such reasoning involves probing logical, ethical and aesthetic, and metaphysical assumptions. Persons are signs or beings who are not tied to the infallible instincts of the animal kingdom, but beings who can control themselves by means of norms and ideals they have come to accept. To make a normative judgement is to criticize. To criticize is to attempt to correct. To attempt to correct presupposes a measure of control over what is criticized in the first place. For Peirce, logic, ethics, and aesthetics deal with three kinds of goodness and persons can begin to understand the nature of this goodness by immersing themselves in these disciplines (Potter, 1967, pp. 8-25).

Peirce thought the higher development of persons within the context of the community of inquiry is characterized by a dialog that gives us the means by which we open ourselves to the pull of ideals. The ideal of concrete reasonableness itself requires a radical openness to what may confront the individual person, either in the guise of another person or of inner thought. In developing the habit of self-correction, the community of inquiry internalizes the disposition never to ignore the different or foreign. To welcome the foreign, the novel, the alternative, is to affirm the connection between concrete reasonableness and creative love.

The higher development of human reason, for Peirce, is agapistic. Agapism is his third general principle of cosmology. It affirms that the principle of evolutionary love operates in the universe as a whole. Agape lets growth develop freely without a predetermined goal but, at the same time, growth is always toward a perfected state of concrete reasonableness. (Here we seem to be on the ground of faith.) Peirce saw all of reality as a continuum. Whatever is, for him, is a part of a continuum. The general habits of nature he saw as moving toward the ideal convergence in which, in an infinite future, the disharmony and unreasonableness that we all experience in the world will be transformed into reasonableness. "Love, recognizing germs of loveliness in the hateful, gradually warms it to life and makes it lovely" (Peirce, 6.289).[5] It is the dialog between persons with different views, different frames of reference, that provides the most important opportunity for this creative process. "It is not by dealing out cold justice to the circle of (either my interlocutors or) my ideas that I can make them grow, but by cherishing and tending them as I would the flowers in my garden" (Peirce, 6.289).

Reason then is a form of love for Peirce. "Reason as a form of love, seeing terms of reasonableness in the irrational, gradually warms it to life and makes it reasonable. What love is in the affective domain, reason is in the cognitive sphere, namely a creative process of generalization" (Peirce 6.289). A genuine community of inquiry manifests this love in a variety of ways: love for the tools of inquiry, love of other's ideas, love of truth, love of each other as persons, love of the ultimate ideal, love of the world. Such a community is never a mere collection of individual selves or individual ideas. It is always a living union of integrated selves. The union of selves that constitutes the community is analogous to the coordination of ideas that constitute an individual personality. In this sense, the community of inquiry itself is a person. Peirce never saw the individual participant as a private sphere. The communicative self for him is the authentic self with its roots not in reason alone, but in agape.

Peirce thought that nature has a purpose. In this sense, he was a Hegelian. He saw nature as evolving and we, as part of nature, are also evolving. The evolution itself is characterized by chance, the brute element, and reason, that is subsumed under agape. It is by means of love that the mind develops and it is mind that makes nature concretely reasonable. Only so far as the cosmos itself is mind, and so has life, is it capable of further evolution. Love for Peirce was creative. It issues in new ways of looking at things. Because we are always in the process of evolving, we experience a need for love as we experience a need for reasonableness in our lives. Peirce envisioned the task of all persons to consist in consciously contributing, by means of their own self-control and self-correction, to the process of nature itself becoming more reasonable. For him, evolution itself is driven by love and such love is circular. It consists of impulses that projects creations into independence and then draws them back into harmony (Peirce, 1.602).

If a person should try to go against reason, experience itself will force a recognition of the necessity for reasonableness. If that person still resists, she or he will self-destruct or be led to live a life of complete bondage. Such a life is characterized by a complete lack of self-control. It is unfree and, in a sense, not human. Yet, we are at liberty to choose how we want to lead our lives. "That is, the person can, or if you please is compelled to make his life more reasonable. What other distinct idea than that I should be glad to know can be attached to the word liberty" (Peirce, MS 675). To be a moral agent implies autonomy, that is, the capacity for self-control.

Without the aspirations, or love of something higher than ourselves, the self will never grow in reason. The moral task is self-regulation in light of just these aspirations – aspirations that we have dreamed up for ourselves with the help of our fellow inquirers. It is as if we are the kinds of beings that must live for something more than ourselves. In so doing, we cooperate with nature itself in becoming more beautiful.

For Peirce then, it is up to us to make the world more reasonable. The *summum bonum* is not action but concrete reasonableness itself. However, it is human action that comes more and more to embody those characteristics which can be called reasonable. As we evolve and as nature evolves driven by the creative powers of love, communal reasoning comes to play a greater role in shaping and directing the future of nature itself. Evolution then is reason progressively manifesting itself. Again, nothing could be more Hegelian. However, Peirce's world is a far more open world than Hegel's. He leaves a great deal of room for chance, human spontaneity, and novelty in this continual evolution. Reason consists in its governing individual events and without those actual events, it would have no reality at all. It also consists in being continually embodied in facts that are themselves always open to interpretation. It follows then that reason can never be fully embodied since no number of events or actual facts can ever fulfill its potentiality.

> *So then, the essence of reason is such that its being can never be completely perfected. It always must be in a state of incipiency, of growth. It is like the character of a man which consists in the ideals that he will make, and which only develop as the occasion arise. Yet in all his life, no son of Adam has fully manifested what there was in him. So, then, the development of reason requires as a part of it the occurrence of more individual events that ever can occur. It requires too all the coloring of all qualities of feeling, including pleasure, in its proper place among the rest. (Peirce, 1.615)*

In this schema of things, all human beings – men, women, and children – hold a privileged and unique place in the world. If reason is the working out of ideas in the world, it follows that to exclude a person from the conversation of persons regarding matters of importance is to hinder the evolution of reasonableness. As children, women, and men in a community of inquiry, persons are capable of cultivating dispositions of tolerance, respect for others, self-control, self-criticism, and self-correction – dispositions that may lead to reasonable actions. Women and children, as well as men, need norms and criteria to guide these actions. It is the discovery or creation of these norms and criteria that we seek when we do philosophy within the context of a community of inquiry. Such philosophizing is deliberation at a highly self-conscious level. It is not an abstract endeavor. It is always related to the universe we experience, the universe which we can come to understand to some degree because we arouse out of it and are forever a part of it. The communal inquiry is the basic stuff of education.

Conclusion: Feminism and Philosophy for Children

Although there is a literature on feminist philosophy of education, one finds little stress on the importance of philosophical inquiry in the formative years of the next generation of citizens. As important as the theoretical work in feminist philosophy, sociology, political theory, linguistics, and literature is, feminist philosophers need to develop a view of education that would assure that the children of today have an opportunity to engage in philosophical inquiry within the context of a non-sexist community of inquiry. Why? Because such inquiry is essential in becoming an active participant in a democratic society while at the same time being able to apply wise norms and criteria when making political and social judgements. It has always amazed me that feminist philosophers have been, until recently, so uninterested in Philosophy for Children as a means to bring about a non-sexist society. If they have found the one particular curriculum that was created unacceptable, I would have thought that they would have been interested in cooperatively creating an alternative curriculum that would find its way into the public and private schools of the world. If Peirce is right, such an education is essential if women are ever to be liberated and if sexism is to be overcome.

People who have been oppressed are often denied access to the education they need to become a strong voice in the dominant society. Peirce was convinced that one needed to study deeply the sub-disciplines of logic, ethics, and aesthetics if one were to gain the tools of autonomous thinking. Philosophy for Children aims to provide children – half of whom are females – with the opportunity to participate in philosophical communities of inquiry where each person is respected as a potential source of insight, regardless of one's sex. The children of today are the citizens and leaders of tomorrow. To the extent that they have been educated to think well, to the extent that they can apply well-thought-out norms and criteria to the judgements they make, to that extent they will be responsible for creating strong democracies where the voices of women are given equal consideration. Such education is essential if one is to think of the possibility of bringing about a world of international understanding and peace.

Philosophy for Children focuses on the doing of ethical, aesthetic, and logical inquiry. It makes possible for young persons the opportunity to see issues from many different perspectives, while at the same time to always consider the normative question – what ought to be. The classroom community of inquiry, guided by the ideal of concrete reasonableness, is a means of preparing children to think in terms of context, criteria, and consequences, while at the same time giving the opportunity to create new norms, criteria, and ideals with which to guide their lives. Such practice aims to create dispositions essential for the formation of responsible children who are able to inquire collaboratively about matters of importance.

Classroom communities of inquiry result in an almost immediate positive consequences in terms of relatedness, participation, relevance, and respect for persons. Feminists have been strong in their critique of traditional philosophy from many perspectives. Keller (1986) and Bordo (1987) have questioned the Cartesian assumptions of philosophy; Lloyd (1984), the male bias of reason that has been handed down through the centuries; Moulton (1983), the adversarial method that philosophers have used to do philosophy; Code (1991), Jagger (1989), Baier (1985), and Ruddick (1989), the separation of epistemology and ethics; Pateman (1989, 1991), McKinnon (1987), and Hawkesworth (1990), the male bias of political theory; and Schor (1982), the emphasis of the general at the expense of the particular. The male bias in philosophy is evident not only in what the discipline deals with, but in what it has chosen not to open for inquiry. Until recently, the perspective of women and children have not been taken into account at all. In summary, feminists have highlighted two major weaknesses of traditional philosophy: (1) lack of relevance to the personal experience of over half the population of the world; and (2) embeddedness in an alienating male-oriented tradition and inaccessibility due to jargon and style.[6] One of the reasons one would think that feminists would find philosophy for children appealing is that it attempts to avoid these negative aspects of traditional philosophy while at the same time laying stress on collaborative inquiry, respect for all persons, reasonableness, relevance, and good judgement. Philosophy for children is an attempt to overcome the dichotomy between practice and substance in philosophy and in so doing revitalizes the discipline beyond what we would have ever thought possible.

Like Peirce, modern feminist philosophy posits that love has an epistemic role to play in the doing of philosophy. It is this same love that enables very different people in a community of inquiry to share an intellectual pursuit in a committed, rigorous, and collaborative fashion. Although some feminists posit that this love is erotic rather than agapistic, like Peirce they stress that it is a source of power – that which drives persons to desire to know, understand, and seek wisdom (see Lorde, 1984 and Ginzberg, 1991). Peirce tells us that we should love the tools of inquiry as we would a new bride. It is love that makes possible a bridge between participants in an international community of inquiry who bring very different world views to the enterprise – a bridge that can eventually be the basis for some mutual understanding of that which makes them similar and that which makes them unique. It is a sense of shared love acting as an epistemic force that can temper individualism and enable many to overcome differences that often block a more comprehensive understanding of the issue under inquiry.

The claim that love is essential for understanding and wisdom is not new with Peirce or feminism. Plato himself eventually came to accept that in the end knowledge required a very purified form of love. It is no accident that, in the *Symposium* (1951), Socrates learns this lesson from Diotoma, the wise woman.

The liberation to be found for all children in doing philosophy well during the formative years of their education is of utmost importance today. Le Doeuff (1991) points out that "the most lively philosophical attitude possible is in harmony with a certain feminist tradition because it provides the possibility of questioning the dominant values of the society and sets up the possibility of opposition and change."(cited in MacColl, 1994, p. 9). Philosophy for Children is not a political ideology. It does not aim to get children to think that they must oppose the dominant values in society. Rather, it aims to give children the tools that they need to think for themselves about what is essential in creating a better world for themselves. Children who do philosophy well know how to question what most people take for granted and to measure what is against what they think ought to be. Such children have been provided with the intellectual tools they need to become potential agents of change for the better. But nothing is guaranteed. If it were, there would be no sense in aiming to develop children's autonomous thinking.

Although we might have many reservations about Peirce's faith in nature's inevitable reasonableness, we assume in philosophy for children that an education in excellent thinking within the context of the discipline of philosophy and the community of inquiry is a necessary first step in the evolution of a more reasonable world. Peirce warned us over and over again: **Do Not Block the Road to Inquiry!!** His own philosophical works laid out much of the theoretical foundation for an education that would aim to transform the classroom into a community of inquiry. Modern feminism is also committed to an education of inquiry in the hope that it will lead to the creation of a more just society. There is a real pragmatic sense in which neither philosophy for children nor feminism can retreat to the postmodern world of the text with its sense of hopelessness and resignation. Even if we do not have Peirce's optimism, even if we do not have his faith in the inevitability of concrete reasonableness, it seems to me that we owe it to ourselves and the rest of nature to act as if the world can be more reasonable, can be more just, given the right education of the future citizens of the world. Such a world would be very beautiful.

Acknowledgements

I would like to thank Philip C. Guin, David Kennedy, Gilbert Talbot, and Richard "Mort" Morehouse for their suggestions and insights.

Notes

1. The journal *Thinking* is available from I.A.P.C., Montclair State College, Upper Montclair, NJ, U.S.A., 07043. The journal *Analytic Teaching* is available from Viterbo College, 815 South 9th Street, La Crosse, WI, U.S.A., 54601.

2. These tapes are available from the I.A.P.C.

3. Susan Bordo in her *Flight to Objectivity* (1987) is a welcomed exception.

4. Also see Vincent M. Colapietro (1989).

5. Also see Carl R. Hauseman (1974). Compare with Allison M. Jagger (1989).

6. I am indebted for these insights to San MacColl (1994). MacColl cites Evelyn Fox Keller (1985), Genevieve Lloyd (1984), and Sandra Harding and Merrill Hintikka (1983). Also see Sandra Harding (1991).

References

Baier, A. (1985). *Postures of mind: Essays on mind and morals.* Minneapolis: University of Minnesota Press.

Bernstein, R. (1965). *Perspectives on Peirce.* New Haven: Yale University Press.

Bordo, S. R. (1987). *The flight to objectivity: Essays on Cartesianism and culture.* Albany: SUNY Press.

Chodorow, N. (1978). *The reproduction of mothering: Psychoanalysis and the sociology of gender.* Berkeley: University of California Press.

Code, L. (1991). *What can she know? Feminist theory and the construction of knowledge.* Ithaca, NY: Cornell University Press.

Colapietro, V. M. (1989). *Peirce's approach to the self: A semiotic perspective on human subjectivity.* Albany: SUNY Press.

Corrington, R. S. (1987). *The community of interpreters.* Georgia: Mercer Press.

Flax, J. (1990). *Thinking fragments: Psychoanalysis, feminism, and postmodernism in the contemporary west.* Berkeley: University of California Press.

Fox Keller, E. (1985). *Reflections on gender and science.* New Haven: Yale University Press.

Fox Keller, E. (1990). *Conflicts in feminism.* New York: Routledge.

Friedman, M. (1989). Friendship and moral growth. *Journal of Value Inquiry, 33* (1), 3-13.

Friedman, M. (1989). Feminism and modern friendships: Dislocating the community. *Ethics, 99* (Jan), 75-90.

Ginzberg, R. (1991). Philosophy is not a luxury. In C. Caird (Ed.), *Feminist ethics* (pp. 126-145). Kansas: University of Kansas Press.

Grimshaw, J. (1986). *Philosophy and feminist thinking.* Minneapolis: University of Minnesota Press.

Harding, S. & Hintikka, M. (1983). *Discovering reality: Feminist perspectives on epistemology, metaphysics, methodology and philosophy of science.* Dordrecht: Reidel Press.

Harding, S. (1991). *Whose science? Whose knowledge? Thinking from women's lives.* Ithaca, NY: Cornell University Press.

Hauseman, C. R. (1974). Eros and agape in creative evolution: A Peircian insight. *Process Studies, 4* (1), 11-25.

Hawkesworth, M.E. (1990). *Beyond oppression: Feminist theory and political strategy.* New York, NY: Continuum Press.

Jagger, A. M. (1989). Love and knowledge: Emotion in feminist epistemology. In A. Jagger and S. Bordo (Eds.), *Gender, body and knowledge* (pp. 145-171). New Brunswick, NJ: Rutgers University Press.

Keller, C. (1986). *From a broken web: Separation, sexism and self.* Boston: Beacon Press.

Le Doeuff, M. (1991). Hipparchia's choice: An essay concerning women and philosophy. Cited in S. MacColl, (1994), Opening philosophy, *Thinking, 11* (38): 4, 5-9.

Lloyd, G. (1984). *The man of reason: Male and female in western philosophy.* London: Methuen.

Lorde, A. (1984). *Sister outside: Essays and speeches.* Trumansburg, NY: Crossing Press.

MacColl, S. (1994). Opening philosophy. *Thinking, 11* (38): 4, 5-9.

McFall, L. (1989). *Happiness.* New York: Peter Lang.

McKinnon, C. (1987). *A feminism unmodified: Discourse on life and law.* Cambridge: Harvard University Press.

Moulton, J. (1983). A paradigm in philosophy: The adversary method. In S. Harding & M. Hintikka (Eds.), *Discovering reality: Feminist perspectives on epistemology, method and the philosophy of science* (pp. 149-164). Dordrecht: Reidel.

Pateman, C. (1989). *The disorder of women: Democracy, feminism and political theory.* Stanford, CA: Stanford University Press.

Pateman, C. (1991). *Feminist interpretations and political theory*. University Park, PA: Pennsylvania State University Press.

Peirce, C. S. (1931-1935; 1958). *The collected papers of Charles Sanders Peirce*, Vol. I - VI, Charles Hartshorne and Paul Weiss (Eds.); Vols. VII - VIII, Arthur Burcks (Ed.). Cambridge, MA: Belknap Press.

Plato. (1951). *Symposium*. Harmondsworth, UK: Penguin Books.

Potter, V. (1967). *Charles Peirce: On norms and ideals*. Amherst: University of Massachusetts Press.

Raymond, J. (1986). *A passion for friends: Toward a philosophy of female affection*. Boston: Beacon Press.

Rorty, A. (1988). *Mind in action: Essays in the philosophy of mind*. Boston: Beacon Press.

Rorty, A. (1976). *The identities of persons*. Berkeley: University of California Press.

Ruddick, S. (1989). *Maternal thinking: Towards a politics of peace*. Boston: Beacon Press.

Scheman, N. (1987). Othello's doubt/Desdemona's death: On the engendering of scepticism. In J. Genova (Ed.), *Power, gender, value* (pp. 113-133). Edmonton, AB: Academic Printing and Publishing.

Schor, N. (1982). *Reading in detail*. New York, NY: Methuen.

Skagestad, P. (1981). *The road of inquiry: Charles Peirce's pragmatic realism*. New York: Columbia University Press.

Spelman, E. (1988). *Inessential woman: Problems of exclusion in feminist thought*. Boston: Beacon Press.

Young, I. (1990). *Justice and politics of difference*. Princeton: Princeton University Press.

CHAPTER 8

Philosophy for Children and School Reform

Dewey, Lipman, and the Community of Inquiry

David Kennedy

There is general agreement among North Americans that our educational system has entered a period of prolonged crisis. The consensus is based on the perception of a growing incompatibility between our educational system and the transitional world for which it intends to prepare its students.

This incompatibility is emerging in all areas of contemporary life such as the economical, technological, and cultural domains. The issue of school reform relates directly to the technological and economic domains. The notorious *A Nation at Risk* (1983) inaugurated the first wave of the current reform in the early 1980s. The report expressed the now increasing apprehension that the economic decline being experienced by the U.S. is directly related to an educational system which has lost the rigor which once guaranteed its world supremacy in markets and in the military. Its architects do not base their policy decisions on the assumption that there has been a shift which makes our schooling system incompatible with world conditions, but that the system has simply lost the rigor necessary to make it work. Its ruling metaphor is one of internal corruption and decline, a loss of an original condition of unity. And hence its focus on uniformity, standard setting, and regulation.

The second wave of current reform, which emerged in the late '80s, bases its proposals on the assumption that the economic, political, environmental, and cultural differences of century's end are differences of kind rather than of degree. It calls for a system of schooling which is restructured rather than just intensified. The old system of education – the system of age-graded classrooms, early tracking, narrowly conceived standardized tests, and inherent pedagogical conservatism and uniformity – is a social and intellectual product of the industrial society and economy of the late 19th century, and will simply not produce individuals able to cope with the new challenges. It has functioned to educate a minority elite for the jobs of industrial and political leadership and management, and the rest to a minimum necessary for filling jobs in an industrialized, mass-production economy, which depended on routinization for its maximum effect (Romberg, 1992, p. 26).

These reformers claim that we are entering an "information age," characterized by a continual reorganization of systems which are increasingly interdependent, requiring skills, not of routinization, but of collaborative problem solving. In a period of accelerating change, students need to be taught to value process over product, which means knowing how to reason well, to work with multiple models, and to think creatively. And just as the universal schooling movement of 1800 aimed to foster national and linguistic unity, the social and cultural aim in the year 2000 is global unity. This means cooperative values, cultural tolerance, and sophistication, the ability to adapt to changing circumstances, understanding learning as a life-long process, and an orientation to the production of new knowledge.

The educational model of second wave of reformers is of necessity an unfinished one, an emergent dimension of a world order even now being born in stormy transition. But we can identify, in this emerging model, elements that have been struggling to be born at least since John Dewey's formulations about schooling, which began almost exactly 100 years ago. Dewey can now be seen to have been speaking prophetically, all through the first half of this century, about the social and economic transformations at its end which would require what he referred to as a "shifting of the center of gravity . . . a change, a revolution, not unlike that introduced by Copernicus," in education (Dewey, 1943, p. 34). In fact, Dewey's educational thought is a dialectical synthesis of the educational philosophy of socialization to citizenship and adaptation to economic and technological ambitions of the state which characterizes the traditional model, and the educational philosophy of the Romantic movement, with its emphasis on the individual and on a pedagogy which relies on the natural unfolding of powers rather than mere socialization.

To understand Dewey as a prophet of the emerging model places the educational theory and practice of Philosophy for Children (PFC) directly in the sphere of the emergence, since Dewey's thought is foundational to, if not the curriculum, certainly to the pedagogy and the educational politics of PFC. The methodology of PFC can be understood as both a fulfillment of Dewey's educational vision and, in the process, a correction or reinterpretation of how that vision might be realized. Matthew Lipman's formulation of the concept of the community of inquiry[1] articulates in a fresh and compelling way the deep structure of Dewey's educational thought, and makes it immediately relevant to current conditions. In this essay I will outline three major foci of the current restructuring movement – pedagogy, the role of the teacher, and school diversity – and show how each is an expression of the Deweyian educational vision. I will also argue that the pedagogy of PFC, in particular the theory and practice of the community of inquiry, offers an exemplary methodology for the accomplishment of the restructuring movement.

Restructuring Pedagogy

The first area targeted by proponents of restructuring is that of teaching, learning, and curriculum development. Second wave reformers call for the overcoming of a limited epistemological and pedagogical model which understands teaching as telling, knowing as being in command of certain facts, and learning as recall. As a result of this limited understanding of the educational process, academic content as it now stands tends to be perfunctory, fragmented, and disconnected from personal meanings. Reformers are in search of an educational model which redefines learning as active engagement in the acquisition of new knowledge, and knowledge itself as deep understanding, rather than the mere storage of information (Elmore, 1990). Central to this new definition is the notion of higher order or critical thinking, or the need for what Lipman (1991) has called complex thinking, by which he means a kind of thinking that is aware of its own processes, self-correcting, and applicable to any content area.

This redefinition of the educational process acts to correct what Lipman (1991), citing Dewey, calls the "stupendous category mistake" of the standard paradigm of education – that is, a confusion between "the refined, finished end products of inquiry and the raw, crude subject matter of inquiry." (p. 15). The standard paradigm considers that "an educated mind is a well-stocked mind," and thus "tries to get students to learn the solutions rather than investigate the problems." (p. 15). The result, as Dewey's classic argument goes, is isolation of the classroom from life, a growing distance between the lived experience of the child, that is, the knowledge children bring to experience, and the elements of the curriculum. The child, says Dewey (1943), "has a question of his own," (p. 148) which, if it is not heard, obliges him or her "to leave his mind behind, because there is no room for it in school." (p. 80).

Dewey's (1943) insistence on building theory and practice on the basis of "the child's own instincts and powers," which "furnish the material and give the starting point for all education," (p. 11) sets us the major task of education, which he refers to as "reconstruction." By this he means finding the educational form which would overcome

> *the gap in kind between the child's experience and the various forms of subject-matter that make up the course of study. . . . it is a question of interpreting them [the various content areas] as outgrowths of the forces operating in the child's life, and of discovering the steps that intervene between the child's present experience and their richer maturity . . . It is continuous reconstruction, moving from the child's present experience out into that represented by the organized bodies of truth that we call studies.*
> *(p. 11)*

Furthermore, for Dewey (1896) "[t]he only true education comes through the stimulation of the child's powers by the demands of the social situations in which he finds himself." (p. 5). This emphasis on the social experience of the classroom as the primary basis for the individual's educational experience is the foundation of Dewey's belief that, in a democracy, education is the fundamental method of social progress and reform. Democracy, in order to fulfill its promise of individual empowerment in the pursuit of a collective ideal, requires laboratories, where its form of life is learned through doing it. So schools which function as participatory, democratic communities, are for Dewey the necessary if not sufficient condition for what Lipman (1991, p. 247), citing Benjamin Barber, characterizes as "strong" as opposed to "liberal" democracy. Only when "nature and society can live in the schoolroom, when the forms and tools of learning are subordinated to the substance of experience" (p. 62) says Dewey (1943), is the possibility of a truly democratic education possible. The school in which democratic practices and forms of life develop best will be a "miniature community," an "embryonic society" – a setting in which "the school itself shall be made a genuine form of active community life, instead of a place set apart in which to learn lessons." (Dewey, 1943, p. 14).

Dewey's vision, associated with American social and political Progressivism, failed to materialize in his lifetime, for complex reasons.[2] But the "second educational revolution" (Farnham-Diggory, 1990, p. 55), which is now being called for by reformers, is directly related to the Copernican shift which Dewey first announced. It construes the classroom as site for "cognitive apprenticeship," (Farnham-Diggory, 1990, p. 56) a complex, situated learning environment, which meets the need of the human brain for rich, varied contexts and meaningful tasks in order to learn well. Students placed in long-range learning situations that are really meaningful to them are best taught by those who can demonstrate more than declarative knowledge or "knowing that" of a given content, but also can model procedural knowledge, that is, problem-solving techniques that may have several statable, heuristic rules of thumb, but which also involve tacit knowledge.

Reformers base this call for more active, interest-centred classrooms on recent discoveries in cognitive science which lead us to presume that learning involves the reorganization of knowledge which is already there in the learner, which in the assimilation of new knowledge, is restructured in complex, idiosyncratic ways by each individual. Good teaching demands a growing understanding of how students organize the knowledge they already have, and the ability to enter the student's world at the point where that knowledge can work for her or him in the further development of cognitive schemes. In addition, knowledge is understood to be a social product, understanding an inherently social process, and growth the mastery of ever-increasing complexity and interdependence.

The Community of Inquiry

The continuity between Dewey's vision and the elements of the cognitive apprenticeship model is clear. Where PFC comes in is that it offers, in the notion of the community of inquiry, an ideal methodology for operationalizing the three major elements just identified: (1) education as reconstruction, (2) learning as cognitive apprenticeship, and (3) the classroom as an embryonic "strong" democratic community. Before showing how the community of inquiry exemplifies all three of these goals, I must briefly outline its educational qualities.

The educational community of inquiry, as formulated by PFC, is both a structure and a process. As a structure, it is a participatory community of discourse, whose function is to undertake a deliberative inquiry, governed by reason, into questions identified by the community itself. As a process, Lipman (1991, pp. 241-243) has recently characterized five of its stages: (1) *the communal reading of a text*; (2) *the construction of an agenda*, that is, the identification of questions which the reading of the text has raised, and a cooperative decision about where to begin the discussion; (3) *solidification*, which includes the articulation of positions and counter-positions, the definition of the terms under discussion, and the search for criteria by which to make sound judgments about the subject; (4) *exercises and discussion plans*, based on the ideas in the text; (5) *further responses*, which may be in the form of creative writing, dramatization, art, or some other modality.

To frame what happens in classrooms in this way leads to a reframing of all the elements of educational practice. The *text*, for one, becomes, rather than a list of bits of received information, organized hierarchically according to the conceptual structure of the discipline it represents, a pretext for the discussion of the meaningful themes and issues which are embedded in it.[3] The community of inquiry also reformulates what *teachers* do in classrooms. Rather than acting merely as operatives who deliver pre-packaged information, they preside over a complex, situated process, involving the acquisition of new knowledge through the group's deliberative inquiry into subject matter which is chosen by students from a selection offered by the teacher. Teachers must become skilled mediators of an ongoing, self-correcting dialog. Teachers in such a model take a fallibilistic rather than an authoritative stance, and demonstrate for their students a thinker no longer held in the tyranny of right and wrong answers. Their goal is not so much that their students master the information within the subject matter of the curriculum, as that they grasp the relationships which form the structural organization of that information.

Along with the text and the teacher, the community of inquiry changes the role of the *student*, who now becomes both more powerful and influential, and more responsible to others. As a participant in a communal dialog, each individual perspective within the classroom is recognized as essential, for without it, the group would not be itself, but some other group. Yet each perspective is now subject to the discipline of the whole group as never before, for the group's ineluctable drive, represented by following the argument where it leads, is in the direction of a coordination of perspectives – an infinitely receding, but constantly beckoning horizon.[4] As the embodiment of that horizon, the community becomes the locus of moral and even intellectual authority, rather than the teacher, who becomes a skilled guide and protector of that horizon, and of the insistence on reasonableness which guards and maintains it.

The community of inquiry as a pedagogical framework and method operationalizes the Deweyian notion of reconstruction, for it creates a collaborative structure of choice and initiative within the classroom, whereby teachers and students share in the identification and pursuit of themes and issues. This makes it possible for students to assimilate the material offered by the curriculum at a level which overcomes, to repeat Dewey (1943), "the gap in kind between the child's experience and the various forms of subject matter that make up the course of study." (p. 11). In the light of the community of inquiry, reconstruction is seen to be connected with that dimension of the cognitive apprenticeship model mentioned above, that is, the construction of new knowledge through the reorganization of schemes, involving assimilation of new knowledge to current schemes, and accommodation of current schemes to new knowledge. The community of inquiry is an ideal framework for this equilibration process, because the knowledge to be acquired through this process is chosen through the initiative of both teacher and students, and in the process of group dialog, each individual internalizes, or "reconstructs," at his or her level of cognitive organization, the knowledge generated by the community.

The community of inquiry is an exemplary form of learning as cognitive apprenticeship. First, it is a complex, situated learning environment. The schematic richness and complexity of the narrative text, and the ability of the group and the individual to choose from the material and pose the questions which are relevant to them, makes of it an abundant, asymmetrical, dialogical context, where the personal and the educational projects have a chance to interact. Through the interaction of the members of the community of inquiry, a thematic context builds which has its own quality, and its own particular requirements.

Second, the community of inquiry models a form of teaching in which procedural knowledge is as important as declarative knowledge. The teacher must be a genuine problem solver, since the process of the community of inquiry itself could be described as a series of problematizations. The pedagogical issue is always how one frames and situates the argument, and calls for or allows the logical move which will, in turn, allow the inquiry to move ahead. The teacher works to create disequilibrium – moderate enough so that it neither bores by being too little, nor intimidates by being too large – in order to allow for the movement of genuine dialog, through which "each argument evokes a counterargument that pushes itself beyond the other and pushes the other beyond itself." (Lipman, 1991, p. 232).

The teacher does this through modelling moves like raising questions of evidence, insisting on definitions, probing for implicit assumptions, pointing out logical contradictions, and so on. All of these moves depend on heuristic and tacit knowledge in order to know when to use them. As the teacher models them in countless specific situations, they and the patterns in which they occur are internalized by each member of the group as a collection of cognitive strategies.

The community of inquiry strikes a dynamic balance between the contribution of the individual and the group to the construction and the distribution of knowledge. Each individual's contribution – even the contribution of silence – is necessarily determinative of the whole, yet the whole, the argument, is followed by each individual where it leads. Thus, each individual perspective both shapes and is shaped by the group's ever-emerging perspective. Knowledge is constructed through the interaction of individuals within the group, and so it is really group knowledge, but that knowledge is, in the very process of its emergence through individuals, internalized by each individual. Lipman (1991), taking from Vygotsky, calls this the "intrapsychical reproduction of the interpsychical." (p. 242).

Finally, the community of inquiry, as a deliberative community that concerns itself with ideas and issues that are identified by its members as important, is the fundamental building block of strong democracy. It is in such participatory communities that democracy becomes in itself an ongoing inquiry into the possibility of a form of social, political, and economic life which balances the rights and responsibilities of the individual and the group in optimal ways. Strong democracy is to be found in the many smaller communities which make up a larger whole, which Dewey called the Great Community. In a classroom which is also a community of inquiry, social and ethical problems and problems of governance are problematized and treated experimentally and rationally, just as any other subject matter would be. Strong democracy in the Great Community depends on learning to be little communities that can function successfully. Commenting on Dewey's vision, Lipman (1991) says: "If we are ever to get that Great Community, we must first have those microcosms in place." (p. 258).

Restructuring Teachers' Roles

The second major area in which advocates of restructuring are working has to do with the conditions of teachers' work in schools. Reformers are calling for the redefinition of teachers as inquirers and decision makers, and of schools as communities which should be shaped and continually reconstructed – by their own members. Part of the crisis of mediocrity of the traditional educational model has to do with the "de-skilling" or "proletarianization" of teachers, which is associated with what Elmore (1990) has called the "technical model" of education. The latter understands itself to be deploying "scientific knowledge" in the service of educational objectives, which are guided by criteria of efficiency, whose primary metaphor is production and utilization of resources. Systematic knowledge about education is gathered by researchers, who then deliver it in so-called teacher-proof packages to the operatives, the teachers, who apply it.[5]

The "professional model" holds, on the contrary, that if teachers expect their students to learn the dispositions and practices of self-initiated lifelong learning and participatory democracy, they must become producers themselves rather than operatives. This requires that teachers change their conceptions of who they are and what they do, and of their relations among themselves. To overcome the structural isolation of teachers' work, teachers themselves must be understood as members of a community in which the meaning and implications of teaching are the subject of ongoing inquiry.

In a school which is a community rather than a bureaucratic outpost, teachers take responsibility for their own actions, and make key individual and collective decisions. They adopt an experimental stance toward their work, and collaborate in the development and the implementation of pedagogical and organizational innovations within their own settings (Raywid, 1990; Sykes and Elmore, 1988). They are encouraged to question existing practices, to create broad structures for participation of all the members of the school community, and to make time available for school-level planning and discussion (Elmore, 1988). Teaching must be reformulated as a communal, not a solitary endeavor.

The Deweyian origins of this argument for the empowerment of teachers are as clear as the influence of his thought in the restructuring of pedagogy. Dewey's fundamental principle – the school as a form of community life – must, if only by inference, indicate the whole school community, not just separate classrooms. The school as the child's "habitat," "miniature community," or "embryonic society" (Dewey, 1943, p. 18) is by definition an adult-child collective, for a child's habitat always includes adults with whom the child is involved in a myriad of ways. In an adult-child collective which is educational, adults function best through practising the same deliberative judgments that they are teaching children to practise.[6]

Dewey's Great Community implies a multiplicity of smaller, diverse communities, all of which have the two major characteristics of democratic culture and society – unimpeded inquiry and free communication (Lipman, 1991, p. 258). "Democracy," he wrote,

> is more than a form of government; it is primarily a mode of associated living, of conjoint, communicated experience. The extension in space of the number of individuals who participate in an interest so that each has to

> *refer his own action to that of others, and to consider the action of others*
> *to give point and direction to his own, is equivalent to the breaking down*
> *of those barriers of class, race, and national territory which kept men from*
> *perceiving the full import of their activity. (Dewey, 1966, p. 87)*

It will be noted that this description of democracy as a process of community formation through a progressive coordination of individual perspectives is analogous to the process of the community of inquiry. Lipman, building on Dewey, calls the community of inquiry "the embryonic intersection of democracy and education. The community of inquiry represents the social dimension of democratic practice." (Lipman, 1991, pp. 249-250). As such, it provides a model, not just for teaching and learning, but for the participation by teachers in a communal process of planning and governance of their own schools. And if we take the same approach to the community of teachers as to the community of the classroom, we ground our communal process in an ongoing inquiry into the structure of relationships which determines our discipline, which in this case is education. Just as in the classroom, it is doing the "philosophy of" the content areas which builds higher order thinking skills; so teachers, through doing the "philosophy of" teaching and learning on an ongoing basis, will experience a higher level of reflection and critical perspective about their work. The same process of group inquiry identified above – the offering of the text, the construction of the agenda, and so forth – can be utilized by communities of teachers in schools to reflect and make judgments about practice, both individually and collaboratively. This is an area in which there are currently no philosophical novels developed, but lacking a fictional narrative like *Harry Stottlemeier's Discovery* (Lipman, 1982), carefully selected texts from the educational literature, the philosophical literature, including the literature of the philosophy of education, and from literature in general could be used as material for facilitating inquiry.

Philosophy for Children offers, then, a model for the practice of ongoing, dialogical inquiry which is necessary to the authentic professionalization of teaching, and to the community-building process at the school level which is a fundamental aspect of the teacher's work in a democratic society. As teachers in individual schools commit themselves to building communities of inquiry, the skills and dispositions developed through their own disciplined dialog equip them to act collaboratively to make key decisions about curriculum and governance, as well as to lead their students in the same process. This is especially important because of the historical struggle between two forms of theory and practice which characterizes North American education. The deep inconsistencies in content, rhetoric, and expectations between the first wave of the current reforms, which calls for an intensification of the traditional model through even greater standardization and centralization, and the second wave, which calls for a new paradigm, both in pedagogy and in governance, is a difference which will not be resolved by a decision from above, but from district to district and school to school. Without a discourse structure in which dialog can take place, the challenge of meshing these conflicting policy agendas will create serious dissonance at the school level.

In analyzing the historical and theoretical basis for the great divide between education as reproduction and education as reconstruction, or the technical versus the professional model, it is easy to convince ourselves that their conflict is insoluble. In reality, each of the thousands of individual schools, with its particular historical and cultural experience, occupies its own location in the conflict, and has its unique impediments to and opportunities for change. The community of inquiry offers a discourse structure which makes a place for the expression and mediation of the conflict of interpretations on the local level. It offers an optimal way of organizing the often tension-charged conversation which must take place between all participants in the school community, including children, if what Lipman refers to as "the Great Leap Forward" in education is ever to take place. Its unique strength is that it offers a form for dialog which assumes conflict rather than avoids it at all costs. The community of inquiry may be characterized as a conflict rather than an order or harmony model,[7] because the argument moves forward through going out of balance. It is disequilibrium which leads to the emergence of new information, and to the reorganization of schemes which allows for new understanding. Thus the community of inquiry offers a form for the continuous but disciplined, rule-governed argument about theory and practice among professionals which the Italians call *discozzione*, and which they consider essential to professional growth. Until teachers feel more comfortable with the kinds of conflict which are necessary to authentic professional collaboration, they cannot be said either to be professionals in any strong sense of the term, or to be preparing children for strong democracy, for the latter depends on a self-critical tradition.[8] The main characteristic of dialogical thinking is that it builds both tolerance of other, conflicting points of view, and the sense of empowerment among individuals – of having the ability to make a difference in one's environment. Tolerance and empowerment both lead to a greater ability to collaborate, and to use conflict in the interests of an ever-emerging consensus. Consensus cannot be administered through top-down bureaucracy. It is just the expectation that teachers **not** communicate, collaborate, argue, and make fundamental decisions about their own practice, and that educational theory and practice be prescribed through a hierarchy which presumes to be doing so on the basis of "technical," hard scientific information, which has led to the atmosphere of intellectual poverty and constraint which characterizes schools. Education will not be transformed until the self-understanding of the teacher is transformed, and that will come about to a great extent by teachers having the opportunity to talk.

Restructuring Incentives

The third major issue for second wave reform has to do with how incentive structures for schools affect educational quality and diversity. Many are claiming that as long as most schooling is provided by state-controlled, centralized bureaucracies, individual schools will have no incentive to respond either to their clients or to the broader public. Critics of the state bureaucracy model work from a free-enterprise economic metaphor, and argue that an industry which is not market-sensitive will be unable to respond to changes in the environment, and consequently will fail. As long as parents and children are without the power to choose among schools which have enough real differences to make the choice more than a meaningless exercise, the level of competition necessary to stimulate innovation, healthy variety, and the ability to meet individual needs will be weak. Thus, the "client model" recommends not only increased parent and student choice among schools, but parent participation in school-site management, arguing that "organizations that have a direct connection with their clientele and a high degree of influence over their resources . . . will produce results that are more aligned with what their clients want and will be perceived by their clients to be more successful." (Elmore, 1990, p. 19). It is expected that allowing the client more influence on the child's education would lead to schools which varied widely in curricular emphasis, pedagogy, attitudes towards discipline, and governance.

Proponents of "site-based management" model, on the other hand, are critical of an approach which takes a "demand-side" as opposed to a "supply-side" perspective on professional knowledge and practice. They argue that, unlike tools, medicine, or legal services, forms of curricula, pedagogy, and discipline which satisfy parents are not necessarily the ones that satisfy professionalism, or that are best for their children or for society. The expert, it is argued, often understands what the client needs better than the client himself or herself. Therefore, they call for a management structure which decentralizes aspects of the existing bureaucracy, but which does not move towards a "free market" in education. Apart from the argument from professionalism, they also tend to understand calls for deregulation and privatization of schooling as representing a dangerous trend toward social and economic fragmentation. Critics of school choice invoke the specter of the withdrawal of the middle classes to private schools, which the poor and underclasses have neither resources or motivation to send their children to, apart from the discriminatory practices they are bound to be subjected to in attempting to do so. This argument against diversification and relative privatization is related to the argument upon which the public schools were first founded, that is, national unity. As universal compulsory schooling was considered necessary to the linguistic and political cohesiveness of the fledgling U.S.A. during the first half of the 19th century, so now it is said to be necessary to maintain a social fabric which is increasingly threatened by racism, ethnocentrism, and economic inequalities.

It is hard to avoid the argument that the intellectual poverty, the crippling mediocrity of vision, and the role rigidity characteristic of American schooling are symptoms, not of educational practice per se, but of the influence of the structure and function of state bureaucracy on educational practice. It is a commonplace of sociological theory that the rationalistic regulation and hierarchical authority structure characteristic of bureaucracy stunt creativity and breed alienation. Bureaucrats, as Joel Spring (1980) has pointed out, "continually seek to expand their roles and increase the importance of their positions. This occurs independently of the general goals of the organization, and in some cases at the expense of those goals." (p. 93). Nor does school choice necessarily imply the abdication of either a funding or regulatory role by state and federal government. Compliance with basic standards of equality of opportunity and even affirmative action established by government agencies, can be maintained by economic incentives in a partially privatized system as well as a fully public one.

Ironically enough, Dewey himself was instrumental in the process of centralization and, by implication, the bureaucratization of education which was a major element in the cooption of the progressive movement by the traditional model.[9] He does not seem to have questioned the assumption that modern, industrialized society demands a centralized, systematic approach to the provision of schooling. In fact, he felt that a centralized system of schools was needed to balance the competitive individualism of American economic system, which contributed to social atomization and mutual alienation. It is arguable that Dewey's trust in the state provision of schooling was the flaw in his understanding which undermined his own vision of schools as embryonic communities. In their assimilation by the welfare state, of which Dewey has been called the "intellectual architect" (Spring, 1980, p. 31), the schools of the first half of the century became at best pseudo-communities, outposts of a rationalized, authoritarian bureaucracy, which was structurally incompatible with local autonomy, participatory governance, and a professional ethic of diversity and innovation.

Dewey may be forgiven for this, especially if his vision of embryonic communities is understood to have been prophetic, pointing to an age – the information age – which had only just begun coming into its own. In fact, Dewey considered ideas and institutions to be historical and social products, and was critical of their reification. He argued that institutions must change as social and economic conditions change, in a process of continual reconstruction (Spring, 1980, p. 29). If the schools changed during the industrial era to adapt to the need for standardization, the change which the post-modern era is calling for may be diversification. This diversification is possible without threatening the social fabric because it takes place in the context of a global centralization of goods, information, and values through technology and infrastructure.[10]

When in our present situation we attempt to predict whether relative privatization of schooling would lead to better or worse schools in general, and to more or less equality of educational opportunity, it makes it easier to understand how Dewey could have misunderstood the conditions which would fulfill his own educational vision. The question of the outcomes of decentralization may well be the educational question of our epoch, analogous to the international question whether the ethnic and regional independence movements now on the rise globally will lead to a more peaceful or a more war-torn world; or the social question whether what is referred to as pluralism in North American culture and politics is an indication of cultural and social decline or evolution.

Ambiguity also results when we try to think about which system of provision and incentives PFC and the community of inquiry would prosper in. Certainly the slow growth of the program in the U.S. over the last five years leads us to wonder if the structural characteristics of the present system are not fundamentally inimical to the structure and processes of the community of inquiry. In a hierarchical, bureaucratic system, PFC and its methodology become just one more technique for teaching critical thinking, and a less popular one at that, because less "technical" and pedagogically systematized. On the other hand, a highly diversified, client-driven educational landscape could very well result in many, many schools which are equally incompatible with the values and pedagogy of the community of inquiry and PFC. It is not hard to imagine even a majority of schools which merely substitute an aggressive, mechanistic, performance-driven model for a mediocre one of the same type. American commercial interests are capable of very quickly designing school "chains," sold to consumers with polished, vacuous media images, boasting curriculum "packages" and a pedagogy even more savagely traditional than that of the public school system, which is at least softened by years of progressive influence.

Such a prospect is very disturbing, but the chance that PFC would fit in even less in a landscape of school choice and diversification is one that it is obliged by its own principles to take. If parents, teachers, and children choose, on a case by case basis, to abdicate their schools to profit-hungry corporations and distorted ideological movements, that is what they must have the freedom to do, if, in turn, schools are to have the freedom to define and govern themselves in strongly democratic ways. The faith of the community of inquiry is in the power of reasonable arguments ultimately to prevail, and in the progressive emergence of truth – in this case, best practices – through participation, collaboration, and community empowerment. Should decentralization lead to educational barbarism, faith in reason exhorts us to believe that the handful of schools which operate democratically will provide models for social reconstruction which will, in the long run, prove the most adaptive to the new age, and therefore increase and prosper. Even if this is not the case, the fundamental differences between the practices necessary for strong democracy to flourish and the practices necessary for bureaucracies to survive are so great that it is logically impossible for the one to make a place for the other without sacrificing itself.

Decentralization – whether complete, in the form of privatization, or partial, in the form of state orchestrated diversification – also creates at least more of a climate for the dialog which is central to second wave reformers' vision. As in the case of the classroom and school as embryonic communities, the community of inquiry offers a discourse model to the community as a whole which includes clients, that is, parents and other interested community members. As at the classroom and school level, the community inquiry provides a framework for reflecting on and transforming practice within a contested, in many places ideologically polarized, tradition. Communities which can agree to at least undertake an inquiry together into the purpose, function, and optimal practices of education, have created a social space for what Elmore (1990) calls "a setting and a mode of discourse in which experts, professionals, and clients argue about and construct the meaning of academic learning." (p. 34). Indeed, the state can do much to facilitate this kind of dialog, through offering models and incentives for setting up educational communities of inquiry within communities. And again, it is PFC which offers a simple, powerful model for the investigation of meanings and relationships among meanings. Whether such communities lead to the level of collaboration which overcomes the politics of ideologs and interest groups is a moot point. The community of inquiry is as vulnerable as any reform which offers genuine change, and which seeks to replace reproduction with reconstruction.

Conclusion

Implicit in the recent reform movements is the coming to a head of the conflict between two educational paradigms. Both are responses to a failure of our schools which seems much more momentous than before, given the economic decline, the dramatic shift in global economies, the explosive growth of new technologies, and the possibility of progressive ecocide. One, called by Sykes and Elmore (1988) the "regulatory response," does not believe restructuring is necessary, but only intensification of existing practices, or, as they put it, "a series of technical adjustments in the regulatory framework of schooling and in the tools utilized to implement the states' directives." (p. 90). The other calls for the adoption by educators of "a new experimental stance toward their work, participating in the creation as well as the implementation of instructional and organizational innovations within schools." (p. 90). What PFC offers to this conflict of interpretations in the form of the community of inquiry is so simple that it is easily overlooked by those in search of packaged, technically facile solutions. The community of inquiry offers a form for a new educational paradigm within the classroom, a new paradigm for collaborative planning within the school as a whole, and within the community of which the school is a part. It does this through the simple reversal which is the major key for productive change: philosophy comes first, not last, in any curriculum. Philosophy here understood is an ever emerging landscape of belief and knowledge, held together and moved forward by a commitment to inquiry. Philosophy as first curriculum holds that understanding the structure of relationships precedes any collection of data; that truth is communal, contested, and emerges through dialog in contexts of use and meaning. It is completely fitting that PFC should represent this hope for late 20th century educational reform, given its profound roots in Dewey's vision of schools as communities, and given the continuity and pervasiveness of Dewey's vision for North American schooling.

Notes

1. The community of inquiry is certainly not an original idea with Lipman. The term is originally C.S. Peirce's, and represents a synthesis of elements of the thought of Peirce, Dewey, Paul Schilder, Josiah Royce, G.H. Mead, Justus Buchler, and Lev Vygotsky. For a discussion of the origins of Lipman's synthesis, see his *Thinking in Education* (1991). See also Ann Margaret Sharp's essay in this collection.

2. These have been definitively addressed in Lawrence Cremin's (1966) history of progressive education.

3. The best textual genre for this sort of process tends to be fiction, because it is schematically rather than conceptually organized. The schematically organized text is – like the community of inquiry itself – dynamic, emergent, and holistic, in that every element has an impact and effect upon every other element. Because it is organized in aesthetic as well as logical patterns, it offers conceptual material in a form which encourages individual appropriation through a balance of critical and creative thinking. A text which can balance the narrative and the expository, Lipman (1991) claims, is the "text of the future." (p. 220).

4. The horizontal character of the epistemology of the community of inquiry is brilliantly discussed by Corrington (1987).

5. Michael Apple (1979, 1983) offers particularly trenchant insight into the ideological aspects of the technical model.

6. Deweyan reformers in the 1920s and 1930s, the heyday of progressive educational reform, were already calling for an administrative system which allowed students and teachers to assume greater responsibilities in the actual management of the schools. The reform initiated by Jesse Newlon in 1922, which became known as the Denver approach, took as its major premise that "No program of studies will operate that has not evolved to some extent out of the thinking of the teachers who are applying it,"

(Cremin, 1966, p. 299) and moved teachers to the very centre of the curriculum-making process.

7. See Chesler and Crowfoot (1975) and Apple (1979) on relevant comments on conflict and order in education.

8. "When a tradition is in good order it is always partially constituted by an argument about the goods the pursuit of which gives to that tradition its particular point and purpose . . . Traditions, when vital, embody continuities of conflict." (MacIntyre, 1984, p. 222).

9. For an account of this gradual cooption, see Cremin (1966, Chapter 9).

10. This seems to be what the slogan "Think globally, act locally" means.

References

Apple, M. (1979). *Ideology and curriculum*. London: Routledge and Kegan Paul.

Apple, M. (1983). Work, gender and teaching. *Teachers College Record, 84*, 611-629.

Chesler, M. and Crowfoot, J. (1975). *Toward a conflict model for understanding the organization of schooling in America* (Report to Northwest Regional Laboratories). Ann Arbor: Community Resources Ltd.

Corrington, R. S. (1987). *The community of interpreters*. Macon, GA: Mercer University Press.

Cremin, L. (1966). *The transformation of the school: American progressive education, 1897-1957*. New York: Viking.

Dewey, J. (1896). *My pedagogic creed*. Chicago: University of Chicago Press.

Dewey, J. (1943). *The child and the curriculum* and *The school and society*. Chicago: University of Chicago Press.

Dewey, J. (1966). *Democracy and education*. New York: Macmillan/Free Press.

Elmore, R. (1988). *Early experience in restructuring schools: Voices from the field*. Washington: National Governors' Association, Center for Policy Research.

Elmore, R. (1990). Introduction: On changing the structure of public schools. In R. Elmore and Associates, *Restructuring schools: The next generation of educational reform*. San Francisco: Jossey-Bass.

Farnham-Diggory, S. (1990). *Schooling*. Cambridge, MA: Harvard University Press.

Lipman, M. (1982). *Harry Stottlemeier's discovery*. Montclair, NJ: First Mountain Foundation.

Lipman, M. (1991). *Thinking in education*. Cambridge: Cambridge University Press.

MacIntyre, A. (1984). *After virtue (2nd ed.)*. Notre Dame, IN: University of Notre Dame Press.

National Commission on Excellence in Education. (1983). *A nation at risk: The imperative of educational reform*. Washington, DC: U.S. Government Printing Office.

Raywid, M. A. (1990). Rethinking school governance. In R. Elmore and Associates, *Restructuring schools: The next generation of educational reform* (pp. 152-205). San Francisco: Jossey-Bass.

Romberg, T. A. (1992). Assessing mathematics competence and achievement. In H. Berlak et al. (Eds.), *Toward a new science of educational assessment*. Albany, NY: SUNY Press.

Spring, J. (1980). *Educating the worker-citizen: The social, economic, and political foundations of education*. New York: Longman.

Sykes, G. & Elmore, R. (1988). Making schools manageable: Policy and administration for tomorrow's schools. In Politics of Education Association yearbook, 77-94.

CHAPTER 9

Philosophy in the Democratic Multicultural Community of Inquiry

Paul F. Bitting

No matter how loudly anyone proclaims his Americanism, if he assumes that any one racial strain, any one component culture ... is to furnish a pattern to which all strains and cultures are to conform ... he is a traitor to American nationalism.

John Dewey

"No sooner do you set foot on American soil," Tocqueville says, "than you find yourself in a sort of tumult, a confused clamor rises on every side, and a thousand voices are heard at once, each expressing some social requirements." (1945, p. 249). The voices Tocqueville describes belong to men and women governing themselves. For some, the sound they make is harsh and discordant, for the confused clamor comes from every American struggling to attain a new or larger piece of the action, or a new or better place in the sun. For others, the sound is a symphony which expresses the well-ordered functioning of the American polity.

Neither the discordant nor the symphonic view is exactly correct. Americans have a common creed, indeed a political religion, which is expressed in the Declaration of Independence, many of Abraham Lincoln's and Martin Luther King's speeches, and the myths which make us a people. The creed gives too much form and depth to the American character for the sound we make ever to be just noise, devoid of order and meaning. We simply have too much in common. Nevertheless, we are also an ambitious people. Americans and American cultural groups all pursue their ends with great energy, and often without regard for the interests or understanding of others. Symphonies require too much coordination of each sound for the cultural and political jockeying characteristic of America to ever have the order, sense, or purpose of a symphony. We are simply too free.

The sound Tocqueville heard is more like improvised jazz, the organized musical chaos indigenous to America. This improvised jazz leaves plenty of room for displays of virtuosity. Our various cultures, for example, constantly blow their own horns. In fact, every culture in America seems to aim at grabbing our attention by being louder or more sophisticated than the competitors whose sound they try to drown. But the horn-blowing requires accommodations. Back-scratching – jiving and staying in tune with others – is absolutely essential for every American cultural group to get ahead. In order to play their solos they have to play with the band.

The music of American democracy is therefore full of much harmony and dissonance, much unity and diversity. What purpose can the music serve to inquiry within educational environments? We live in an age that has highlighted the cultural experiences of others. Airplane travel allows cultures to collide; television brings strange and alien imageries into our homes. Yet our temperament has tended to reduce cultural experience out of the picture of inquiry. We so easily become entrenched in our own views of the world that we exclude those of others. This occurs despite the fact that our media bombards us with different experiences daily. But our attitude has a tendency to be passive. This is because philosophical inquiry is not at the heart of the appreciation of other cultural experiences. In this essay I will argue that understanding the cultural experiences of others is an important part of philosophical inquiry. I will go on to suggest that understanding the cultural experiences of others is a hallmark of maturity, that is, of what it means to be an educated person. My objective is to present an argument which establishes a direct link between a conceptualization of multiculturalism, which includes an enhanced capacity for viewing entities in the world from a multiple of perspectives through exposure to and understanding of the experiences of others, and what it means to be an inquirer in a democratic environment.

Culture and Persons: A Conceptual Relationship

Revolution occurs in a society when a gap develops between the culture and the social structure, leaving the institutions exposed and unsupported in the consciousness of the people and in their feelings, emotions, and aspirations.

The culture of a society, as I am using the term, is that structure of meaning, the spiritual soil and climate on which people and institutions depend for their nourishment, health, and vitality. We cannot simply create an institution at will without regard for the culture on which it must depend. Whenever the culture of a society ceases to support and to sustain its existing institutions, either they or the culture must be reformed, for social structures can be maintained by force only for so long. Like all dead things, they disintegrate in time. Thus, culture is a structure of meaning on which people and institutions depend for spiritual nourishment, health, and vitality.

It is clear that the culture of a society is most intimately related to the structure of the consciousness of the people. It was developed out of the long commerce of the people with reality. It may have begun in the dim past with beings not yet persons who became persons only at a certain stage of cultural development. Indeed one cannot be a person, in the full sense of the term, merely by being biologically generated by human parents and physically maturing. A horse biologically generated and physically nurtured for a short time can go on to become a mature horse without ever contacting another horse after birth, and will live the life of a horse. But a person has to be culturally generated and nurtured (Adams, 1975, p. 8). Under their own development, if they could physically survive, humans would, no doubt, come to have rudimentary experiences, memory, and imagination, and perhaps in a more advanced form than other animals because of a greater native intelligence. They would perhaps develop some rudimentary semantic tools, but not enough to extend their semantic powers to the point that they would have distinctly person-like modes of consciousness. Without language and symbols to deepen and to structure their subjectivity, without beliefs, myths, and theories to organize their consciousness into a unity and to form an image of the self and the world, one would not be an "I", a person capable of moral, religious, and artistic experiences and intellectual thought. The person's centre of gravity is not in its biological being, but in its selfhood. This appears to be the truth underlying the claim that people are not animals among other animals, but spiritual beings and are thus culturally dependent.

American Democracy as a Multiculture

The term democracy has been applied basically to political affairs, and dominated by implications arising out of the basic principle centred around the will of the majority. However, contemporary tendencies have been to extend the meaning of democracy beyond its political connotations. Deeply rooted in the new tendency is the idea that democracy aims at the social as well as the political. Dewey, for example, stressed that democracy is more than a form of government. It is a form of associated living, and it is these forms of association that bind and enrich us, and result in a vital education, society, and government (1916, p. 87).

Democracy also has its beliefs, myths, and theories. It has its language, symbols, mores, and values; they are revealed in manners, dress, and attitudes. In its social and ethical aspect, democracy signifies a belief in the value of each person. Rich or poor, of whatever race, nation, or religion, all persons are to have absolute worth.

Democracy's concept of "inalienable rights" was a beginning in moving democracy from a social and ethical principle to a political imperative. When John Locke spoke of the "natural rights of man," he was referring to human rights that are embedded within the very texture of reality. When Thomas Jefferson asserted that rights are "inalienable," he meant that alienating them is not unlike defying a basic law of nature.

To actualize the purposes and direction of the democratic way of life, governments with their various bodies (legislative, executive, and judicial) must be established. In a modern democracy this power (to choose and control government) is vested in the people as a whole by means of universal suffrage. Thus, "majority rule" becomes essential as a methodological procedure.

There can be no greater wrong, however, than to confuse the expedient of majority rule with the principle that the majority is always right and that the minority must therefore conform. Tocqueville (1945), in his very insightful analysis of nineteenth century democracy, questioned:

> When an individual or a party is wronged in the United States, to whom can he apply for redress? If to public opinion, public opinion constitute the majority; if to the legislature, it represents the majority and implicitly obeys it; if to executive power, it is appointed by the majority and serves as a passive tool in its hands ... However iniquitous or absurd the measure of which you complain, you must submit to it as well you can. (p. 271)

The germ of Tocqueville's concern may be found in the ideas of Rousseau who exalted the practical notion of the "general will." Consensus as a reflection of the "general will" being seen as a principle of perfect truth, it followed, according to Rousseau, that the minority must accept the decrees of the majority:

> The general will is always well-meaning and always tends toward the public good. . . . There is often a great difference between the will of all and the general will. The latter looks only to the common interest, while the former looks to private interest and is only a sum of individual wills. If the people always decided on the basis of adequate information, and with no discussions among the citizens beforehand, the general will would always result from the larger number of small differences and the decision would always be right. (1974, pp. 26-27)

Democracy has not accepted the totalitarian fears of Tocqueville as exemplified through the "general will." On the contrary, the rights of minorities to differ is its fundamental thesis in our times. Tocqueville's reference to the possible "tyranny of the majority" is limited by the right of the minority to dissent from the majority. Democracy's essential tendency is to permit the greatest possible divergence compatible with its basic principles. Thus, democracy, in all aspects, tends toward diversity and pluralism.

Donna Gollnick highlights a number of political and social changes of recent decades which reflect this diversity and pluralism in American democracy. She reminds us of the 1964 Civil Rights Act passed by Congress declaring that discrimination based on race, color, national origin, or sex was prohibited (1991, p. 2). She goes on to emphasize the inclusion of students whose first language was not English through the passage of the Bilingual Education Act. She continues, "legislation to support sex equity in the schools further extended the application of civil rights to another oppressed group. The Ethnic Heritage Act of 1972 supported the development of curriculum materials on different ethnic groups." (Gollnick, 1991).

As a result of hard fought battles over many decades, and the subsequent political and social changes, the multicultural nature of American democracy is now generally recognized as its organizing principle. We are now beginning to view variety as the spice of life. We are slowly learning that differences among groups in modern democracy are resources to be tapped, rather than a problem to be solved. Indeed the unique feature of the democratic way of appropriating the reality has been formed by the interaction of its various subsidiary ways of appropriating reality. Its language, myths, symbols, legends, art, music, ethics, and normative social and political thought all show the effects of the commingling of diverse cultures in one nation. As Diane Ravitch (1990) suggests, paradoxical though it may seem, "America has a common culture that is multicultural." (p. 7).

What might it mean to say that the modern democratic culture is a multiculture? What is being claimed here? At rock bottom I would say that this observation signifies the recognition of the existence of a variety of perspectives on reality. That there are multiple structures of meaning and each structure must be judged, critiqued, or evaluated from within that perspective. Therefore, the designation of a culture as a multiculture is to recognize that that selected between groups must be viewed as fundamental enough to be capable of producing values, beliefs, and dispositions that contribute to significantly different outlooks on the world.

With these conditions in mind, we may further identify what multiculturalism expresses. We can start with its descriptive use. As a descriptive term, multiculturalism refers to the co-existence of distinct groups semantically structuring meaning and appropriating reality in distinct ways, but within a common social system. Such a descriptive use makes no judgments about this situation for it is employed simply to record the fact that different groups are able to live together in a way that allows the society to accomplish the basic functions of producing and distributing goods, defining social arrangements and institutions which determine collective goals, and providing security.

But multiculturalism may also be used normatively to express a social ideal. Because education, in its distinction from schooling, is primarily a normative concept, as I will argue later, it is this use of multiculturalism which most interests me here. As a social value, the concept goes beyond the descriptive sense to emphasize the individual and social value of freedom of association, the so-called "democratic ideal." That is, a multicultural society is commonly portrayed as a cooperative venture for mutual advantage; everyone profits from a variety of groups expressing different structures of meaning. Thomas F. Green (1966) expressed this point most eloquently:

> *The view is that any society is richer if it will allow a thousand flowers to blossom. The assumption is that no man's culture or way of life is so rich that it may not be further enriched by contact with other points of view. The conviction is that diversity is enriching because no man has a monopoly on the truth about the good life. There are many ways diversity is further valued because it provides any society with a richer pool of leadership from which to draw in times of crisis. (1966)*

Green (1966) develops this position by observing that the values of multiculturalism entail two further assumptions:

> *In the first place it means that there must be contact between the divergent groups in society. A household may be richer for including persons of different aspirations, values, dispositions, and points of view. But these differences will not be enriching to any particular individual unless he talks with, eats with, or in some way has an exchange of views with those who are different. The value of diversity implies contact between persons, and not simply incidentally, temporary, and casual contacts. Secondly, this fundamental value implies that the diversity which is enriching is not itself endangered by the contact which is valued. The diversity must be sustained through contact.*

Thus, in its normative aspect, the concept of multiculturalism has a very real advantage over monoculturalism. To see this advantage, it may be helpful to consider a concept borrowed from inquiry into the nature of a form of group interaction referred to as "situational leadership." According to this concept, different situations require different abilities from the person who leads the group, so that as the group moves from problem to problem, different members of the group will lead when their competencies are needed and make way for another member(s) when the situation has changed. In similar fashion, the multicultural person and, by extension, the multicultural society should be able to adapt to a changing environment more quickly than a monocultural person, or society, in that a variety of perspectives are available to meet the new situation. However, Green's second point becomes crucial when one realizes that this advantage can be nullified unless the society and its institutions are constructed to allow these different perspectives to express themselves. Individuals within the society must be exposed to them in order to learn from them. If these various semantic structures of meaning have no influence in our institutions, if they cannot be heard, then their richness will be of little use to the individual and to the society as a whole, and the major advantage of multiculturalism will be lost.

I have thus moved from a concept of culture as a way of semantically relating to and appropriating the world and, secondarily, the world as semantically appropriated in the shared experiences and aspirations of the people with their accumulated knowledge and wisdom, to democracy as a multiculture, that is, accepting a variety of ways of semantically relating to and appropriating the world. Such multiculturalism, I have argued, has advantages and thus should be fostered. But fostering the norms of multiculturalism is not a matter of genetics; it is a matter of philosophical inquiry and transmission across generations. Therefore, the concept of philosophical inquiry within the context of educational institutions promoting the "democratic ideal" becomes crucial to this analysis.

Philosophy Within the Multicultural Community of Inquiry

The problem of understanding and transmitting how I and others semantically relate to and appropriate the world is not one that lends itself to the methods of scientific investigation nor to a practical problem-solving approach under the guidance of scientific knowledge. It calls for the kind of understanding and critical judgment that is relevant to the inner development and inner direction of individuals, institutions, and societies. It calls for refined and highly developed humanistic methods of cultural analysis and criticism that will lead to personal, cultural, and social reorientation and reorganization from within. Here I shall explore the contribution and viability of humanistic inquiry, especially philosophic, to cultural understanding and reconstruction as well as the contribution and viability of multiculturally-oriented communities to humanistic, especially philosophic inquiry.

The analysis of culture I have provided presents us with massive problems. The problems concern our cultural ways of semantically relating to and appropriating the world and therefore affect every aspect of our lives. Mistakes made at the cultural level distort our efforts to know and to cope with reality. In addition to a general undefined feeling that something has gone wrong with our way of life, such mistakes generate intellectual perplexities which drive us to philosophically examine the troubled spots in our culture. So we have a right to ask, "what, if anything, can we expect from philosophy?"

Like all value entities, the value of philosophy can be viewed both intrinsically and extrinsically. Intrinsically it can provide some measure of philosophical understanding and enlightenment for those who study it and develop responsible, disciplined methods of philosophical thinking. No one who has ever achieved such understanding and enlightenment will deny that they are among the intrinsic values of the human spirit. They give depth to one's being. Without philosophical understanding of the culture within which we operate and a critical philosophical view of the world as knowable through it, we are enslaved by our culture and our uncritical assumptions about it and the world. And it is to that extent that we are provincial in mind and spirit. Such philosophical self-criticism and the enlightenment and understanding thereby obtained are essential for a true liberal education.

In addition to the intrinsic value of philosophical understanding and its importance for a deepened and enriched selfhood, philosophy has an important "therapeutic" function. An individual or a culture with serious philosophical difficulties in their or its fundamental assumptions or views suffers from an illness that limits their or the culture's efforts to understand correctly their world. Philosophy, in its work to expose and to clear up such difficulties, is concerned with wisdom: philosophical wisdom, not moral wisdom or other common varieties that provide guidance for solving our ordinary daily problems, but wisdom about human powers and the structure of the world that guide us in our efforts to know and to cope with reality and to live the life that's good. Thus, "cultural therapy" is the practical side of pure philosophy. It is what philosophy, apart from its intrinsic intellectual value, is good for.

Thus, it is through philosophy as cultural therapy that we are able to evaluate and assess our cultural assumptions and beliefs. "Belief" is not a scientific concept; that is, it is not an empirical concept grounded in scientifically refined sensory observation. It is grounded in self-knowledge and the understanding of others in a communicative, intersubjective relationship. A belief, by its very nature, involves meaning. It has a semantic dimension. It is about something. It can be given linguistic expression or articulation. It is offered in propositional form. The sentence that expresses it is declarative. A report of the belief would be in the form "I (or they) believe(s) that . . .," where the blank would be filled in by a clause that would, if by itself, express the belief. A belief stands in logical relationships to other beliefs, statements, perceptions, and so forth. It may logically entail others, contradict some, and be logically supported or corroborated by others. To ask why one believes something is to ask for reasons, evidence, grounds for so believing. A belief may be appraised as rational or irrational, as logical or illogical, as justified or unjustified, as true or false, and the like. Thus, a belief is not simply an event among other events, nor even a disposition among other dispositions, to be simply described and explained scientifically. It is not something to be described in terms of concepts grounded in the sensory discriminations of a scientific observer, but in terms of the concepts that constitute the belief itself. It is not something to be explained in terms of scientifically discovered causal conditions, but in terms of its logical place in the semantic field that constitutes the mind of the person whose belief it is. To understand and to explain a belief, one must know the mind of the person whose belief it is in an extra-scientific way; not in an observational way, but in a communicative, intersubjective way in which there is a sharing of concepts, thoughts, and semantic contents in various logical forms. This is the philosophic way of knowing as distinct from the scientific approach.

Such philosophic ways require a democratic environment. If we approach the beliefs of a person or a people in this way, any attempt to alter them would not be through the manipulation and control of their scientifically discovered causal conditions, for that would be to understand and to treat people under the categories of things rather than those of people having intrinsic worth and therefore would be, by the nature of the approach, dehumanizing and undemocratic. A philosophic approach would require that the people be approached as people, as rational agents, who are capable of reflective, critical assessment of their cultural assumptions and beliefs in light of evidence and logical considerations. Mulvaney (1992) calls such a philosophizing environment the "nursery of the democratic ideal, where teacher and student share a cross-generational issue of profound human significance, suggest alternative formulations of the question, and hint at possible answers, in a climate of mutual respect and toleration." (p. 93).

When such an environment is also multicultural, we have students sharing cross-cultural issues of profound human significance, suggesting, as Mulvaney says, alternative formulations of the question, and hinting at possible answers, in a climate of mutual respect and toleration. It is here that such an environment makes its contribution to philosophical inquiry. At the heart of multiculturalism is the conviction that diversity is enriching rather than harmful. Any attempt to semantically appropriate reality from a multiple of perspectives, whether within the context of academic disciplines or simply lived experiences, makes it clear that human behavior is not single-minded or single-sided. What appears to be missing in this sort of easy single-mindedness is a multidimensional model of persons and reality. The multidimensional perspective allows, and even forces, us to seek meaning and understanding in a variety of ways, and from diverse viewpoints. The inquirer, having appropriated this broad-based perspective, develops the disposition to approach differences in a healthy and mature manner. Not only do they respect differences of perspective, they actually seek them out.

Thus students philosophically inquiring into the meaning of work in literature would emphasize and elicit from their culturally diverse peers the different effects and interpretations the work may produce in different students. We then may discover that the most interesting aspect of the literary work may not be what the author intended but the many possible effects it can have on the reader. Experiences of this kind lead to richness of insight. Thus, Young Pai (1992) offers at least two ways in which the philosophical environment is enriched by such diversity:

> One is that human life becomes much more interesting, stimulating and even exciting when there are many varied ways of thinking, feeling, expressing, acting and viewing the world. Secondly, and perhaps more importantly, given the range in kinds and complexity of human needs and wants, the more alternative problem-solving approaches there are the more likely we are to find solutions which may enable us to live our lives in an increasingly effective way. (p. 4)

To say that the appropriation of multiple perspectives through the fostering of a multicultural community of philosophical inquiry can be enriching is not to say that all perspectives are equally acceptable. It is here that philosophy as cultural therapy does its work. Cultural patterns can be judged in terms of the effectiveness with which they enable the members of that culture to appropriate reality and to deal with their problems. This implies that some cultures may be more efficient than others. Similarly, some cultures may be more maladaptive and self-defeating than others and that those cultural practices which tend to be self-defeating are in need of philosophical therapy and need, as a result, to be modified, abandoned, or even prohibited. We should not consider the use of deranged and self-defeating patterns as merely a matter of applying different but equally valid cultural norms.

Thus, it is through philosophical inquiry that we therapeutically address the maladies, pitfalls, and derangements of our self-defeating cultural and multicultural practices. And it is through the ideal environment of the multicultural community of inquiry that we enrich our philosophical understanding of the world.

Conclusion

I have argued that philosophical inquiry is best practiced within the context of a social ideal. This social ideal can be measured by the extent in which the interests of the social group are shared by all its members, and the fullness and freedom with which it interacts with other social groups. I have argued that this type of ideal has and can be labeled "democratic" and requires an environment that is multicultural. Such an ideal begins with the individual and seeks to prepare the person for a harmonious existence within a pluralistic society. Thus it offers a concept of inquiry for self and cultural awareness. I make no claims for originality here. It has a tradition which can be traced to the ideas of the Greek philosopher Socrates. It can be formulated through the Socratic contention that the "unexamined life is not worth living." The concern of such philosophical inquiry in such an ideal environment is to enable the inquirer (as student) to establish an understanding of their own acquired cultural ideas, beliefs, and assumptions with their limits and to show them how their cultural upbringing constrains or consummates who and what they are. In a word, the achievement proper to such inquiry in such environments is self-knowledge through the understanding of others. Aided by thought about principled action such inquirers learn to shape an image of themselves for themselves. Culture, as I have argued, is the lens through which we view and judge the world. If we have not had the opportunity, as Dewey (1916) warns, "to escape from the limitations of the social group in which we were born" (p. 20) our culture can become a blinder to other ways of thinking, feeling, and acting. The inability to view the world through broader cultural lenses may prevent an understanding of the world in that broader context. This inability often makes it difficult for us to be fully functioning persons in that broader context.

References

Adams, E. M. (1975). *Philosophy and the modern mind.* Chapel Hill: The University of North Carolina Press.

Dewey, J. (1916). *Democracy and education.* New York: Macmillan Publishing Co., Inc.

Gollnick, D. (1991). Multicultural education: Policies and practices in teacher education. Unpublished paper.

Green, T. F. (1966). Education and pluralism: Ideal and reality. Twenty-sixth Annual J. Richard Street Lecture, School of Education, Syracuse University.

Mulvaney, R. J. (1992). Conversation, dialogue, and dialectic: A response to Paul Bitting. In J. Cogleton (Ed.), *Creating a multicultural education conversation* (pp. 92-97) (Proceedings of South Atlantic Philosophy of Education Society). Chapel Hill, NC: South Atlantic Philosophy of Education Society.

Pai, Y. (1992). A conversation about multicultural education: Three troublesome notions. In Joseph Cogleton (Ed.), *Creating a multicultural education conversation* (pp. 1-12) (Proceeding of South Atlantic Philosophy of Education Society). Chapel Hill, NC: South Atlantic Philosophy of Education Society.

Ravitch, D. (1990). Multiculturalism: E pluribus plures. *American Scholar, 59* (3): 337-354.

Rousseau, J.J. (1974). The social contract. In L. Barr (Trans.), *The essential Rousseau.* New York, NY: New Amsterdam Collection Inc.

Tocqueville, A. de. (1945). *Democracy in America,* 2 vols., Phillips Bradley (Ed.). New York: Alfred A. Knopf, Inc.

CHAPTER 10

Critical Theory, Post-Modernism, and Communicative Rationality

Ronald Reed

Papers about critical theory, if they are to refrain from approaching book length, must make certain assumptions, must stake out certain areas for discourse, and leave out or ignore others. In this essay I will examine a small, though obviously significant, feature of Habermas' critical theory, that is, his notion of communicative rationality, especially as it is played out in Robert Young's (1991) *Critical Theory and Classroom Talk*. I will also look at critical theory as an example of modernism and an antagonist of post-modernism. Curiously, the latter task may prove most amenable to solution and so, I will start there.

Modernism, as well as post-modernism, is as much a faith as it is a coherent set of articulated, developed, and justified propositions. That faith, especially as it relates to education, is expressed in Kant's *On Education:*

> It may be that education will be constantly improved and that each succeeding generation will advance one step toward the perfecting of mankind. . . . It is only now that something may be done in this direction, since for the first time people have begun to judge rightly, and understand clearly, what actually belongs to a good education. (Cited by Young, 1991, p. 10)

A primary characteristic of the faith, as the preceding quote shows, is a belief in evolutionary progress from a worse stage to a better one. Concomitant with that belief is the claim that there are discernible standards and criteria that can be used to distinguish better from worse. These standards and criteria are objective, in the sense that they can function across contexts and it is possible and worthwhile to discover standards and criteria that can be of use in evaluating the contexts themselves. Put in the language of the modernist/post-modernist dispute, the modernist faith claims that there is a meta-narrative to which narratives must conform and by means of which they can be evaluated. Without the existence of the meta-narrative, so the modernist argues, one is condemned to the (mindless) cultural and ethical relativism that is the post-modern condition.[1]

Now, the pragmatic dictum is that *all differences make a difference* or, stated negatively, if the difference does not play itself out in terms of some significant action, then it is merely "verbal," or "theoretical." If one assumes, and in a *fin-de-siecle*[2] epoch this is a trivial assumption, that no clear meta-narrative has emerged, one must, if one is a modernist, paraphrase Kant, that we are getting closer to the establishment of such a meta-narrative. Why *must* one assume that we are getting closer to the establishment of a meta-narrative? The answer, in large part it seems to me, revolves around the pragmatic dictum: if we do not assume that we are getting closer, both that progress is possible and that we are progressing, then we, especially those in education, will fall into the trap of cultural relativism. We will spend our time pushing a bare-bones, back-to-the basics curriculum, stripped of value and significance. Or we will be reduced to imposition and indoctrination – exercising (political) power over children to get them to do and think and feel what we wish them to without having any clear ethical mandate for such exercise. Stated in such a way, it is clear that the "must" relates to the behavior of educators – if we do not believe this then we will do something unseemly to children. Our beliefs will make, if we are modernists, a positive difference and a negative one, if we are post-modern.

Surely, however, this is treating a psychological or contingent relation as if it were a logical or necessary one.[3] Certainly for some educators, and perhaps for the vast majority of educators, a belief in educational progress, a belief in the eventual discovery of the meta-narrative is a necessary condition for continuing to *act* as if educational progress were possible. Without that belief, many, if not most, educators would despair of educating and would content themselves with training and behavior management. But there are some educators – William James might call them the tough-minded – who like Sisyphus, in Camus' classic retelling of the Myth,[4] are condemned to perform a task in which real progress is precluded, in which the stone will always betray Sisyphus, but who continue on with the process and, recalling Camus' imagery, do so with grace and joy.

Critical theorists – most notably Habermas and Robert Young – do speak the language of modernism. They do involve the spectre of cultural relativism, and they do write as if an Enlightenment-like belief in progress, in perfectibility, was a necessary condition for significant educational reform. Again, I have tried to show that that amounts to a category mistake – treating a psychological matter as if it was a logical one. One could argue, à la Kuhn (1970), that although paradigms are not absolute (they are cultural constructs) it is possible to make progress *within* a paradigm, or, à la Rorty (1980, 1989), that although there is no meta-narrative, it is possible to construct better (richer, more evocative, more useful, and so on) narratives. Very simply, the argument is that there is no entailment relation[5] between modernism and critical theory; a postmodernist interpretation and/or use of critical theory is not oxymoronic.

To return now to the narrow point mentioned at the beginning of this essay, that is, the notion of communicative rationality, for Habermas, rationality is, just as it is for John Dewey, a transactional event between or among persons which exists in and is sensitive to a situation or a context.

> *How should we use the term "rational"? Rationality has less to do with knowledge as such, Habermas asserts, than the manner in which knowledge is used. If we consider the circumstances in which we speak of something as "rational", we see it refers either to persons or to symbolic expressions which embody knowledge. To say that someone acts rationally, or that a statement is rational, is to say that the action or statement can be criticized or defended by the person or persons involved, so that they are able to justify or "ground" them. . . . Rationality presumes communication, because something is rational only if it meets the conditions necessary to forge an understanding with at least one other person. (Giddens, 1985, p. 98)*

Rationality involves a form of conversation among persons who exist within a situation. As those persons talk among themselves, as they begin to agree to this claim, to assert this and not that, as they become familiar with each other, and with each other's presuppositions, certain properties begin to emerge. One of those properties, for Habermas, is that of rationality. At some point, if we are talking well, if communication is taking place, we can begin to utter claims of validity – this is true, this is defensible, and so on. We can, as the modernist might say, begin to speak objectively or, as the pragmatist might say, begin to assert with warrant.

Now, let us make some assumptions. Let us say, using Habermas' terminology but arguing as much from John Dewey and Young's *Critical Theory and Classroom Talk*:

(1) Validity is always a public matter. Validity occurs as groups, in effect, convince themselves of the truth of some proposition. In a one-person universe, questions of validity could not arise.

(2) As publics shift, as the paradigms which hold publics together shift, so too will validity claims shift. Validity at t_1, and this is

where a post-modernist understanding of critical theory is so suggestive, is not necessarily the same at t_2.

(3) While it may be logically possible that validity could occur by happenstance, it is typically a function of communicative competence, that is, members of the public have sufficient knowledge, interest, and wherewithal to engage in the conversational matrix, figure out the rules implicit within the matrix, and ultimately know how to make themselves understood and how to understand others.

(4) Communicative competence is not something that exists "untethered." It is always heavily context-dependent. This is not to suggest that there are ultimate standards of validity, but only that certain groups might in fact be more practised at communicating than others, hence certain groups might have a better chance of establishing validity than others.

(5) Communicative competence involves something as slippery as the conveying of meaning; it involves a situation in which two persons or a group of persons come to understand something (some preposition) and, at the same time, come to understand themselves. As validity emerges, the public, of necessity, must pay attention to the conversational matrix that differentiates this public from others. For example, when validity emerges in mathematics, mathematicians come to know themselves as acting *as* the public of mathematicians and not as the public of artists. Given the slipperiness of communicative competence, it is not the sort of thing that can be mechanized, nor reduced to a set of formalized procedures. Also, it is not the sort of thing that can be legislated. The language of describing communicative competence involves words like "invite," "nurture," or "coax." "Mandate," "enforce," or "demand" seem to reflect a basic category mistake, a basic misunderstanding of the nature of communicative competence.

The question now, if we make the assumptions suggested above, is the following: What *sort* of classroom restructuring will "flow" from trying to act upon those assumptions? Will the restructuring be small, piecemeal, and reformist in nature – the sort of restructuring that can take place without much basic change to the system *or* does it involve large, widespread, and deep change, the sort that is more revolutionary than reformist? The rest of this essay will involve an attempt to answer the question of "sort."

As critical theorists, we are concerned with questions of validity. We understand (see categories above) that education must be active. It is something that is not done *to* students but done *by* them in consort with their colleagues. It occurs when inquirers have an adequate knowledge base and know how to inquire in such a way as to extend that base. It occurs when, in effect, the community of inquiry is effective, when individuals are in a position where they can inquire well. As we have seen, or more precisely as the preceding assumptions strongly suggest, inquiry (which, if successful, yields communicative competence, which in turn, yields validity) and the success of inquiry is always context dependent. But consider how many contexts are involved and how deep is the dependence.

> *When we speak of the historical nature of inquiry we are referring, in part, to the fact that contexts change over time and with them, inquiry changes. One aspect of this change is generated by the emerging outcomes of inquiry itself. Each new discovery changes the baseline for future inquiry. This is true of communities of inquiry, such as physics or astronomy, but it is also true for individuals. The more we know, the more we can know. And inquiries are not carried on in total isolation from other changes and developments, or developments in other areas of inquiry. Politics influences lines of inquiry, through either funding change or indirect influence. In a similar way, the personal life of individual learners provides an environment for their learning. At one stage in a person's life they may be very interested in religious inquiry, at another in academic learning. During a personal crisis they may not be interested in deliberate inquiry at all, even though they may be learning a great deal. (Young, 1991, pp. 21-22)*

One can imagine a reform-minded teacher, disillusioned by a banking mode of education who comes to the conclusion that (a) her or his students are not learning the required material (or are learning it poorly, or in shallow fashion, or in some other undesirable manner) and assumes (b) that there must be a better way to teach the material at hand. One can imagine that teacher attempting to arrive at canonical knowledge by novel methods, methods different from the traditional ones, by "community of inquiry" methods.

Here, of course, is precisely where a significant problem occurs. The tradition (traditional education) assumes a canon and a special kind of canon. For the traditionalist there are a limited set of essential skills, dispositions, and facts that have to be passed on to students in the course of their schooling. The canon is subject to change and, at times, that change can be rapid and sweeping, for example, the computerization of the curriculum over the past ten to fifteen years. Still, for the most part, the canon is amazingly stable with history, language arts, and geography texts reflecting more a bridge of sorts between generations (a bridge that might be commended by conservative critics like Bloom and Hirsch) than a reflection of the current theorizing of members of those disciplines. Simply put, canonical change is typically slow, relatively stable, and when change does come it is more often a function of change in the needs of business and industry than of advances within disciplines.

If, on the other hand, one took inquiry within communities seriously, if one saw validation as a goal of communities of inquiry, and understood communicative competence as a necessary condition for the achieving of that goal, one would, of necessity, be forced into a radically different understanding of the canon. One would not, in the manner of leftist critics of the 1960s, such as Neil Postman and Charles Weingartner, have to give up on the notion of the canon altogether. One would, simply, have to recognize the contextual nature of the canon itself. If validity changes from community to community and if the community that is the school is always sensitive to both the natures of its individual members and to the larger community from which they come, then the canon will reflect those changes. As, for example, the larger community's base line changes, so too will the school's. As, for another example, the special (special to that school or that classroom) dynamics change, so too will the canons which emerge from those dynamics. The sort of change, then, that critical theory entails is significant, thoroughgoing, and revolutionary. It involves both a shift in the model of the classroom and the nature and role of the canon. And along with that, of course, goes a rethinking of the role of the teacher, the teacher-student relationship, and so on.

A final question arises. There are critical thinking programs in existence which attempt to do what that reform-minded teacher attempted to do: act melioristically and introduce a community of inquiry model within the existing school structure without necessarily changing that structure. Would it not be worthwhile to use that approach, as many teachers do today, to teach the traditional canon? That question is far too complex to answer in the space remaining. All that we might do is recall to mind some of the advice of that most melioristic of American philosophers, John Dewey (1916): "Only persons, parents, and teachers, etc., have aims, not an abstract idea like education. And consequently their purposes are indefinitely varied, differing with different children, changing as children grow and with the growth of experience on the part of the one who teaches." (p. 107). To the extent that we accept the canon as given and not the result of the inquiry of persons in community, we are acting in an aimless fashion. In other places, Dewey labels such aimless actions as "dumb" and "unintelligent."

Notes

1. From the modernist perspective, relativism is mindless precisely because it denies the existence of standards and criteria which are necessary for thinking well about issues of value.

2. Fin-de-siècle is a term used to describe the feeling of weariness and unease with claims regarding ultimate truths. That unease typically comes at the end of things, at the end of centuries.

3. This is like treating the relations among emotions as if they were equivalent to the relations among propositions in an argument in logic.

4. Albert Camus. *The Myth of Sisyphus* (New York, NY: Random House, 1991).

5. Modernism is not a necessary condition for critical theory.

References

Dewey, J. (1916/1966). *Democracy and education.* New York: Free Press.

Giddens, A. (1985). Reason without revolution? Habermas's *Theorie des kommunikativen Handelns.* In R. J. Bernstein (Ed.), *Habermas and modernity* (pp. 95-121). Cambridge, MA: The M.I.T. Press.

Kuhn, T. (1970). *The structure of scientific revolution.* Chicago: University of Chicago Press.

Rorty, R. (1989). *Contingency, irony, and solidarity.* Cambridge: Cambridge University Press.

Rorty, R. (1980). *Philosophy and the mirror of nature.* Oxford: Basil Blackwell.

Young, R. (1991). *Critical theory and classroom talk.* Avon, England: Multilingual Matters Ltd.

Section III

Pedagogical Possibilities in Philosophy for/with Children

CHAPTER 11

Creating a Meaning-Centred Environment

Linda Nowell

Newspaper headlines continually remind us of the problems facing our society, in particular, problems affecting our children. We are confronted daily by stories of drug abuse, poverty, teen-age pregnancy, gang violence, weapons in schools, and juvenile crime. Within these stories blame is bandied about, resulting in "accusing fingers" pointing not only at the breakdown of the family and "traditional values" but also to the inadequacies and poor performance of our educational system.

From a historical perspective, civilizations have placed an enormous responsibility on the schools to solve the problems that plague society (Cremin, 1990). The present social and political climate attests to this belief. Within this context this essay will focus on the notion of the school as an agent for social change, the political implications that this notion carries, and the impact Philosophy for Children can have in bringing about change.

In Article five of "My Pedagogic Creed," John Dewey (1981) writes:

> education is the fundamental method of social progress and reform. All reforms which rest upon the enactment of law, or threatening of certain penalties, or upon changes in mechanical or outward arrangements, are transitory and futile. (p. 452)

Put another way, Dewey sees the educational system as the means by which society changes or redirects itself. However, in order for changes to occur, in order to shift its direction, the members of that society not only must desire the changes, they must also see the meaning behind them. We need only recall the Era of Prohibition, to cite just one example, to realize that changes imposed upon the members of a society from without are doomed to failure. For Dewey (1916), the school is the agent of communication, the means by which the individuals of a society come to have an "enlarged and changed experience," – how we come to understand ourselves, others, and the world in which we live. Moreover, it is for Dewey (1916) the only sure "method of social reconstruction" (p. 5). Yet, Dewey (1981) sees "a tragic weakness in the present school" (pp. 415-419 and p. 459) and it is what many contemporary scholars see today (Reich, 1991) – an attempt to prepare future members of society in an environment which does not nurture or develop any sense of "social spirit," an environment in which individuals have no sense of connectedness, or community, to the world outside of the classroom (pp. 415-419, 459).

Although there are those who would disagree, the educational system is not a neutral process. It either functions as an agent of conformity: the means by which the younger members of the society not only are "nurtured and cultured" into the traditions and customs of the society but are also indoctrinated into the thinking of that society; or it acts as an agent of change: the means by which individuals learn how to deal "critically and creatively with reality and discover how to participate in the transformation of their world" (Shuall, 1981, p. 15).

At present, our society seemingly demands change. We need only listen to the political rhetoric or read the volumes of commission reports, in particular the National Education Goals that were adopted in 1991, to believe that our society wants a citizenry who is able to function well within society. Moreover, it seems that society wants individuals who critique and question the policies, practices, and beliefs of the society. Yet, when we examine the proposed reforms, when we examine how these reforms translate into practice, a different picture emerges. It appears that what many individuals want, especially those in positions of political and economic power, is a citizenry who is manageable and who values the status quo. In order to justify this claim I offer two case studies.

I.

In the summer of 1991 I taught critical thinking[1] at a fine arts camp sponsored by the *I Have A Dream Foundation*.[2] The seventh and eighth grade students participating in this program are labeled "at-risk"[3] and attend urban schools, primarily in the Polytechnic, Southeast, and Northside areas of Fort Worth.

As I observed and listened to my students during camp, I recognized attitudes and behaviors that some scholars (Paulo Freire, 1981; John Goodlad, 1984; Henry Giroux, 1993; Jonathan Kozol, 1967, 1975, 1981, 1985, 1988, 1991; Peter McLaren, 1989; and Catherine Walsh, 1991) describe as not only typical of schools with high ethnic populations but are also exhibited in many middle-class schools. The students in my two morning classes sat slumped over their desks; their eyes focused on the floor, they felt uncomfortable facing each other (the desks were arranged in a circle); they resisted my attempts to engage them in any kind of discussion or conversation (they responded with silent shrugs or whispered "I don't know"); and they rarely questioned me or each other. On the other hand, the students in my afternoon class continually insulted each other, spoke over each other, and resisted any attempts at working with each other. Furthermore, these students not only were disruptive during camp, they were "in trouble" at school and at home. The majority of these students are labeled as "special needs," many of them living in group homes, attending special schools, and some awaiting legal action.

Subsequently, society demands that something be done and, in response, intervention programs, like this one, are implemented; yet the problems continue. Critics blame the schools and, in turn, the schools blame society, especially the lack of support they receive from parents. In one sense the critics may be right; as I look into the faces of my students I see in them what Paulo Freire (1981) calls the "character of the oppressed." Oppressed people view themselves as "good for nothing," "incapable of learning," and "lazy and unproductive." They feel like "things and are convinced of their unfitness" (p. 49).

Freire contends, and Dewey, I think, would agree, that this sense of self is inculcated by an educational system, and for our purposes we can label the system as traditional education or, as Freire refers to it, banking education, that values the accumulation of information, a content of information that many have argued that all "educated" people should know.[4] Moreover, the information or knowledge is seen as something that not only accurately represents the world, it can also be deposited or transmitted clearly and precisely from one individual, namely the teacher, to another, the student. The student's task, then, is to passively and mechanically store, memorize, and repeat that information. It is a system that emphasizes individual achievement and performance in an atmosphere that conditions individuals in precise behaviors: seeking right answers, conforming to the values, including policies, procedures, and practices, of those in authority, in particular administrators and teachers, and reproducing the known (Goodlad, 1984). Likewise, all talk is channeled through the teacher, who the students view as a "storehouse of knowledge" and the "dispenser of academic praise and blame" (Reed, 1985, p. 231).

The relationship that this system fosters among students, in particular individuals who are considered "at-risk," is one of intellectual, social, and emotional isolationism (Fine, 1989). Rarely are students encouraged to listen to each other, to question each other, to follow on the ideas of each other. This isolationism is further reinforced by the "physical restraints of the group and the classroom"; by the "flat, neutral emotional ambience" of the classroom; by the "kinds of questions the teacher asks" – as well as the answers she or he expects; by the "nature of the seat work that is assigned and by the format of tests and quizzes" (Goodlad, 1984, pp. 241-2). The sense of self that is inculcated is one of impotence. Consequently, individuals are unable "to perceive critically the way they exist in the world *with* which and *in* which they find themselves" (Freire, 1981, p. 71). They come to see the world as static reality and their lives as "fated and unalterable." As a result they give up and accept the "role imposed upon them" (Freire, 1981, p. 71). These are students who, too often, are poor, who are African-American or Hispanic, and who are labeled as underachievers (Kozol, 1967, 1975, 1985, 1988, 1991; McLaren, 1989; Walsh, 1991). They are passive participants who barely "get by," who struggle to finish school, who struggle just to exist (Oakes, 1993). Moreover, they are often tracked into courses that prepare them "for a life of temporary, dead-end, underpaid, undignified, and menial jobs" (McLaren, 1989, p. 152).

On the other hand, there are others, like my afternoon class, who are disruptive, destructive, and continually vie for control of the classroom. They realize that they have no control over their lives; they sense that the situation has reduced them to "things," and in struggling to escape this "death-affirming" climate they react (Freire, 1981, p. 55). Yet, their actions are not an attempt at restoring control to their lives, or to the lives of others, but rather their actions are an attempt to be like their "oppressors," to have the power to oppress or to control others (Freire, 1981, p. 33). These are the students who are seen as "trouble-makers," who, the system declares, will never amount to anything and who are "weeded"[5] out of the system in order to make the environment more manageable for those whose resistance is one of passivity (Carnoy, 1989; Oakes, 1993).

Freire (1981), again, points to "banking" education as reinforcing this mind-set in students as well as in society. Since this type of education does not value collaborative learning, individuals do not see their "place in the world" because they have been shown that individuals are "independent, isolated, abstract, and unattached from the world" and, as objects in isolation, they are unable to comprehend or explain the way individuals "exist in the world" (p. 69). Consequently, they are enslaved in a system that renders them powerless – not only in their ability to question their position in society but, just as important, their ability to change their world.

Yet, there are critics (Hirsch, 1987 and Bloom, 1987) who argue that the problems facing education are a result, in part, of the philosophy and practice that characterized the 1960s and 1970s, and that part of the solution lies in returning to a more "traditional" educational system. However, the second case study appears to point out that, although the educational system has introduced what could be called "innovative practices," the underlying foundational structure has been the "traditional" model.

II.

The Sunday morning, April 14, 1991, edition of the *Fort Worth Star-Telegram* carried a sobering headline: "When Babies Die." The article, four and a half pages, detailed the alarming statistics that "one out of every 45 Black babies born in Fort Worth" dies before their first birthday. Although the information was not surprising to me, I was interested in people's reactions to the article. I conducted an informal survey of 100 people[6] who attend church in a predominantly older and ethnically and economically diverse neighborhood. What surprised me more than their reactions to the article was the fact that 45% of the respondents stated that they did not see or notice the article, although the majority of this group stated they read the paper on a regular basis.

Only 18% of the respondents saw and read the article. Their reactions ranged from "concerned" to "surprised" to "what I expected." In addition, they cited "a lack of education, a lack of parental involvement, and the attitudes of the poor" as the primary causes of this problem. Furthermore, they stated that solutions to this problem would have to come from the educational system.

This survey was not intended to produce any significant statistical findings, nor did I expect any startling revelations; however, as I read the comments section of the survey I noticed what seems to be a disturbing line of thinking. The group wrote that the poor were in this condition because "they lacked a desire to work, that there are jobs for those who want to work; the poor must be educated to a different set of values and morals; they must change their standards or expectations." These comments seem to imply that the fault lies with the victim, although this group probably would not refer to the poor as victims, that they should be able, in the image of Horatio Alger, to pull themselves up by their boot straps. As one individual stated, "the article insinuates that society is to blame for not doing more. I totally disagree, I think we do too much as it is." One might expect such attitudes from a more "monied" group; yet these are the comments of a group that is older, educated, but not wealthy, at least not by U.S. standards. Again, this survey is not intended to reflect the views of the majority of Americans; however, we need only read the "op-ed" page of any newspaper across this country to believe that these are, indeed, the views of a great many Americans.

We are forced, then, to ask what fosters these attitudes, what would cause people to ignore so serious a problem, or to see the problem as only a concern, and then to dismiss the problem as the fault of the victim. Freire, again, points to the "traditional or banking" model of education for reinforcing this mind-set, a mind-set that believes if individuals persevere, work hard, then success, regardless of the environment in which they live, will be theirs. Jonathan Kozol, likewise, not only points to "traditional" education as inculcating this mind-set, he condemns it.

One of the most compelling aspects of Kozol's books are the stories of individuals who reflect the hopelessness and desperation of people, and in particular, children, sentenced by a society that is "anesthetized to their plight" (1975, p. 12). He criticizes our schools for not "educating good people, but educating people to be good citizens" (p. 27), citizens who have been indoctrinated by our educational system to be "ethical incompetents" (p. 12). He finds a citizenry that is skilled: they can "tell of challenges, refer to agonies, and comment on difficulties;" yet their "hearts are dead and their consciences are in exile" (p. 32). As Kozol states, "school is the ether of our lives, the first emaciation along the surgical road that qualifies the young to be effective citizens, alert to need, but tempered as to passion, cognizant of horror, but well inoculated against vigorous response" (p. 39).

Although Kozol is often criticized for his harsh judgments of society, especially the educational system, Dewey (1981) would argue that the disparity Kozol cites as savage not only threatens the very life of society, but if "acted upon destroys our democracy" (p. 455). Dewey (1916) states that an "undesirable society is one that internally and externally sets up barriers to free intercourse and communication of experience" (p. 99). A society that not only changes, but values change that promotes its improvement, will "have a type of education that gives individuals a personal interest in social relationships and control, and the habits of mind which secure social changes without introducing disorder" (p. 99).

If we accept Dewey's claim and if we desire – as reflected in the National Education Goals – to improve existing schools, to create a new generation of schools, to recognize that learning is a life-long process, to ensure that *all* children come to school ready to learn – then we must ask ourselves how can this be accomplished. Moreover, and maybe the more important question, given the research findings of noted scholars like John Goodlad, "why has change *not* occurred?"

In trying to understand the latter we can again look to Dewey (1976). He states that "democracy is the faith that the process of experience is more important than any special result attained" (p. 260). In other words, democracy is not an end in and of itself, but rather a means by which individuals can have an enhanced and enriched experience, a "more humane experience in which all share and all contribute" (p. 265). Yet, what interferes with this process, even in existing democracies, and can ultimately halt the process, is when the "means" become the "end," when society fixates on the gains, whether they are economic, political, or social, that are already attained. Consequently, society protects these gains at all costs and, if need be, imposes them upon its members (Aronowitz & Giroux, 1993). Dewey (1976) notes that this notion is the basis for "every autocratic and authoritarian scheme of social action" (p. 260). The notion further suggests that the "needed intelligence is confined to a superior few, who because of inherent natural gifts are endowed with the ability and the right to control others" (p. 260). We would not be hard-pressed to see an analogy to the present educational system. The teacher is seen as the expert and ruler of the classroom (but only within the classroom), not only laying down the rules and procedures but directing the ways in which they are carried out. Students have limited participation and, again, that participation is directed by the teacher. Likewise, the teacher has limited control and participation, receiving mandates as to what to teach, when to teach, and how to teach from superintendents, local and state boards of education, and other "special interest groups," in particular the business community (McLaren, 1989).

Dewey (1976) states that the "very fact of exclusion from participation is a subtle form of suppression. It gives individuals no opportunity to reflect or decide what is good for them" (p. 259). Moreover, he sees this form of "coercion and suppression" as "more effective than overt intimidation. When it is habitual and embodied in social institutions it seems the normal and natural state of affairs" (p. 259). This produces individuals who not only are unaware that they have a right to participate, they are not even "conscious of restriction" (p. 259). Again, this is evident within the schools. As Apple (1989), Giroux, (1993), McLaren (1989), and others point out, many of the reform proposals are considered "teacher proof." The teacher is not expected to think or act as a scholar but only as a technician. As such, the teacher is stripped of her or his power to actively influence and shape the direction and political structure of the system. Students, on the other hand, suffer the same, or worse, fate – they are seen only as products or objects of the system. Reich (1991) presents the metaphor of the assembly line: students are the raw materials that are shaped and fashioned; they move, as if on conveyor belts, from grade to grade following a planned sequence of subjects and activities; certain facts, at each stage, are poured into their heads; standardized tests are routinely administered to measure how many facts have stuck. Within this model, children who have the greatest capacity to absorb facts are placed on a rapid track through the system; children who have the least capacity for fact retention are placed on the slowest track. And those children who prove to be "product defects are taken off-line and retooled" or discarded (p. 60). Moreover, if we look closely at the "assembly line" we notice that those children who are on the rapid track tend to be white and upper-middle class, while those children on the slowest track, as well as those who are retooled or discarded, tend to be poor African-American and Hispanic males (Kozol, 1967, 1988, 1991; Fine, 1989; Oakes, 1993).

In order to restore Dewey's (1976) notion of democracy, "the power of pooled and cooperative experience" (p. 259) requires a radical restructuring of the educational system, in particular, it requires remaking the classroom into one that values meaning – a community of inquiry.[7] Dewey (1981) reminds us that it is through the school that the complexities of our experiences are mined. In other words the school serves as a "laboratory in which life is tried out" (p. 337). In order to accomplish this we must first rethink the role of the disciplines (subject matter); rather than mere repositories of information, they must be viewed as active avenues of inquiry. But in order to nurture that inquiry "we have to drastically slow things down and parse things out" (Reed, 1992, p. 21). In other words, the amount of information presented in the classroom must be limited so that students have ample opportunity to think about and talk about what they are inquiring into and, more importantly, to question the significance of that inquiry. Moreover, the curriculum would not be something that is "imposed upon the child," rather it would emerge "from the community's own inquiry" (p. 22). But Dewey (1916) is not advocating doing away with courses. For Dewey, subject matter represents the "ripe fruitage of experiences like theirs," not "perfection or infallible wisdom," but the working resources the teacher utilizes to aid students in making sense of their experiences (p. 182).

Secondly, as Giroux (1993) points out, the teaching relationship would be seen as a scholarly endeavor where teacher and student, talking and learning from one another, would not only discover and invent meaning, they would also gain practice in coming to reasoned judgments about what to think and how to act. Dewey suggests that the teacher's role is not to "impose certain ideas" and knowledge into students, but rather as a member of the community she or he "selects the influences," the experiences, the students will have and then aids them in interpreting and understanding those experiences.

The following example may help clarify the preceding discussion: a group of East Harlem students were involved in a comparative study of judicial systems. During their study the students' interest turned toward the riots in Los Angeles that broke out following the Rodney King verdict. The students argued that our judicial system had failed to treat King justly. At this point the teacher could have allowed the discussion to have a very narrow focus – Rodney King; however, she moved the discussion to a wider focus, translating the students' interest from a particular case to a general one. Simply, she helped the students see that their real interest was in the notion of what is justice and what is fairness. From their inquiry into the nature of fairness and justice, the students concluded that the verdict in the King situation was indeed unjust and unfair. Furthermore, these students then decided that some kind of action was called for, but rather than reacting, the students critically considered the issue and the responses they thought would be the most effective. As a result, these students, East Harlem students, held a forum in which the school heard the issues and they then decided that they would participate in a march in Washington, D.C.[8]

Dewey, as well as other scholars, believed the school could and should be a place that puts a premium on thinking well, that values inquiry, and that encourages the child "to mine his or her own experience in a systematic and intense fashion." (Reed, 1992, p. 21). We are, then, compelled to ask, "how do we create that environment?" Again, Dewey suggests that change cannot be mandated. We cannot demand that individuals value an endeavor, whether it's inquiry or technology, and expect that they will do it or do it well. Only, when they are immersed in an environment in which certain responses are called for, in which the desired attitudes, dispositions, skills, and knowledge bases are nurtured and developed, only then will individuals, namely teachers, begin to remake their practice.

In order to understand the environment Dewey is suggesting, we can look to the writings of Matthew Lipman who, later with Ann M. Sharp and Frederick S. Oscanyan, formulated a notion of community of inquiry that is unique to Philosophy for Children and one that sets it apart from the traditional model of the classroom.

Within Philosophy for Children the community of inquiry is more than the creation of an open environment. It is an environment in which teacher and student, as co-inquirers, try to make sense of issues they find interesting and problematic. The inquiry, for the most part, is done publicly — usually being with the common experience of reading a chapter from one of Lipman's novels, although other narratives can be used — and through a linguistic medium that at times is dialogical and at other times conversational. The ideas and questions posed by the community not only provide the agenda for the discussion, they also provide the foundation for building the curriculum. As teacher and students engage in this scholarly endeavor, the children not only are "sensitized to and gain practice in the art-like endeavors of setting significant problems and experiencing the force of those problems" (Reed & Witcher, 1992, pp. 209-210), but the intellectual habits of "acting critically, fair-mindedly, reasonably, and imaginatively" are also nurtured and developed (Sharp, 1987, p. 39). It is this kind of environment that led the East Harlem students to act as they did.

However, it is here that a problem emerges, a problem Dewey would see as critical. Philosophy for Children, a program that focuses primarily on teachers and children in primary and secondary school classrooms, relies on teachers seeking out the program, teachers who find the traditional methods of teaching problematic. For Dewey (1981), the teacher plays a critical role in bringing about social change. He views the teacher as "a social servant set apart for the maintenance of proper social order and securing of right social growth" (p. 454). In order to accomplish this, the teacher must be sensitive to the context of the present society, its strengths and weaknesses, and select the "influences which shall affect the child and to assist him in properly responding to these influences" (p. 447). This places an enormous responsibility on teachers, a responsibility, Kozol (1981) argues, that they are unable to undertake. He sees teachers so indoctrinated by the system that they are "impotent" to effectively bring about the change that is needed (p. 3). However, another solution may be suggested by focusing our attention on our colleges and universities, in particular, our schools of education. Rather than criticizing teachers for being preoccupied with teaching the basics, for emphasizing the retention of information, and for being overly didactic, we should realize that teachers replicate in their classrooms their own educative experience. In other words, they teach as they were taught. Consequently, if we want teachers who see education as a life-long experience, who value inquiry, who realize that information, technology, and other "innovative" practices are only tools in aiding children to make sense of their experiences, then we will educate our future teachers, as well as the professional development of our present teachers, in an environment that fosters inquiry into issues that they see as significant.

Again, we can return to Philosophy for Children and, borrowing Lipman's "methodology," begin with the community of inquiry. For our purposes this community would be comprised of prospective teachers, university faculty, clinical faculty (public school teachers), administrators, children, parents, and community members, with at least one member who is knowledgeable and experienced in the nature of a community of inquiry (for purposes of clarity within this section, this individual will be referred to as the facilitator).

The community would begin with the reading of a narrative and, in this case, the narrative would come from scholarly works, such as *Democracy and Education* (Dewey, 1916), from case studies of children, teachers, classrooms, and communities, from literature (both fiction and non-fiction), and from the community's own research. From the narratives, the facilitator would solicit the ideas, issues, and questions that the community finds important or problematic. Rather than beginning with the mechanics of lesson plan preparation and delivery, classroom management, and, at times, the student's specialization, the community would inquire into those "issues" that they see as significant. For example, instead of lectures, seminars, and videos on "Effective Classroom Management," the community might inquire into what is "discipline." They might read and consider Dewey's (1981) statements that

- *the child should be stimulated and controlled in his work through the life of the community.*

- *the discipline of the school should proceed from the life of the school as a whole and not directly from the teacher. (p. 445)*

In this case, inquiring into "discipline" might also lead the members of the community into inquiring into the role of the teacher, the nature of the subject matter, the relationship of the informal environment (home/neighborhood) to the formal environment (school), the definition of "education," and the social and political structure of schooling.

The facilitator would aid the community's inquiry by pointing out that certain topics seem to have a logical priority over others, by facilitating progress within the conversation, by helping the members to understand each other, and by nurturing a willingness to "reconstruct what they hear from one another" (Sharp, 1987, pp. 42-43). Likewise the facilitator and/or other community members would then present skills, facts, and methods, not as isolated entities, but as tools to aid the members in furthering the inquiry.

Within the community each individual would bring a unique perspective and as the members talk, listen, and learn from each other and then reflect upon what is said, their individual perspective would be enhanced and, at times, changed – again, a willingness "to submit their views to the self-correcting process of further inquiry" (Sharp, 1987, pp. 43). Through this process the community would come to see knowledge, not as something "out there," but rather as a social element "rooted in human interest, activities, and conditions" (Benjamin & Echeverria, 1992, p. 77).

It is here that the cyclical nature of the community of inquiry would become evident. As the members take this "knowledge" back into the classroom, they would apply it, reflect upon it, and evaluate it within the context of their students' lives and, as new experiences are had, the process not only would begin again, but as the community reflects upon this knowledge they would act to change and transform those policies, practices, and structures that prevent individuals from claiming their education.

This essay has attempted to put us in a position to reflect upon our attitudes toward educational reform and the societal changes that reform would entail. We must ask ourselves if we truly desire a citizenry in which all individuals are educated for full participation – that all children, regardless of their race, sex, social, or economic status, are given the type of education that allows that participation. Or is Kozol's indictment of us true, that we choose to protect our "privileged position," that our pursuit of excellence in education, of superiority both in economic endeavors and in national and international standing has been bought at the expense of a certain segment of our society? As Reed (1992) states,

> It (the conservative argument) says, in effect, that you deal with the situation as you find it and that you educate and achieve excellence where you can and you train and warehouse where you must. And what you wind up with is a two-tiered system in which minorities get trained and whites get educated. (p. 22)

The conservative argument follows a rather pessimistic line of thinking – that social and economic factors have a tremendous, and often fatal, impact on the academic success of the marginal members of society, in particular poor African-American and Hispanic children and, to a certain extent, they are right. A child who is hungry, abused, and homeless is not going to be successful in school, especially if her or his success is measured on some form of standardized test. But as I read of Freire's work with Brazilian peasants, of Kozol's work with inner-city children in Boston, and as I work with urban children, I find another hunger, one that, if satisfied, enables them to survive and, it is hoped, thrive in these devastating conditions. That hunger is a hunger for meaning.[9] This is not to imply that transforming classrooms into communities of inquiry exonerates us from passively accepting the social, political, and economic structures that forge their physical, emotional, and intellectual poverty; rather, it should burn us to the marrow of our bones and move us to action.

In the end, what we say and do, and how and on whom we spend our money and expend our time and energies says a great deal about who we are and what we value. To extol excellence in education while at the same time continuing policies and practices that favor one segment of society and exclude other segments, in particular the poor and non-whites, "is a covert admission of the racism and inequity that makes that excellence possible" (Reed, 1992, p. 22).

Notes

1. For the purpose of this paper, critical thinking is the ability to think for oneself – an individual who is sensitive to context, is respectful of criteria, and is self-correcting.

2. The foundation is modelled after Eugene Lang's program. Mr. Lang offered scholarships to the 1981 sixth grade graduates of his alma mater. But he also recognized that these individuals needed more than financial assistance; they needed people who would talk to, listen to, and encourage them. Mr. Lang employed a young man to act as a mentor to these students. Programs that emulate Mr. Lang's program provide each child with a mentor.

3. "At risk" denotes any student who is in danger of dropping out of school.

4. E.D. Hirsh has probably written more about this topic, or is more widely known than others. His book, *Cultural Literacy* (1987), details what every educated person should know. This book was followed by a series of books, primarily targeted at parents, on what a child should know at each grade level. For additional read-

ing and response to Hirsch (1987) and Bloom (1987), see Stanley Aronowitz and Henry Giroux (1993), and Benjamin R. Barber (1992).

5. This is a term that frequently was used by teachers, primarily white male teachers, in middle schools and high schools, as they discussed their students from urban elementary schools.

6. Demographic information for the 100 people surveyed (only 80 people responded): 33 males and 47 females; 5% of the respondents are aged 20-29 years, 10% are 30-39 years, 15% are 40-49 years, 15% are 50-59 years, 28% are 60-69 years, 20% are 70-79 years, and 2.5% are 80 and older; 97% own their own home; 99% graduated from high school and 35% have post secondary degrees.

7. On the connection between Dewey and the community of inquiry, see L. Nowell (1993).

8. In May, 1991, I visited Central Park East High School in Manhattan and was privileged to sit in on this class.

9. Cornel West (1993) presents a strong case for this in his powerful work, *Race Matters*. I also suggest that "meaning" played a tremendous part in how individuals in Los Angeles reacted to the Rodney King verdict and how the East Harlem students reacted.

References

Aronowitz, S. & Giroux, H. (1993). Schooling, culture, and literacy in the age of broken dreams: A review of Bloom and Hirsch. In H.S. Shapiro and D.E. Purpel (Eds.), *Critical social issues in education* (pp. 305-329). New York: Longman Publishing Co.

Apple, M. W. (1989). *Teachers and texts*. New York: Routledge.

Barber, B. R. (1992). *An aristocracy of everyone: The politics of education and the future of America*. New York: Ballantine Books.

Benjamin, M. & Echeverria, E. (1992). Knowledge in the classroom. In A. M. Sharp and R. F. Reed (Eds.), *Studies in philosophy for children* (pp. 64-78). Philadelphia, PA: Temple University Press.

Bloom, A. D. (1987). *The closing of the American mind: How higher education has failed democracy and impoverished the souls of today's students*. New York: Simon and Schuster.

Carnoy, M. (1989). Education, state, and culture in American society. In H. A. Giroux and P. McLaren (Eds.), *Critical pedagogy, the state, and cultural struggle* (pp. 3-23). New York: State University of New York Press.

Cremin, L. A. (1990). *Popular education and its discontents*. New York: Harper & Row.

Dewey, J. (1916). *Democracy and education*. New York: The Free Press.

Dewey, J. (1976). *The moral writings of John Dewey*. James Gouinlock (Ed.). New York: Hafner Press.

Dewey, J. (1981). *The philosophy of John Dewey*. John J. McDermott (Ed.). Chicago, IL: The University of Chicago Press.

Fine, M. (1989). Silencing and nurturing voice in an improbable context: Urban adolescents in public school. In H.A. Giroux and P. McLaren (Eds.), *Critical pedagogy, the state, and cultural struggle* (pp. 152-173). New York: State University of New York Press.

Freire, P. (1981). *Pedagogy of the oppressed*. New York: Continuum Publication Co.

Giroux, H. (1993). Teachers as transformative intellectuals. In H.S. Shapiro and D.E. Purpel (Eds.), *Critical social issues in American education* (pp. 272-277). New York: Longman Publishing Co.

Goodlad, J. I. (1984). *A place called school*. New York: McGraw-Hill.

Hirsch, E.D. (1987). *Cultural literacy: What every American needs to know*. Boston: Houghton Mifflin.

Kozol, J. (1967). *Death at an early age*. Boston: Houghton Mifflin Co.

Kozol, J. (1975; 1990). *The night is dark and I am far from home*. (revised edition). New York: Simon and Schuster, Inc.

Kozol, J. (1981). *On being a teacher*. New York: Continuum Publication Co.

Kozol, J. (1985). *Illiterate America*. New York: Anchor Press.

Kozol, J. (1988). *Rachel and her children*. New York: Crown Publishing, Inc.

Kozol, J. (1991). *Savage inequalities*. New York: Crown Publishing, Inc.

Madigan, J. (April 14, 1991). When babies die. *Fort Worth Star Telegram*.

McLaren, P. (1989). *Life in schools*. New York: Longman Publishing.

Nowell. L. (1993). Thinking the classroom. In *Analytic Teaching, 14* (1), 39-44.

Oakes, J. (1993). Tracking, inequality, and the rhetoric of reform: Why schools don't change. In H.S. Shapiro & D.E. Purpel (Eds.), *Critical social issues in American education* (pp. 85-102). New York: Longman Publishing Co.

Reed, R. F. (1985). Discussing philosophy with children: Aims and methods. *Teaching Philosophy, 8* (3), 229-235.

Reed, R. F. (1992). Cultural pedagogy. *Analytic Teaching, 12* (2), 19-22.

Reed, R. F. & Witcher, A. (1992). Restoring the connection between education and philosophy: Matthew Lipman and philosophy for children. In J. Van Patten (Ed.), *Profiles in higher education* (pp. 209-210). New York: The Edwin Mellen Press.

Reich, R. B. (1991). *The work of nations*. New York: Alfred A. Knopf.

Sharp, A. M. (1987). What is a community of inquiry. *Journal of Moral Education. 16*, 1, 37-45.

Shuall, R. (1981). Forword to *Pedagogy of the oppressed* by Paulo Freire.

Walsh, C. (1991). *Pedagogy and the struggle for voice*. New York: Bergin & Garvey.

West, C. (1993). *Race matters*. Boston: Beacon Press.

CHAPTER 12

Incorporating Philosophical Discussions within a High School Literature Curriculum

Glynis Ross

Teaching, as I am perfectly willing to tell anyone who will stop to listen to me, is my greater passion in life. I love spending time in classrooms with kids. This sounds sentimental and idealistic. It isn't. I know myself to be a faculty teacher given to all sorts of inadequate, human responses to the overwhelming burdens of my work – responses which I theoretically deplore. I am not nearly as innovative or energetic as I would like to be or can imagine the possibility of being. In short, I am like most teachers I know – someone who strives to be a dedicated and creative professional and sometimes, less frequently than she would like, succeeds.

This disclaimer is a necessary preamble to what follows. I am about to attempt to describe a project I designed and implemented in 1989. It was an effort to do philosophy with high school students – to be precise – my English literature students. The journey toward the designing was a lengthy one which began, although I hadn't known it at the time, with my own unhappiness as a pupil in school. I must emphasize that this was not the misery of a brilliant, insightful student chronically under-challenged by the syllabus of the 60s. Rather it was the vague malaise of a child who failed to grasp why we were learning much of what we were learning or how one thing connected to another, the diffident dislike of a child who although she was a relatively model student, didn't really understand why or how her marks appeared on her report card or why certain pieces of knowledge were deemed by vague and important personages to be vital to her academic growth, others pleasant extras, and still others not relevant to her at all.

The pattern continued at university where I continued to perform (an appropriate description) at very competent level in arts, the wonders of science now beyond me, and continued to fail to grasp what was missing in my education and finally, in my teaching, a profession I had known I wanted to pursue since I was the smallest of small girls. My actual teaching experience, first with elementary special education, subsequently with high school foreign languages, German and French, and then with high school literature, was what uncompromisingly compelled me to begin asking a series of hard questions about both what we teach children to do in school and why. I cannot claim that these were by any means original or astonishing questions. They were the natural responses of a reasonably intelligent person who was learning to think critically about the contradictions inherent in the establishments in which she had spent all but the first five years of her life. As a special education teacher, I was forced to begin to see the existence of a relentless hidden curriculum in school, an agenda which kept certain children conveniently in the basement. As a high school teacher, I watched as the monotony of the schedule kept students pacing through the halls and through their subjects without having the luxury of time to explore the various connections among the subjects they studied or to come to recognize the value or place of critical thinking in and across their curriculum. I was forced to recognize the diverse and fiercely competitive nature of high school for those who could compete, its inexorable, unquestionable rightness for those who couldn't.

With every passing year I became more and more distressed, more aware that if I were to continue to live with myself in the classroom, I needed to do something to change what I saw and indeed actively perpetrated. The long and short of it was that after a great deal of rumination and plain old procrastination cleverly disguised as rumination, I went out in deliberate search of concrete solutions to what I had targeted as the principal problem in high school education – its failure concertedly to cultivate in children the ability to think critically and compassionately about the world in which they were citizens; its failure by implication to prepare them to assume intelligent and concerned responsibility for the world they would inherit. Recognition that identification of the problem and attempting to implement something of a solution are worlds apart sent me on a quest for help that ended, one branch of it anyway, in the office of John Portelli, one of the editors of this collection. Our lengthy talks persuaded me that wondrous possibilities for helping children to become ethical, critical thinkers could be uncovered by doing philosophy with them. It was John and I who became familiar with the considerable work done by Matt Lipman, Ann Margaret Sharp and Frederick Oscanyan, but the philosophy novels Lipman had developed did not seem appropriate either to my students' interests or to the core curriculum I was obliged to follow. So I began to think about how I could use the literature I was required to teach to engage students, not just in literary criticism, but very deliberately in philosophical dialog about the meaning of their world, about how to live a good life together in it.

That is what this essay is supposed to talk about – how I did it, how successful I wasn't, what I learned, and what I would do differently. But now it is three years later and I am finding it terribly difficult to compose an information paper about the work I did. Part of that reluctance inevitably stems from having already written a fairly extensive thesis about it and being naturally somewhat sick of the whole thing and very sick of talking about "myself-as-if-I-were-not-me." But that isn't all of it or even most of it. I want to say that although I went looking for some better answers to my questions about the nature of ethical teaching, I ended up (as is, I suppose, fairly predictable) with many more unavoidably political questions and my hesitant responses to those, in direct consequence, compelled me to make some radical changes in my teaching life. The work I do now and the children with whom I work are radically different from what I did in my comfortable middle to upper middle-class high school in 1989. Even as I unfolded the thesis which discussed the results of my effort to do philosophy with high school students in a community of inquiry, I felt diffident and worried. And now I feel infinitely less sure of the lasting value of what I claimed to be doing. Make no mistake; I do not write now from the position of a teacher who having fallen off her donkey on the way to educational Damascus gets up to tell all to the unenlightened; further, I want it clearly understood that if an educational radical at all, I am a most reluctant crusader. The fact is that I have great reservations about the transferable value of what I did, that I began to feel trepidation even as I wrote about it all and that the feeling, far from having subsided, has indeed solidified in such a way that I cannot write with blithe and breezy confidence about the considerable success of my effort at doing philosophy with high school students. It is no reflection on that wonderful group of children at all that I learned far more from the enterprise than they did and that the knowledge changed me significantly. So instead of talking about what they may have learned, what I shall attempt to do is first to outline the program I put together and explain the rationale, and then, because what I do now is a direct consequence of my own cumulative discoveries throughout that naïve effort to help children discover, explain a little the irony of how formally doing philosophy with high school students for one year, in an effort to make life richer for them and me, led me forcibly away from a place, when I thought about it at all, I had probably thought only retirement would take me.

That September, when I set out to do my study, as always, I was assigned to teach five literature classes – two grade twelves and three grade elevens. I had already decided that since I was hoping to video tape our discussions and transcribe them for analysis, one class was as much as I could realistically expect to handle of this cultivated effort to do philosophy. Five from which to choose seems generous, but the reality was that each of the grade twelve classes contained 39 persons and one of the grade eleven classes, 41. A class period for literature was 45 minutes long. Discussion being critical to the success of the enterprise, these larger classes, for all intents and purposes to them, were eliminated from consideration. In the end, after carefully explaining my purposes to them, and my very deep commitment as teacher to the twin notions of critical and caring thinking, I asked the smallest of my grade eleven classes, a group of 23 students, to consider whether they would be willing to work with me. They agreed. I was to note in my thesis that there was "some politely masked scepticism on some veiled faces; they seem to ask whether I really believe *they* really believe there is any choice" (p. 44), but for the most part, I recall they were eager, even excited at this possibility of something new in their school day.

I tentatively entitled the course we were following "A Philosophical Approach to Literature" and described it to my students as "a series of philosophical discussions on a variety of issues and problems that arise out of the short stories and articles that we will read together."[1] I then presented them with three course objectives to consider,

1) To analyze and to clarify philosophically, selected problems and issues which the student group identifies in the works we read.

2) To discuss various considerations and viewpoints of these issues and to evaluate critically these different positions and their supporting arguments.

3) To encourage and help all members of the group to form their own views and reasons for them with regard to the issues raised.

There were and continue to be very specific questions that it was and is my aim as teacher/student to explore, and these too I shared with my students:

1) Can students learn with some consistency to ask philosophical questions about the literature they read? Can they come to some tentative, reasoned conclusions in response to their own questions?

2) Can they learn to recognize in their reading the issues that best give rise to philosophical questions?

3) Can they be motivated to continue probing below the surface of thought (perhaps even beyond the formal inquiry classes) to develop, to *want* to develop clarity in their thinking and reasonable support for beliefs held?

4) Can they learn that this is best done cooperatively in a community of inquiry through which they pursue together the best answers to the questions they raise and the best reasons for those answers?

5) Can they learn to distinguish between two dispositions: "anything is within the realm of questioning" and "any opinion's fine"?

6) Can they come to a better understanding/appreciation of literature through their communal effort to see it philosophically?

I recall wondering whether through this process, the students might move some distance toward accepting me, their teacher, not as Giver of Points to whose cavalier whims they must unthinkingly cater but as a member of their community; whether if I attempted to model reasonableness and consistency as best I could myself and if I established these ideals in our classroom, *they* would be encouraged to *be* rational and consistent and to see the intrinsic value in these dispositions, despite the difficulties inherent in acquiring them.

> *Why be rational? It's all so complicated. Why not just do what you're told, accept what most people think, and leave it at that? The most direct answer I can think of giving this person is that the rational method — the method of inquiry — is the only one that will help human beings become fully persons, capable of autonomous action, creativity and self-knowledge. It's the only method I know that will help one devise means to attain the ends that one thinks are meaningful and worthwhile. It's the only method that will enable one to make predictions and to live a self-fulfilling, morally satisfying life. In a circular way the satisfying life involves living the life of the method itself which presupposes rationality. (Sharp, 1987, p. 42)*

The essay from which this quotation is borrowed was inspired or, perhaps more accurately, provoked by the apparently complacent confidence of a young teacher who informed Ann Margaret Sharp, after only seven days, that her study group had become a community of inquiry: "It took work . . . but we got there" (Sharp, 1987, p. 37). By the conclusion of my thesis work, I was beginning to understand what a long and difficult process that is, what far off ideals these aims and objectives are and yet still, I am correspondingly certain that . . .

As the process continues

    year after year

focus must always be on the improvement

    of the inquiry itself

in its relation to the problems

    under discussion.

It is this education

    and only this kind of education

that will enable children

    to think for themselves

in an objective, consistent

    and comprehensive manner. (Sharp, 1987, p. 38)

I do not know to what degree my students understood my intentions even as they accepted them. Nor am I sure whether they saw as worthy of internalizing what, in theory, they may well have understood. What evolved, what we created together was complex and remains indeed somewhat murky despite its having had many lovely moments of thrilling light and I hesitate to suggest that any of my group went away profoundly changed by our work. But more on that later.

The Readings

Compiling a satisfying and satisfactory list of readings for the program was a serious challenge. It was my aim to strike a judicious balance between short stories, a compulsory component of the grade eleven English curriculum, and purely philosophical articles, each of which could somehow be ordered so that they were sequential – so that a naturally developing sense of philosophical issues might conceivably emerge. As well, I wanted at least some of the stories and articles to engage the imagination even as I wanted them to arouse the intellect:

Puzzlement and wonder are closely related. Aristotle says that philosophy begins in wonder... Bertrand Russell tells us that philosophy, "if it cannot answer so many questions as we would wish, has at least the power of asking questions which increase the interest of the world, and show the strangeness and wonder lying just below the surface even in the commonest things of daily life." (Matthews, 1980, p. 2)

I recall wanting to compose a list out of which at least something could inspire a sense of strangeness and wonder in each child if the child so chose. That is the primary reason, too, why I opted for short works rather than for a novel study. There is much to be said for Jonathan Jacob's view that if one is examining literature for its philosophical content, "novels or book length treatments are superior to short stories – because of the details of development of character" (Jacobs, 1987, p. 301). But all too often, I had met the abortive experience that a novel to which *I* was convinced my students would be inescapably drawn produced apathetic yawns or sullen resistance or indignant incredulity. Such initial reactions can so easily color everything that follows. The potential for an early and permanent negative bias was not a risk I felt I could afford to take and I came down on the side of variety. In retrospect, I am compelled to say that one serious limitation of our discussions, despite my effort to order the material I did choose in such a way that it encouraged the building and interweaving of ideas, was the lack of cohesiveness and layering which are characteristic of an evolving series of good discussions about a good novel.

In any event, I finally selected and arranged twelve pieces so that if the students saw it that way, we could move from consideration of the nature of what it is to be human to the nature of what it is to be a morally *responsible* human. I did not indicate to the group that there was anything special about the order and although I set down for my own records issues which I thought might potentially concern them, I did not share these ideas with the class. I was and continue to be very much concerned that wherever possible and appropriate, students' understandings and inter-ests dictate the agenda. In essence, what I was striving to do was to set a flexible agenda, a starting place which I hoped to avoid making into an entrenched order of operations – that, after all, stood in obvious contra-diction of my frequently espoused conviction that students are best able genuinely to think philosophically when they identify from the work they are considering their *own* sources of wonder and puzzlement. To give authoritarian voice to that schedule seemed to be pretty loud conviction out of my own mouth and considering my purposes, fallacy and incon-sistency would be – well, inconsistent. And so this ordered list of rich stories and articles was given to the students, while what created wonder for me was withheld.

1. "Robot Dreams" – Isaac Asimov

   What is it to be human? To aspire? What is life? What is reality? What is a dream?

2. "Getting to Williamstown" – Hugh Hood

What is life? death? What is awareness? What is aspiration? What is the essence of the individual? How long does that essence exist? What is God? What is faith? Can there be awareness after life?

3. "The Essence of Marigold" – Elizabeth Brewster.

   What is mind? What is identity? What is objectivity? What is truth? What can we recall with accuracy? Can we know anything as it 'really is'? What really is?

4. "The Rocking Horse Winner" – D. H. Lawrence.

   What is reality? What is mind? What is knowledge? Where does it come from? What kinds of knowledge are there? Can we ever know what has not yet happened?

5. "Of this Time, of that Place" – Lionel Trilling

   What is reality? What is sanity? insanity? Are these definitions relative? What is understanding? What is knowledge? What is conscience? What are rights? responsibilities? What is justice?

6. From "the Meditations and Selections from the Principles of Rene Descartes"

   What is self? Is the mind separate from the body? What is body? What is soul? Does it have its own existence? What is identity? When and where does 'self' begin? Can one know one's 'self' objectively? Can anyone?

7. "The Tomorrow Tamer" – Margaret Lawrence

   Does this 'self' have rights? How are we to determine rights? Are all understandings of the world valid? What counts as valid? What is progress? What is freedom? What is justice? What is morality? Can values be true for everyone everywhere or are they relative to the person and societies that formulate them?

8. "A Modest Proposal" – Jonathan Swift.

   What are responsibilities? What are rights? What is prejudice? What is 'assumption'? What constitutes a reasonable/unreasonable assumption? What is justice? What is ethically/morally right?

9. "Propaganda in a Democratic Society" – Aldous Huxley

   What is democracy? What is propaganda? liberty? freedom? What are a citizen's responsibilities and rights in a democracy?

10. "The Indispensible Opposition" – Walter Lippmann

    Why is opposition necessary? What is the function of a gadfly? What is liberty? By what standards may we judge a society?

What are society's responsibilities to the individual and vice versa?

11. "Keegstra's Children" – Robert Mason Lee.

What is the responsibility of the teacher to his/her students in a democratic society? What is the difference between inculcation and indoctrination and how may we know? What is the difference between indoctrination and education and how may we know?

12. "The Apology of Socrates" – Plato.

What is the responsibility of the teacher in a democratic society? What is it to be righteous? Why be righteous? What is an ideal? What is 'good'? What is 'evil'? What constitutes education in a democracy? How do ideals shift into fanaticisms?[3]

The Procedure

The solution offered by Socrates – involving young people in a process of inquiry which entails dialog and the inculcation of habits of inquiry – is an educational solution. It presupposes that the tools of inquiry can be taught and that children are rational persons capable of eventually forming communities of inquiry in which they begin to discover for themselves certain things they have to take into account; impartiality, comprehensiveness, the relationship of parts to wholes, the relationship of ends to means, and the role of ideals and context in discussing philosophical and ethical issues (Sharp, 1988).

I told the students in my study group that I would like the course to run as a discussion seminar and that each week, one of the readings on the list would be assigned for consideration in our discussion. I told them that I expected them to have read and thought about each weekly reading prior to discussion and, partly to ensure that they did this, partly to develop some feeling of community and shared experience, I asked them to sit with me in a circle and take turns reading the selection aloud prior to gathering leading ideas and holding a discussion. Already achingly aware from long experience of what a dreaded event oral reading for an audience is for many of my students, I introduced them to the concept of "pass," so that anyone who felt for any reason that he or she did not wish to read when the time came, had a simple, formal out. There were students who chose not to read a single time and others who seized their turn to read at length, and as enthusiastically as they could. Something of a forerunner, the oral reading, in retrospect, enunciated quite clearly just who would participate and the manner of their participation.

Once the reading was completed, the next step was to collect the leading ideas. These could take the form of statements or questions; they could be very specific to the story or more broad and general; they might be a collaborative effort or the concern of one individual and we went on collecting them and recording them until no one had anything else to say. I tried hard to emphasize that an idea didn't have to be enunciated as a "finished product," that it could be a fragment of a thought, a glimmer of a notion, tentatively expressed or held, that we as a group could then try to give shape and focus until its original author felt his or her intention had been expressed as concisely as possible. The originator of any idea always had final jurisdiction over any suggestions, adaptations, or proposed additions which others might regard as related ideas. To my delight, my students readily accepted this notion of oral drafting without any apparent self-consciousness, but once again I must say that dominant proposers of leading ideas very readily established themselves and I grew increasingly concerned that their organization of the menu of leading ideas necessarily determined the main course of our discussion. So it was that I changed the gathering procedure from a whole class effort to a small group enterprise. To this end, I divided the students into four evenly distributed sections in each of which there was a chairperson of my choosing, confident but not domineering, who solicited and helped refine ideas while a secretary recorded them for presentation to the whole class. Here many of my shyer students felt freer to voice their positions and to help clarify others. Even so, there were those who chose to make almost no contribution, even though each student should have come to the session with at least one concern in mind, for I required that after each oral reading and before the gathering of leading ideas, each student write a reaction to or reflection on the assigned reading. In about three hundred words, each was to try to address the question "Where do I stand with regard to this reading?" For a number of the twenty-three, 300 words was not adequate but for others, this task was an exercise to be done as quickly, as briefly and as prosaically as possible. I should also add that the most articulate and thoughtful writers were not always the most confident speakers and vice versa.

Once a composite list had been compiled by the whole group, we examined it together for patterns – to see if there was one dominant, common concern, as was quite often the case, or whether perhaps one issue, strikingly original and intriguing, attracted us more than others. Our discussion topic was chosen by consensus and students then had the evening prior to the discussion itself to consider their positions and, very importantly, the reasons for their views.

I did speak both about the benefit to the group as a whole if everyone in it were an active participant, but I hope I made it abundantly clear that there was no notion of forcing spoken participation upon them by means of holding marks like Skinner's pellets of food in front of them in exchange for the number of times they mindlessly pushed the lever of participation. I tried to stress that it was the quality of one's questions and comments – that is, active and voluntary participation which suggested serious reflection both on the readings and on the issues raised in the reader's mind, their honest concern with asking searching questions of their teacher, their classmates, themselves – that determined the success of any discussion. I did not, I think now, give enough time to the legitimate value of silent participation. Ah, hindsight! What wisdom comes with it! I was very careful to establish that one of the guiding principals of a community of inquiry was that each member participate critically and searchingly, *not* destructively, whenever she or he felt there was something important to be said. I would *lead* the discussions and ask clarifactory, exploratory, or critical questions, when appropriate, in an effort to help them build on *their* understandings. My role, for the time being, I wanted them to see, was strictly this: to help them build, to help them uncover the assumptions which held them back, and to help them come to some rational understanding of their world; not to offer, except admittedly through the powerful means of procedure, my own world view. (It goes without saying that I was to discover the clay not just of my feet but of my entire person!)

For the actual discussion itself, I asked that the group sit around the tables in the classroom in a large circle. This was largely to facilitate our being able to look at each other when we were talking but the videotapes reveal that, for the largest part of the time, the students mostly looked at me when they were speaking. Old habits are hard to break. I also asked that each session someone take responsibility for recording the names of those who signalled that they wanted to speak. Again, there was a very practical reason – the constant waving of hands is not conducive to concentrated discussion. Whenever possible, as their turns came, students were asked to explain whether their points were related to previous ones and how, or whether the point was a new one. As well, I suggested that because the wait could sometimes be long and the conversation intense, we all jot our thoughts down quickly so as not to forget them and to stay focused on the discussion. There was to be no rude or inappropriate interruption, but if they felt an issue had not been adequately explored, they had a right to continue examining it before a new one was introduced. As much as they could, they were to focus on each other's ideas rather than what they thought mine might be.

Above all, I wanted the idea of discussion class to be appealing rather than threatening, particularly to those students whose hearts were struck with terror at the thought of public utterance. Ideally, all of them would eventually feel comfortable with the notion of participating when they felt they had something to say. Ideally, all of them would come to feel not only that they had something valid to say, but that the group itself depended on their contribution; that in fact their absence on any given day would be noted, not simply as a black dot on the computer attendance sheet, but because we genuinely missed them. And lots of them were, but as with oral reading and brainstorming, in discussion too, there were leaders and talkers and there were some followers who sat in respectful silence or inattentive silence or sullen silence; both the silence and its quality were critical. By high school certainly, and now I think long before, it is not only ethical or controversial *issues* about which children have preconceptions and prejudices, but also about their very roles as individuals in the drama of the classroom and, by extension, I am afraid, their roles as citizens in the world. It was only after the program drew to a close and I was left with reams of journal entries and pages of transcripts from the discussions to contemplate, that I began to consider very seriously the possibility that, for me at least, essential as I thought them to be, the dual tasks of helping children think critically about their potentially destructive and taken-for-granted assumptions about *themselves* as gendered persons of particular class and race and of helping them think critically about the *world* which had fostered in them these views, was infinitely too complex to accomplish or even approximate accomplishing in the daily 45 minutes I was allotted.

In an effort to give further opportunity to my silent partners to clarify their thinking and, as well, give my more forceful but not necessarily more profound participants an opportunity to further reflect on the quality of their thinking, I required a second reflection submitted each week after the discussion; a reaction to the discussion itself, one which attempted to resolve unfinished thoughts in the mind of the writer or deal with the conclusions to which we as a group appeared to have come. Once again, a number of students took this task very seriously and engaged themselves in genuinely philosophical dialog while others tossed it off perfunctorily at the last minute or regarded it as the superfluous rehashing of a dead subject and neglected to do it at all. This second reflection drew the unit to a close and signalled the beginning of another.

A week before the first reading, I distributed a handout detailing all this information as a proposal for procedure. I wanted my students not only to *listen* to my ideas but to *read* them, critically to *assess* them, to be sure they knew what I was asking of them and to understand that I was entirely willing to change any aspect of it which they could reasonably demonstrate to me needed anything from minor tinkering to drastic reorganization. There were few questions, no suggestions. I told them that I would be audiotaping the first three sessions for transcript purposes and then, when they felt more comfortable with the whole process, videotaping the rest; that only formal discussion would be recorded. Again, no one raised an objection. Indeed, I think many of them were rather taken aback with the idea of being study subjects and one person volunteered to be the camera person when the time came. I told them as well that I would like to quote from their reflections in my thesis when the time came but that I would ask permission before I used anything that they had written and that I would tell them both what I wanted to use the piece for and why. Once again there was no difficulty, they indicated that this was a fair request on my part. Finally I told them that, in my own mind, everything we did was subject to revision; that if they were to truly to evolve as a community of inquiry, *they* must take responsibility for shaping and sculpting themselves by adding guidelines which suited their specific needs and deleting others which served them poorly, by constantly keeping their own watchful eye on their individual and collective progress.

And once again, a number of them listened seriously, conscientiously, and critically while others were and remained unsure of their own abilities, unable or unwilling to articulate or defend an opinion, apparently content to leave control in the hands of others who must surely know best. Still others saw it as an interesting variation on just one more teacher's game, the rules of which it became a challenge meticulously to case and unravel, to get the marks to get to the university to get the job to support the affluent lifestyle they dreamed about and had coming to them. This assessment may appear to ring with hollow cynicism but I mean it really as an admission that, in the system of which I remain very much a part, such divisions are all pervasive and they come from a long entrenched tradition. There were many times during this study that I was sorely tempted to throw up my hands in despair, to acknowledge, however reluctantly, that if the order wasn't at all necessarily what it *ought* to be, it was nonetheless embedded *and* immovable. Sometimes, indeed, I think it is far easier to buckle under the relentless coercion of the apparently inevitable. It is at such times that I remind myself once more that the twelve weeks the study officially ran were, in the face of their twelve years in school, very little seeds.

Rereading now, I am struck by the self-righteous flavor of what I have just said. I have given not nearly enough credit to the wonderfully lively minds of my much-loved students and I appear to suggest that my not so humble offerings were all that stood between them and categorical defeat of their capacity to think with critical compassion by the Entrenched Status Quo. I never cease to amaze myself! What I ought to say is that armed with all these disclaimers and appeals, we set out on our adventure together, beginning, with unintentional irony, with "Robot Dreams" and that I got a great deal of joy out of it as well as the worry and frustration which seemed to predominate here.

I said at the outset that this study was directly responsible for a dramatic change of direction for me and indeed it was. I now find myself, after a year away from school altogether, a year in which to reflect and consider, teaching grade six in an elementary school whose population is largely drawn from a trailer court and low-rental housing units. I have 29 students, three of whom are special needs and many more of whom, in a less demanding environment, would be so deemed. We do philosophy every day and we use *Harry Stottlemeier's Discovery* as the basis of our discussions. Matthew Lipman would be happy to know that the children love the book. We have sustained hour long discussions on a variety of topics including "what is thought?", "what is real?", "what makes me, me?", "are my mind and body separate?", and "what is a right?" and we have begun to explore the world of syllogisms. Watching them uncover the magic and power of their own minds, individually and collectively, is one of the most moving experiences I have ever had.

The first inkling that this was where my study would lead me came as I was analyzing a particularly heated discussion among my grade eleven students about the nature of democracy and whether the schools of a democracy operated in a way that was conducive to preparing a new generation of concerned and intelligent citizens. The consensus was that they didn't and perhaps Matthew's shrewd analysis best gives expression to their view:

> *Matthew: I think it's a question of power . . . Once you're an adult, you don't want to give up the power, you know, like school boards, administrators, something like that. You have the power to control things and*

> *they know, adults have been teenagers before, without influence or something, they just don't want to give the power up. They've gone through it and they now think it's their right to be the ones with the ultimate say.*

Although they agreed that there was a hidden curriculum at work, there were a number of them who argued that for many students, this was a necessary evil. Ariana expresses this view:

> *It would be ideal for everyone to choose their teachers and their principal but really, if most students got that right of the ability to do that, they would take advantage of it don't you think? They would probably find the easiest teachers and the hard teachers or the strict teachers, nobody would want those teachers.*

I asked if she thought that genuine interest and a sense of responsibility might prevail over self-indulgence and she replied, "maybe a minority but a lot of people would take the easy way out." John Portelli, who was visiting that day, pointed out that it was in the best interest of an individual who was interested in a particular subject to choose the best teacher and Ariana responded "*I* would but not all students are like that!" A little further on in the discussion, David made this claim:

> *Right now in school, there's a lot of people who don't want to be here. If they had the choice, they'd be elsewhere and these people should have the choice to leave or not. And if they left the people who wanted to stay would have a better atmosphere to learn in. That's why I think streaming is right . . . .*

Ariana was not happy with this laissez-faire notion:

> *Just one question. All these people who don't want to learn, obviously, their jobs aren't going to be as good or as well paid because they aren't as well educated and they might start collecting unemployment and stuff like that and it's going to come out of our taxes. I'm just making another point. Could we be creating a bigger problem?*

It is not *at all* my point that these very comfortable and capable children are elitist snobs any more than I am suggesting that all children must be forced to enjoy the pleasures of abstract thought. Rather I want to establish that *I* learned that my students' vulnerable receptiveness to our view of knowledge and power is a matter of verifiable fact and what I chose to do with that knowledge was a matter of ethics. And it seemed, continues to seem to me, that my aim was truly to foster in children a lifelong habit of critical compassionate thinking about themselves, their fellow students, the world around them, and their place in it, I could not possibly say in my insulated little high school struggling daily in forty-five minute blocks of time, with my own complacency and our collective assumption that what *is, ought* to be. Maxine Greene speaks to this sense far more eloquently than I can:

> *We do not ask that a teacher perceive his or her existence as absurd; nor do we demand that he or she estrange himself or herself from the community. We simply suggest that he or she struggle against unthinking submergence in the social reality that prevails. If one wishes to present oneself as a person actively engaged in critical thinking and authentic choosing, one cannot accept any "ready-made standardized scheme" at face value. One cannot even take for granted the value of intelligence, rationality, or education. Why, after all, should a human being act intelligently or rationally? How does a teacher justify the educational policies he or she is assigned to carry out within his or her school? If a teacher does not pose such questions to himself or herself, he or she cannot expect the students to pose the kind of questions about experience that will involve them in self aware inquiry . . . .*
>
> *If one is immersed and impermeable, one can hardly stir others to define themselves as individuals. (Greene, 1988, p. 189)*

And so I find myself not an older, wiser teacher of philosophy in literature, but rather once again a neophyte, who having recognized her inescapable responsibility as a political actor in the world of school, continues to believe in the power of philosophy to help children work intelligently and humanely through the political problems they face. And I would argue that the younger *all* children begin and the more conducive their classroom environment is nurturing a community of inquiry, the more likely we are, if indeed that is what we want, to create a generation of critical compassionate citizens.

Notes

1. Responsible for a syllabus consisting of two modern novels, one modern drama, one Shakespearean tragedy, a broad selection of poetry, creative writing, language usage, and media studies, I felt that focusing on short stories allowed us the greatest potential for flexibility and variety.

2. This is not to suggest that I am always or even frequently successful!

3. It is the mark of the malaise of which I initially spoke that I look at this list now with the angst of one who recognizes its indisputably white, western, male focus and didn't when she composed it. So much for the claim of leaving students free to locate their understandings. As, I think, yet another white western male, Antonio, said in *The Merchant of Venice*, "I have much ado to know

myself." My list now would be substantially more inclusive; the fact that it wasn't is even scarier than it is embarrassing.

References

Greene, M. (1988). Teacher as stranger. In W. Hare & J. P. Portelli (Eds.), *Philosophy of education: Introductory readings* (pp. 187-200). Calgary, AB: Detselig Enterprises Ltd.

Jacobs, J. (1987). A *novel* approach to ethics. *Teaching Philosophy, 10* (4), 295-303.

Matthews, G. (1980). *Philosophy and the young child.* Cambridge: Harvard University Press.

Sharp, A. M. (1987). What is a community of inquiry? *Journal of Moral Education, 16* (1), 37-45.

Sharp, A. M. (1988). Philosophical teaching as moral education. In W. Hare & J. P. Portelli (Eds.), *Philosophy of education: Introductory readings* (pp. 275-284). Calgary, AB: Detselig Enterprises Ltd.

CHAPTER 13

The Community of Inquiry and the Euthanasia Trial

Reenie Marx

This essay discusses the ways in which I have applied the principles of the community of inquiry and Philosophy for Children in an innovative project developed for secondary students of moral education.

A. Background and Description of the Euthanasia Trial

The Euthanasia Trial, which I developed in 1983 and refined over nine years of classroom practice, is a four-month long project developed for senior high school students. When I first began the project, I had no knowledge of Philosophy for Children or the community of inquiry. The Trial[1] began as a kind of qualitative research project. I had a sense of the questions I wanted to explore, a beginning notion of how to pose the questions, and a working knowledge of the students who would be involved in the project. Like many enterprises of this nature, the results of the first *experiment,* or Trial, enabled me to perceive problems I could not have anticipated in advance. Finding the solutions to these problems has been an unending process of discovery and understanding.

My experiences in the first several Trials demonstrated clearly that discussions alone were incapable of developing students' thinking skills, and without an ability to perceive biases and hidden assumptions and project the implications of certain lines of thought, neither the lawyers nor the jury could do an effective job. What the community of inquiry has provided is a forum which enables me to develop both the cognitive and affective skills students need to master the challenges posed by The Trial. Through Philosophy for Children, I have learned the language of philosophical thinking and the techniques for imparting this type of thinking to my students.

Matthew Lipman correctly observes that, "[i]f the community forms the context with which the process begins, it also characterizes the product with which it ends." (1991, p. 138). The ability to work collaboratively with other students is both a means and an end in The

Euthanasia Trial. The *Introduction* phase employs the community of inquiry form and Philosophy for Children principles to teach students methods of collaborative inquiry and logical reasoning. In the *Trial Preparation* phase, while half of the students are using narrative and dramatic techniques to prepare for their roles in the trial, the other half are being schooled in the community of inquiry form and principles of philosophical dialog to prepare for their role as jurors. The climax of these preparations is a day long trial, in an actual courtroom, in which students act upon their emotional and intellectual understanding to present their arguments and arrive at a verdict. Following this *experiential* phase they return to the community of inquiry in the classroom for the final *Reflection and Summation* phase.

The Euthanasia Trial is built on the assumption that two factors are essential for learning to take place: experience and reflection. Without experience, students receive only unassimilated bits of knowledge which they will soon forget. Without reflection on their experiences the inherent learning potential is lost, as critical connections remain unseen.

As a teacher I have long recognized the truth in Dewey's assertion that educators far too often ". . . supply ready-made ideas . . . [but] do not usually take much pains to see that the one learning engages in significant situations where his own activities generate support, and clinch ideas — that is, perceived meanings or connections" (1966, p. 160). The Euthanasia Trial attempts to remedy this problem by creating a learning situation in which students' own activities result in the perception of meaningful relationships. This reflects Dewey's theory that "only by wrestling with the conditions of the problem at first hand, seeking and finding his own way out . . . [does a student actually] think" (1966, p. 160).

The subject of euthanasia is a fascinating web of moral, social, legal, medical, personal, and religious concerns. However, teaching students *about euthanasia, in an abstract, hypothetical way* is contrary to both Dewey's concept of learning through experience, and the moral theories of Gilligan (1977), Noddings (1986), and others. Gilligan believes that it is "only when substance is given to the skeletal lives of hypothetical people . . . [is it] possible to consider the social injustices which their moral problems may reflect and to imagine the individual suffering their occurrence may signify or resolution engender." (1977, p. 512).

Each Euthanasia Trial is based on one of three stories, which are largely recreations of actual cases. Just as the characters in the Philosophy for Children novels give life to abstract logical principles, so the characters in each of the stories used in The Euthanasia Trials give substance to hypothetical moral dilemmas.

> To the extent that children become involved in the plot and critically reflect upon the actions of the characters, taking into account the complexity of the situations in which they find themselves and the consequences of their actions, to that extent they are involved in a process that can result in a heightened moral sensitivity . . . (Lipman, Sharp & Oscanyan, 1980, p. 176)

In the courtroom, students use dramatic techniques that fall somewhere between scripted and live theatre. The roles, which they have spent weeks developing, parachute them into the circumstances, motives, and history of their characters' lives, thus enabling them to explore the profound ways in which contextual factors, such as age, gender, class, and culture shape the meaning individuals make of their experiences.

Another similarity between the Philosophy for Children novels and the stories that unfold in the courtroom during The Euthanasia Trial is that both ". . . afford an indirect mode of communication that, in a sense, safeguards the freedom of the child." (Lipman et al., 1980, p. 174). The characters in The Trial stories permit students to "try on" different moral or philosophical points of view, without the risk of being personally identified with that viewpoint by their peers. The distance that this fictional technique permits leaves students ". . . free to interpret and eventually decide for themselves which philosophical view makes the most sense to them . . ." (Lipman et al., 1980, pp. 174-175).

B. The Community of Inquiry and The Euthanasia Trial

As soon as students learn that they will be putting on a full length trial, in a real courtroom, on an actual euthanasia case, and that they will be responsible for all of the various roles, the circle has been drawn. The next step is to concretize that sense of community; this is done by rearranging the classroom to facilitate the formation of a community of inquiry. The physical arrangement of a classroom has both symbolic and practical importance. If all of the students are seated in rows facing the teacher, the message is that the only one whose opinions really matter is the teacher. The physical inability of students to see, and often to hear their peers reinforces the point that students can learn nothing from one another.

In contrast, the community of inquiry, which uses the circle as a physical and symbolic beginning place, erases the distinction between the teacher as the dispenser of knowledge, and the student as the *tabula rasa*. Instead, "the teacher is a learner, and the learner is, without knowing it, a teacher . . ." (Dewey, 1966, p. 160). The circle also conveys the message that, "in making moral judgements we consider other people to be on an equal footing with ourselves." (Wilson, Williams & Sugarman, 1967, p. 77).

In a circle the class faces inward, perceiving both its wholeness and its individual components. The community of inquiry affirms that each student is an individual and at the same time a part of the class. This concept is later reflected in the courtroom where each student has to articulate his or her own unique view of the moral dilemma. Yet only when all of the information and viewpoints are combined in a meaningful and inclusive way are students able to arrive at a satisfactory verdict.

In Lipman's recent book, *Thinking in Education* (1991), he attempts to analyze the notion of the community of inquiry by breaking it down into stages. Stage one is the offering of the text; stage two is the construction of the agenda; stage three is the solidifying of the community; stage four is using exercises and discussion plans; and stage five is encouraging further responses (Lipman, 1991, pp. 241-243). Using this view of the community of inquiry, the first step after rearranging the classroom is the offering of the text.

The texts used in the *Introduction* phase of The Trial consist of numerous articles and short videos that introduce students to some typical and atypical cases, as well as some of the medical and legal facts related to euthanasia. Students begin to learn about the potential consequences of life-support machines, various definitions of death, beliefs about the sacredness of a life, a person's right to self-determination, and the role and responsibilities of doctors in our society.

Although the acquisition of facts is secondary to the process of inquiring, these community of inquiry discussions are not mere aimless meandering. "It is a process that aims at producing a *product* – at some kind of settlement or judgement, however partial and tentative this may be" (Lipman, 1991, p. 229). As students begin to articulate some initial opinions on the issues, the goal is to encourage them to offer logical reasons, to search for hidden assumptions in their own and each other's viewpoints, and to perceive the implications of their views.

The agenda, which Lipman describes as the second stage, is essentially "an index of what students consider important in the text . . ." (Lipman, 1991, p. 242). Each class, or community of inquiry, tends to choose somewhat different aspects of the articles and films to discuss. These are written down and displayed on an overhead transparency so that everyone can see the areas which the community is interested in discussing. The order in which the topics will be discussed, as well as the length of time spent on each one, are then determined by the community itself.

Setting the agenda leads students to consider the procedural rules which will govern their discussion. Often disagreements and tensions will arise as to who should speak and when, or how long a topic should be explored. One unique feature of the community of inquiry is that discussions relating to procedural details are not treated as a distraction, or divergence from the *real* purpose of the discussion, but are recognized as an essential step in the actual formation of the community. It is here that students begin to resolve their problems in a way that assures the integrity of the group. Practising certain moral behaviors such as mutual respect, tolerance, and fairness helps to assure the success of their collaborative enterprise. These skills will then be carried into the small inquiry groups which are used in the second phase of The Euthanasia Trial.

Once students have decided upon certain procedural rules, they can begin to move into what Lipman calls the third stage, solidifying the community. This is the critical stage in which students learn the cognitive skills they will need to prepare for and put on their own trial. They must become increasingly sensitive to meaningful contextual differences – for example, is a Jehovah Witness' decision to refuse a lifesaving blood transfusion an act of suicide? What reasons, criteria, generalizations, and examples can be employed to help articulate the areas of disagreement and thus further the quest for understanding?

The teacher's craft at this point rests not in his or her knowledge of the facts pertaining to euthanasia, but in the ability to foster collaborative inquiry among the students, to identify and praise their efforts to build on each other's ideas by asking useful questions or offering counter-examples or alternative interpretations. It is also imperative that the teacher model the cognitive skills, such as assumption finding, generalizing, and employing reasons. Moreover, all of this must be done in the spirit of a fellow inquirer, lest one overwhelm students' budding efforts to find their own answers, and assume increasing responsibility for their own process of inquiry.

It is this emphasis on inquiry and self-correction that probably most distinguishes the community of inquiry from a myriad of other models for guiding student discussion, stimulating critical thinking, or encouraging cooperative learning. Ann Margaret Sharp writes:

> Inquiry . . . is seldom a solitary matter. It is generally pursued by groups of individuals with similar objectives, . . . who share information . . . respect one another's views and opinions and offer reasons for their views. . . . When such a group reflects in a self-corrective manner upon philosophical issues, it can be called a community of inquiry. . . . (Sharp, 1984, p. 3)

C. The Jury as a Community of Inquiry

Another area of The Euthanasia Trial which relies heavily on the techniques and philosophy of the community of inquiry is the preparation of the jury. For the first six years of doing The Euthanasia Trial the jury was consistently the most difficult group to prepare. It was evident from the very first Trial in 1983, that without training in critical thinking and discussion skills, the jury could not function without a great deal of teacher input, which was contrary to the inherent goals and philosophy of The Trial. Finding the *time* to train a jury, however, while also attending to the lawyers and witnesses, and more importantly, finding a *method* for doing it, were problems that took years to resolve.

The first breakthrough occurred in 1987 when external circumstances necessitated combining two Secondary IV (Grade 10) classes of students who normally would have each put on their own trial. One class became the lawyers, witnesses, and judge, the other class became the jury. Suddenly there was classroom time to focus exclusively on the jury, without the constant pressure to be available to the lawyers and witnesses.

The second part of the solution came through a graduate course in Philosophy for Children, taken at McGill University in 1988, in which I learned about the community of inquiry. The training I received in conducting philosophical dialogs provided me with the tools to train a group of students to function as a jury with the least amount of teacher interference.

Hence, for the past four years there has been only one courtroom trial, which combines two classes of students. One class serves as the jury, the other as the lawyers, witnesses, and judge. Since the minimum requirement for a trial is at least 14 students with strong reading, writing, and verbal skills to serve as lawyers, witnesses, and judge, the principal criterion used to decide which group will serve as the jury is academic ability.

Every solution generates new problems and this solution is no exception to the rule. One problem is that by imposing the role of juror on a student, one loses the tremendous advantage in giving students a role in the decision-making process. A second problem is that there is a real danger that capable students may, in a sense, be penalized simply because they are in a class with predominantly less capable students.

Without detracting from the gravity of these potential consequences, I still believe that the current solution offers the best learning opportunities for the *majority* of students. Alfred Binet said that "the art of education consists in finding small, well-graduated tasks which shape the character of the child and progressively give him courage." (Pollack & Breuner, 1969, p. 206). The current solution recognizes that there are variations in students' abilities and needs, and tries to use these variations to help find the kinds of learning tasks that will challenge the student, without overwhelming him or her.

The training students receive as jurors in the community of inquiry specifically addresses certain cognitive deficiencies and provides students with valuable skills which can then be transferred to other subjects. Matthew Lipman attests to this transference of cognitive skills developed in philosophical dialogs.

> *The integration of thinking skills into every aspect of the curriculum would sharpen children's capacity to make connections and draw distinctions, to define and to classify, to assess factual information objectively and critically, to deal reflectively with the relationship between facts and values, and to differentiate their beliefs and what is true from their understanding of what is logically possible. These specific skills help children listen better, study better, learn better and express themselves better. They therefore, carry over into all academic areas. (Lipman, et al., 1980, p. 15)*

The social health of the class is another important area to assess before beginning a Trial. In discussions, are they able to listen to their peers, or are they easily distracted? When asked for reasons, are they defensive, argumentative, or unkind to other members of their class? The lawyer and witness group require a certain level of social functioning in order to work effectively in small groups with minimal teacher guidance. The *Introduction* phase may enhance these skills, but there is not enough time to provide remediation if these skills are below average. For other students, however, learning to become a *community*, let alone a *community of inquiry* is a major achievement. Perhaps the most significant quality each student can learn is "caring." Ann Margaret Sharp describes it this way.

In a real sense to care presupposes a willingness to be transformed by the other — to be affected by the other. This care is essential for dialog. But it is also essential for the development of trust, a basic orientation toward the world that accounts for the individuals coming to think they have a role to play in the world, that they can make a real difference. Further, the world is such a place that will receive not only their thoughts but their actions. Trust, in turn, is a pre-condition for the development of autonomy and self-esteem on the part of the individual participant. (Sharp, 1991, p. 32)

When a class is informed that they will be the jurors, the decision is delivered not in the spirit of a consolation prize. What is stressed is the importance of their role; they are the ones who will have the power to decide the outcome of the trial. Their challenge is to learn how to do this in a responsible way in order to come to a fair decision. As jurors, each one of them will have an opportunity, and an obligation, to help the group as a whole come to a verdict. In the process, they may discover the value of their own thoughts, and those of their classmates as well. By the date of the trial they will be able to run their own jury, and put their learning into practice.

This is the spirit in which the jury is appointed. In the sense that the roles are assigned without consultation, the process does smack of the-teacher-as-authority model. Yet the spirit in which the challenge is set forth comes straight out of the community of inquiry model.

There are many specific mental acts which a juror must perform. For example, jurors must try to expose errors in other jurors' thinking, must be willing to acknowledge errors in their own reasoning when a valid counter-argument is presented; and must be capable of perceiving the bias in both prosecution and defense arguments. Jurors must also be able to synthesize the evidence and arrive at an agreed-upon version of the events. Finally, they must be able to make inferences about the law, and apply the legal criteria to their specific case. Moreover, all of these sophisticated thinking acts must occur in a social framework which is easily threatened by emotional outbursts, peer pressure, and an unwillingness to reassess one's initial stand on an issue. Clearly, a jury needs to learn how to think both critically and collaboratively.

Jury training for The Trial begins with the "text" of *Twelve Angry Men* (Lumet, 1957). This movie, starring Henry Fonda, provides models of both good and bad reasoning, and shows the way in which a jury functions as a community of inquiry. Henry Fonda's character, for example, shows concern and respect for all the members of the jury, as well as for the jury process itself. Unlike some of the other jurors, he is willing to take the time to conduct a full *inquiry* and critically examine all of the evidence. In contrast, the character played by Lee J. Cobb has already decided, before any discussion, that the defendant is guilty, and steadfastly refuses to consider any alternative interpretations of the events.

The film also helps students get an idea of what a jury does and what skills and attitudes contribute to, or detract from, the process. Once again, the specific topics the class chooses to discuss after watching the film are determined by the needs of the class; their questions set the agenda. Regardless of the topics chosen, these discussions permit students to encounter and resolve some of the procedural issues which will arise in their work as a jury.

After students have had several class periods to experience their current level of dialog, it is time for a "Discussion Discussion" (Kyle, 1984). These meta-discussions give students an opportunity to reflect on their procedures, discover what is and is not working, and make changes that reflect their observations. According to Lipman it is important to exercise "care for the procedural principles of inquiry . . . ," because they become the means by which a child's moral judgement is improved (Lipman, et al., 1980, pp. 186-187).

In the initial phase of jury preparation, the group tends to require substantial involvement from the teacher. This involvement takes the form of modelling and encouraging the expression of alternative view-points, clarifying and explicating students' arguments or statements, pointing out implications and hidden assumptions, and noting consistency or inconsistency in students' reasoning.

After several classes, students are encouraged to take a more active role in guiding their own discussions. One technique for accomplishing this is *mini-discussions.* One student will raise a new idea for discussion and be permitted to call upon six students who wish to comment on the idea. This enables the student to practise some of the behaviors he or she has observed in the teacher. Mini-discussions not only provide students with increasing responsibility for managing their own discussions, they also greatly enhance student to student communication.

The "texts" used throughout this period consist of a variety of cases and essays on various aspects of euthanasia. The goal is to provide students with a broad understanding of the way each of the parts, medical, legal, social, and moral, fit into the whole.

As students become more capable of conducting their mini-discussions, they are given two sample cases for deliberation. The teacher's role in these deliberations is to provide input where necessary, but principally to increase student responsibility for the inquiry process.

D. Reflection and Summation Phase

After their day in court, students return to the classroom and reassemble as a community of inquiry. The first several discussions tend to focus largely on the jury decision. The group which contained the lawyers, witnesses, and judge is always eager to view the videotape which is made of the jury deliberations. This videotape provides students with a visual transcript of the decision-making process. Viewing the "text," they can reflect on which factors most influenced the jury's decision. It is an opportunity to perceive the consequences of their choices, to reflect on errors of omission or commission.

In the class of jurors, the videotape is equally important because it provides an opportunity to stand outside of the experience and exercise the self-corrective quality so typical of the community of inquiry. Jurors are encouraged to find errors in their reasoning, to see whether or not the inquiry procedures were applied correctly, and to evaluate how well they collaborated as a jury in reaching their decision.

Sometimes the questions raised in these discussions can only be answered by referring back to a specific individual's testimony or cross-examination. Because the videotape also includes the entire trial proceedings, students can check certain details or listen to the nuances in a witness' tone of voice or choice of words. These discussions continue until the group is satisfied with their understanding of why and how the verdict was reached.

A second round of discussions allows students to explore the affective lessons which were learned through the experience. They may reflect on how their groups worked, their feelings towards their character, or the moral dilemmas raised in the trial. One of the signs of a class' growth as a result of The Trial is their ability to have discussions such as this which clearly require a great deal of mutual trust, sensitivity, and respect for each member of the classroom community.

Perhaps the most important objective of *Reflection and Summation* phase is to enable students to create what Dewey calls a "map." This logical statement of their experience "summarizes and arranges, and thus separates the achieved results from the actual steps by which they were forthcoming..." (Dewey, 1956, p. 19). The value of this logical rendering of their experience

> ... is not contained in itself; its significance is that of standpoint, outlook, method. It intervenes between the more casual, tentative, and roundabout experiences of the past, and the more controlled and orderly experiences of the future. It gives past experience in that net form which renders it most available and most significant, most fecund for future experience. (Dewey, 1956, p. 21)

The "texts" used in these final discussions include excerpts from many well-known authors in the field. These readings assist students in making logical sense of their experience in part by providing them with the language to express their ideas more clearly. The readings also help students integrate their views into the broader perspective of our society. One contrast between these community of inquiry discussions and those at the *Introduction* phase is that students are more capable of understanding and assessing many of the moral and philosophical arguments because of the experiential knowledge they have acquired in putting on their own trial.

Another subtle difference in these discussions is that the emphasis is less on inquiry and more on developing a tentative conclusion, or "qualified decision" about euthanasia. Shaver and Strong define a qualified decision as "one that takes into account the possible negative consequences of a policy or action to be supported, and the circumstances under which you might change your mind and support a different value" (Shaver & Strong, 1976, p. 104). In other words, students do not merely deduce a position from a single value; they must show how their viewpoint represents a trade-off between competing or conflicting values. For this reason, the student's position on euthanasia at the end of The Trial tends to be far more logically consistent than his or her initial stance.

E. Tentative Conclusions and Implications

Recognizing that moral development is a lifelong process in which formal education plays only a limited part, a moral education teacher must ask herself or himself, "what can, or ought, one strive to impart to one's students?" In answering this question for myself, I have come to believe that one part of the answer lies in making students aware of the power of reflection. One of the implicit goals of The Euthanasia Trial is to demonstrate to students that reflection upon one's personal experiences is the key to change. Without such reflection we are prisoners of our own habits; with reflection we can learn from our mistakes and change those behaviors which are destructive to ourselves or others.

A second lifelong insight which The Trial seeks to impart to students is that other people's viewpoints can enrich and deepen our own. By teaching methods of collaborative inquiry, students may learn a tolerance, open-mindedness, and appreciation for others that will nurture their future moral and intellectual growth.

A third part of my answer is to teach students to think more logically, articulate more clearly, and listen more attentively. If The Trial accomplishes even some of this, it provides students with a method of problem solving which can be useful throughout their lives. Moreover, by teaching them to be more self-corrective in their discussions with others, they may also become more critical thinkers in themselves.

The final part of my answer is that a moral educator can help students to recognize that neither logic nor feelings alone are enough of a guide when it comes to moral decision making. Rather, what is required is a harmonious blending of these two capacities, a kind of dialog between one's thoughts and emotions. By dramatizing the moral issues in each Euthanasia Trial, I hope to awaken students' sense of compassion and caring. By teaching the principles of philosophical discussion, I try to provide students with the means to reason, judge, and critique their emotional responses. Thus, an individual may come to see that when it comes to complex moral decisions, reasoning must always be leavened by caring, and caring must always be balanced by reason.

Notes

1. Whenever "The Trial" is capitalized, it refers to the entire model and includes all phases of the Euthanasia Trial. When the word "trial" appears without capitalization it refers only to the actual courtroom experience in which students enact their own trial.

References

Dewey, J. (1956). *The child and the curriculum* and *The school and society* (Combined Edition). Chicago: University of Chicago Press.

Dewey, J. (1966). *Democracy and education: An introduction to the philosophy of education* (Free Press Edition). New York: The Macmillan Company.

Gilligan, C. (1977, November). In a different voice: Women's conceptions of self and morality. *Harvard Educational Review, 47*(4), 481-517.

Kyle, J.A. (1984). Managing philosophical discussions. *Thinking: The Journal of Philosophy for Children, 5*(2), 19-22. (Reprinted from *Analytic Teaching, 3*(2), 13-16). [Revised unpublished manuscript, 1987].

Lipman, M. (1991). *Thinking in education.* Cambridge: Cambridge University Press.

Lipman, M., Sharp, A.M. & Oscanyan, F.S. (1980). *Philosophy in the classroom.* Philadelphia: Temple University Press.

Lumet, S. (Director). (1957). *Twelve angry men.* [Film]. Unlimited Artists.

Noddings, N. (1986). *Caring: A feminine approach to ethics and moral education.* Berkeley & Los Angeles: University of California Press.

Pollack, R. & Breuner, M. (Eds.). (1969). *The experimental psychology of Alfred Binet.* New York: Springer Company.

Sharp, A.M. (1991). The community of inquiry: Education for democracy. *Thinking, 9* (2): 31-37.

Sharp, A.M. (1984). Philosophical teaching as moral education. *The Journal of Moral Education, 13*(1), 3-8.

Shaver, J. & Strong, W. (1976). *Facing value decisions: Rationale building for teachers.* Belmont, CA: Wadworth.

Wilson, J., Williams, N. & Sugarman, B. (1967). *Introduction to moral education.* Harmondsworth, Middlesex, England: Penguin Books Ltd.

CHAPTER 14

Yes, Teacher, First Graders Can Do Philosophy

Sharon G. Palermo

Yes, Teacher, first graders can do philosophy – and they can do it with serious interest!

Some of my own work in Philosophy for Children involves six and seven year-olds actively engaged in philosophical discussion stimulated by picture books from the trade market. I have seen first graders think logically, sustain a train of thought, imagine circumstances from points of view other than their own, make distinctions, provide evidence, and wonder imaginatively about phenomena outside their immediate percep-tions. I have seen them intent on philosophical investigations.

The following discussion is drawn from a particular study which I conducted for my master's thesis in critical thinking in young children. It shows that young children think concretely and abstractly as the situation and subject matter require. If, for instance, we were discussing the evidence to prove how a baby owlet in one story was killed, concrete phenomena were discussed. On the other hand, if discussing the connec-tion between motivation and blame in the same story, abstract informa-tion was given. Children understood what was necessary to illustrate their points.

Making Distinctions

Children were able to see distinctions in various kinds of situations, some of which were of an abstract nature. One of the more interesting cases involved the story, *It Could Always be Worse* (Zemach, 1976), in which a man is advised to take increasingly more animals into his already crowded house so that he will see how much worse it can be. We were discussing what happened to the house. Did it become smaller, or did it only seem to become smaller? Some of the children claimed that the house had actually become smaller, but when Mark asserted confidently that the book had never said such a thing, I searched for a particular passage in the book and found, "the hut seemed smaller and the children grew bigger." Laurence was able to explain the distinction between seemed smaller and was smaller: "Seemed smaller is like there's more things in the house, so it feels like it's smaller 'cause there's so much things in it, it feels like it's shrinking."

Laurence's ability to make this statement implies several things. First, he was able to imagine the physical difference between the house with and without the animals in it and apply those differences to the abstract concept of the difference between reality and illusion. He was able to see how what was happening actually impinged upon a person's state of mind and to hypothesize about why the house seemed smaller, or, in reverse, to hypothesize about how the house would feel if there were more animals in it. While the distinction he made seemed simple enough at first, on analysis, it's clear that Laurence was operating with a well-developed ability to think in abstract terms and to formulate and test an hypothesis.

In another, somewhat different, handling of reality and illusion, Tommy was trying to explain whether or not Donald Duck is "for real." He had established a distinction between reality and fantasy in relation to story books. Something can be for real for the purposes of the story, but in fact, it didn't happen in real life. As an extension of this, he made the claim that Donald Duck is for real, "only if they're on movies and they're cartoons." Tommy was not able or willing to explain this further: "Oh, don't ask me to explain the . . . difference between real people and cartoons. Don't ask me that," but he has a clear enough understanding of those nuances to make his original statement. He then went on to say that Donald Duck costumes at Walt Disney World are both real and not real in different ways. He was dealing with the philosophical distinction between real and not real, which in this case has to do with physical existence in the world and, possibly, the idea of viability. Donald Duck costumes are made of real touchable materials and exist in an entirely sensorial way. Yet the abstract character is made up (to use a child's term) and could not exist on its own. Tommy was defining and making comparisons about different aspects of the same phenomenon. He could see Donald Duck costumes from different perspectives and apply different criteria to those perspectives.

What is the distinction between a lie and an exaggeration and can a six or seven year-old see that distinction? This would seem an important question in getting the author's full meaning from the story, *Liar, Liar, Pants on Fire!* (Cohen, 1985), in which a new boy comes to school and tries to gain attention by lying about his belongings. The story is of a realistic and didactic nature, indicating that the author certainly believes children can grasp that distinction. Yet it is an entirely abstract concept, not based on any physical phenomenon, but rather on the concepts of motivation and intent.

I questioned and led the children extensively to help them make this distinction, feeling that it was crucial to understanding the story. They had considerable difficulty with it and I finally gave them a fictional example of how I had been caught speeding and, to get out of it, told the policeman I had a sick child to take to the hospital. I asked if this was different from saying something like, "I'm so hungry, I could eat a horse." Laurence was the first to respond after this, saying, "the car one's lying – and the other one was exaggerating . . . because . . . you're so hungry you feel like you could eat a horse." In qualifying his statement with *you feel like*, Laurence was getting at the very question of motivation which is so crucial to the distinction between lying and exaggerating. He is beginning to understand and articulate the point of view of the person speaking and how that point of view affects that person's actions. The distinction can be made even finer if we add the element of intent which Laurence was able to do with help from me:

> *Sharon: Does it have anything to do with what I wanted the other person to believe?*
>
> *Laurence: Like, um, you have to make the other people believe you needed to go fast.*

Though it was a struggle, he managed to handle these very abstract ideas with competence and increased understanding as the discussion went on.

Seeing other points of view

Sometimes the children showed excellent readings of other people's or the story characters' points of view while at the same time making important connections and distinctions or looking at broad philosophical implications of the stories. In the story, *Mooncake* (Asch, 1983), Bear thought he had taken a rocket to the moon, but had actually fallen asleep in the rocket during the count-down. He awoke after the snow had fallen, but he had never seen snow before. Therefore, his perceptions of the world around him when he woke up were crucial to his interpretation of where he was. The children picked up on this and in their leading ideas, Carrie mentioned that she would like to discuss, "when he eats the snow." Later, Bobby said, "How come he doesn't know what snow tastes like?" Tommy immediately saw a connection between Bobby and Carrie's statements and said, "that's the same as Carrie's." Though we will never know exactly what Carrie meant, Tommy's inference that she meant essentially the same as Bobby was a good one. All three of the children seemed to understand the hypothesis of the story that if Bear didn't understand his surroundings, he was likely to think he was in a foreign place. In addition, Tommy had been listening carefully and understood Carrie's imprecise language well enough to make the connection between her and Bobby's statements.

In a similar instance, Laurence enlightened us on the sun's point of view in *What the Moon Saw* (Wildsmith, 1978). Showing every indication that he fully understood the world from Sun's perspective, Laurence interpreted her statement, "I believe there is nothing I haven't seen," to mean, "he [she] didn't miss anything. There are hundreds of kinds of houses and he [she] saw every one. She saw every kind of house." Laurence based his understanding partly on the early sections of the book which laid out some of the things of the world which Sun was capable of seeing. Yet his explanation went a step further than Sun's. He was able to put it in more everyday language that all of the children could understand. Not only was he able to take Sun's explanation and essentially make it his own, but he expanded it through the use of examples and added the concept of omni-vision.

In *What the Moon Saw*, it is entirely possible that children might focus on the specifics of what the sun and moon could see: plain lions, small villages, round balls, and so on. Yet Laurence was able to begin understanding and talking about the broader and more abstract philosophical dimensions of the story by stepping into Sun's shoes and interpreting her meaning.

Again, in the story, *Bradley and the Clock* (Palermo), Laurence was able to step compassionately into Bradley's shoes. In this story, Bradley tries valiantly to understand how time and the workings of the clock relate to his daily life. He notices that the hands of the clock seem to make pie-like pieces and decides that is why the clock is round. In his final statement in the book, Bradley asked, "Whoever heard of a square pie?" Several of the children had trouble with this, saying that there are indeed square pies and I asked if they thought Bradley was being silly. Laurence jumped to Bradley's defense and said, "No. No, maybe he didn't ever see a square pie." With this statement, Laurence accepted two possibilities at once: that there may be square pies but that Bradley may not have seen one. His explanation showed an understanding of Bradley's store of background knowledge and his further comment, that Bradley asked his question because "the clock looked like it was cut into pie pieces," indicates his understanding of the stimulating force behind Bradley's statement. Laurence certainly understood what made Bradley tick!

Making Inferences

Laurence helped us with our discussions by making relevant inferences from the stories several times. He was able to pick out a flaw in a discussion about whether or not the house in *It Could Always be Worse* had become taller. While others were discussing what had happened to the house, Laurence stopped to think about what was happening to the characters and suddenly realized that the man in the story had to keep going back to see the rabbi. Laurence brought this to our attention when he noted that if the house had become so tall as to reach the moon, the man would not have been able to get down to see the rabbi: a fascinating and reasonable inference based on careful attention to the story and the meshing of different bits of information, and the imaginative wonderment of what life would be like if we lived up around the moon.

Bobby brought a very different interpretation to this same story than did the rest of us. His belief was that when the animals went into the house they stretched the walls and ceiling up. Most of us thought that this was a rather outlandish suggestion, but Bobby argued his point cogently for an entire half-hour session and based some of his arguments on quite reasonable and abstract inferences. He looked toward the rabbi for evidence of motivation in telling the man to take the animals into his house. He asked a question concerning another's point of view: why would the rabbi do that? He hypothesized an answer: because the animals would cause the house to stretch and it would get bigger and be easier for the man to live in.

Tommy addressed the issue of motivation, also, in conjunction with the story, *Why Mosquitoes Buzz in People's Ears* (Aardema, 1975). He asserted that it was no one's fault that the owlet had died because, though Monkey jumped on the branch, "the branch was dying and it just fell." Therefore neither Monkey nor Mosquito meant to kill the owlet. It was a victim of unfortunate circumstance. Tommy seemed to change his mind the next day, however, when he suggested that Mosquito, who set off the entire chain of events, had done so by telling a lie. Further, Tommy looked at Snake's knowledge and intentions when he entered Rabbit's hole and determined that Snake was not to blame for scaring Rabbit and continuing the chain of events. Snake was simply trying to hide in the hole and did not know that Rabbit was there. Tommy was able to separate important facts from implications and make connections between motivation and blame. These are abstract concepts which we would think are inaccessible to children under classical developmental theories. It is interesting, however, that adults in our society almost universally try to teach young children the difference between doing things by accident and doing them on purpose. We often don't clue in to the inconsistency between our teaching and our professed beliefs. It seems that in this case, at least, our teaching is based on the better understanding. Tommy has handled these ideas comfortably.

Being able to infer meaning from other sources goes beyond what we would traditionally expect to see in children at the turning point between pre-operational and concrete operational thought. According to Piaget's system, they are just beginning to understand others' points of view, they are just beginning to show flexibility and reversibility in their thought, and they are supposedly far from the ability to look at things purely abstractly. While there are many instances in my transcripts in which the children have not been able to fully express their meaning verbally, many of the statements that they have made imply an excellent ability to think abstractly. Would a child, for instance, be able to pick out the flaws inherent in a procedure whereby a person's guilt is decided through a vote? Carrie suggested this procedure in establishing who was to blame for the owlet's death in *Why Mosquitoes Buzz in People's Ears*.

Laurence immediately picked up on this and said, "how about if the one that did it won't say if he did or not?" and "Maybe the person that really did it didn't go to the place where they been called." It is not entirely clear what Laurence meant by these statements. What is clear is that he was uncomfortable with Carrie's suggestion and that he thought it would be important for the guilty party to be there. He suggests in his statements that an important reason for this might be that that person could supply evidence or even, possibly, self-defence. If he were not there, he certainly could not speak for himself. Laurence could have been thinking in terms of justice, or simply in terms of providing evidence. In either case he has noted and expounded upon a significant flaw in the suggestion and has seen it from the point of view of the accused party.

Classifying

One of our early sessions dealt with the story of *Frederick*, (Lionni, 1967), the little mouse that brought warmth and color and poetry to his friends in winter. In conjunction with this story we were trying to establish the difference between mind and body by determining their specific inclusions, that is, what things are in the mind and body. As a group, we had decided that colors and warmth were in our minds because we think of them. Later, however, Bobby said that only ideas are in our minds. "Only ideas are in your mind?" I asked. "Yeah," he said, "because words, they're not in your mind, but you think of something and that makes an answer." Bobby was expressing his view of how ideas produce words, implying both a relationship and a distinction between the two which has not been firmly established in adult philosophy. But as a group, we continued when I raised the question, are colors and warmth, therefore, ideas? Laurence said, yes, they are because you have to think about them to see them and, by doing so, established clear criteria for an abstract classification system. He was able to see similarities between colors, warmth, and ideas. They are all things that you have to think about – things that are in our minds. Though this is a far more complicated classification task than the visually concrete ones often given to young children (4-legged animals vs. 2-legged animals, squares vs. triangles), Laurence and Bobby handled different aspects of it with relative ease.

Another instance of a child establishing criteria for a category occurred in our first session when Tommy was considering some of the guesses the children had made while trying to figure out what was at the centre of a package that was wrapped in many layers. For a moment he had forgotten that we were talking about the final contents and focused on the individual layers. He remembered that one child had guessed the contents to be soap. He suggested the relevant criteria for a layer when he said, "It couldn't be soap because you couldn't open soap and reclose it and put something in it. It's impossible." He was able to describe a certain characteristic of soap, weigh it against the necessary conditions for a layer and make a logical deduction based on that comparison.

Providing Evidence

In conjunction with the story, *Mooncake*, we were trying to establish the criteria which Bear should have utilized in figuring out if he was really on the moon. Bobby had argued effectively that Bear should have seen the grass and trees and known that these things did not exist on the moon. But Tommy noted that Bear had been sleeping beyond the time when the snow fell and when he awoke, the world was white. This was a significant element in the credibility of the story and Tommy saw the connection between Bear sleeping and the snow falling as the important bit of evidence that it was. Because the world was different when Bear awoke, he thought he had blasted off and gone to the moon. Tommy imagined two situations at once – Bear awake and in the grass and Bear asleep and in the snow – and made a relevant comparison between them.

During another part of this same discussion, the children were wondering why Bear didn't remember the snow when he saw and tasted it. A couple of arguments had been suggested to explain this while Laurence sat patiently allowing everyone their turn to speak. Finally he pointed out a flaw in the entire discussion when he said that "bears hibernate in winter. How could they taste snow if they go to sleep in winter?" Laurence had thought back to the book's passage, "Bear had never been awake in winter," or perhaps to his own store of knowledge and applied that information to the conditions necessary for Bear's perceptions.

In all our discussions, as behooves critical thinkers, we stressed the importance of providing evidence for the opinions we expressed. In conjunction with *Why Mosquitoes Buzz in People's Ears*, we turned explicitly to a discussion of the nature of evidence and how it works to establish proof. To help the children get an intimate grip on the concept I asked them if it would be fair for me to blame one of them if our class mice were stolen. Laurence provided the alternative possibility that a robber might have done it. I pushed him to pursue the problem further:

S: *Well how would we know the robber had done that?*

Laurence: *'Cause you might see some of, he might have muddy shoes and you could follow the mud on the floor.*

S: *But maybe one of you kids came in with muddy shoes. It could have been one of you.*

Laurence: *Oh, he would have bigger footprints.*

S: *Oh, I might know it wasn't one of you if there were bigger footprints leading to the mouse cage?*

Laurence: *You had to measure our foots to get the footprints.*

With the stimulation of my questioning and restating, Laurence was able to think out some specific kinds of evidence to look for and a way of analyzing that evidence. Several minutes later, he used the understanding he had gleaned from this discussion to bring us back to the problem of Owlet's death: "In the story they have evidence because . . . he [Iguana] told everybody it was Mosquito's fault because he was bugging him and Mosquito was saying things that weren't true," and, "He's [Mosquito] the one that made the iguana put sticks in his ears that made the snake go into the rabbit's hole." Laurence showed his ability here to transfer his understanding of one situation to an analogous one. He saw the need for evidence in general and was able to pick out specific evidence to accuse Mosquito.

Sustaining Arguments

For the most part, the children did not tend to sustain arguments on their own over the course of a session when others strongly disagreed, whether or not those arguments were valid. Our discussions tended to be convoluted, jumping from one aspect of an issue to another with me making the greatest effort to keep things on track and to keep questions arising. Bobby was the one child who became involved enough in his ideas to keep pushing them forward despite considerable opposition. Part of the reason for this may be that we found his opinions so interesting and unusual that we had many responses to them. Another reason is that Bobby's personal commitment to his ideas necessitated his own continued response and contributed to an inability to see other points of view.

In conjunction with *Frederick*, we asked the question, "is warmth in your body?" Bobby said, yes, warmth is in your body because the sun gets in your ears and warms you. By way of drawing out his idea and suggesting an unlikely implication of it, I noted that that meant to me that there is a little tube running from your ears to the rest of your body which carries the sun. Bobby was quite clear and unhesitant in noting that this was not at all what he meant, but rather that the sun shines and that "those shines" [rays?] stay in and warm you. Bobby had rejected an idea which he probably felt was outlandish in favor of one for which he may have seen concrete evidence. Sunrays can be seen in floating dust particles and in pictures in story books. His term *those shines* indicates this realistic sensory approach to sunrays. I made a counter-argument to his sun-in-the-ears theory by suggesting that girls with hair covering their ears could not get warm. This did not daunt Bobby: the sun could get through those tiny spaces between the hairs. Bobby followed through on his original argument very logically. He maintained the same logical thread several minutes later when the discussion turned to the question, "is the sun in your mind?" Here, Bobby viewed the mind as a very concrete thing, associating it perhaps with the brain, and said, as he gestured to his head, yes, the sun is in your mind for the same reason that it is in your body. The sun can shine both up and down and, therefore, it shines up to your mind.

Tommy and Stuart had both suggested that the sun warms you by warming your skin. Bobby had at first rejected this idea, but came later to accept it. There is no clear indication as to why he did accept it. We can only assume that he weighed the evidence silently, or it simply made enough sense that it became a part of him. But rather than allowing this to weight against his own view, or to sit unexamined in contrast to it, he incorporated the two very logically together. The sun warms the outside of your body by shining on your skin and the inside of your body by entering your ears.

It is interesting that Bobby seemed to equate warmth and sun when he began talking about the sun being in our bodies rather than warmth. No one seemed to notice this equation and it is worth wondering about the entire phenomenon. What caused Bobby to treat these two ideas as one? They are both concrete physical entities with distinct differences, though they both have abstract qualities about them. The sun is so far, so bright, and so hot, that we can only experience it from a great distance and can never look at it directly. It is really the sun's warmth and light which are actually concrete to us in that they are experienced directly through our senses. But warmth, in another sense, is a much more abstract idea than is sun. Sun is a specific physical entity which can be located and localized in space and observed through two senses, sight and touch. It is much more difficult to talk about warmth as a specific phenomenon. It can be observed through only one sense, touch, and dissipates in ways which often make it very hard to localize. Indeed, if we do actually locate warmth, it is usually in terms of another specific thing rather than warmth itself. The room is warm, and so forth. When we speak of warmth as its own entity, we do so in the abstract, as an emotional warmth rather than a physical warmth.

"Warmth" in the physical sense and "sun" are strongly tied together. Alone, they each present unique conversational tendencies: warmth must be associated with a thing and sun is experienced mostly through its two effects of warmth and light. This accounts for the strong association in conversation, and the tendency to equate warmth and sun. The effect is nearly as strong, I think, for adults as it is for children. We can see how easily I let the equation pass in this conversation. I could have done this purely to allow the conversation to continue in its vein or in hopes that other children might question it. However, my memory of the event is that, in fact, I didn't even notice. What would classical developmental theory say about this? That Bobby made this association because of his very strong tie to the concrete and inability to think of either warmth or sun in abstract terms or separately from each other? His argument itself is certainly based on very specific concrete behaviors. It is an argument that no adult would make, but Bobby is unlikely to have run across any specific explanation for how the sun does warm us. In fact, the only explanations that I know of are also very concrete and physical, just different from Bobby's. So perhaps Bobby's explanation of events has nothing to do with being specifically object bound, but rather, with the nature of the phenomena.

Bobby put forth a more vehement and equally unbelievable argument during our discussion of *It Could Always be Worse*, but he carried it through with originality and great effort to add supporting evidence.

It was Bobby's contention throughout the discussion and in the face of strong counter-arguments, that the animals stretched the walls and roof of the house to make it bigger. This belief follows logically from Bobby's understanding of the situation. When faced with the discovery that the man's house seemed too small, Bobby's likely first reaction was that he needed a bigger house. Thus, he theorized that the rabbi's reason for telling him to take the animals into his house was that those animals would stretch the house and make it bigger. One could only believe that this would work, however, if one were ignorant of the stretchability of walls and roofs. This is a concept which Bobby seemed to have missed prior to the discussion and it is not brought up by others until well into the discussion.

Bobby also had another reason to back up his view. An illustration in the book showed the moon coming through a window. With the idea already in mind that the house needed to be taller, this provided a reasonable piece of evidence that it did grow. Though the drawing is whimsical, it is assigned a strong reality by Bobby in support of his view. He did not stop to think that perhaps it was just a humorous drawing to go with a humorous story. But why should he? Indeed, we were taking the discussion quite seriously, so Bobby had every reason in that context to take the pictures seriously.

With plenty of counter-evidence from the rest of us, Bobby actively constructed other rationale to support his belief. Laurence stated that it would be impossible for the house to get so tall because the man would not then be able to get down to see the rabbi. But Bobby suggested that he could have used weights to pull him down. Bobby did not think out the implications of this statement: if the man used weights, he would fall and hurt himself. But he thought creatively, using rudimentary logic and trying out ideas without fear or rebuff.

Later, Laurence and Tommy said that the house seemed smaller because it was so crowded when the animals were in it. At first, Bobby indicated agreement with this, but when I provided an analogy, "It's like if we filled up this rug with more and more and more kids, it would get so crowded it would seem like the space you were in was very tiny, right?", he went back to his original position, making my analogy into his. He said that the kids would push out the chairs surrounding the rug just like the animals would push out the walls of the house. Clearly, Bobby was so convinced of his position that other points of view were really difficult to see.

Carl and Laurence argued that if the house got taller it would get skinnier, not wider, because the walls would stretch up and be pulled in. Bobby by now was very ego-involved and upset and did not consider this possibility at all. It is clear that his personal investment in the subject had gotten in the way of his ability to examine his beliefs or consider opposing evidence. But in spite of his inability to accept other possibilities in this case, Bobby presented a strong and steadfast argument with sufficient evidence to make it plausible. He had the rabbi's motive, the presence of the moon, and the effect of squeezing many things into a small space.

Thought most of us were bound to the familiar observation that houses do not stretch, Bobby seemed to be thinking in imagery and going beyond his range of past experience. His strong visual imagery and lack of convincing experience regarding the nature of houses allowed him a very personal and wondering approach to this story. He was thinking independently.

Perhaps a comment should be made on the use of literature in philosophical discussions. I did not anticipate the difficulties caused by the illustrations in this book when I chose to use it, nor did it occur to me that anyone would imagine that the house had stretched. Perhaps, if we are using a book to discuss philosophical issues, issues which we wish to have taken seriously, we should make sure that the book is written and illustrated in a realistic vein to avoid confusion. On the other hand, fantasy provides all sorts of interesting issues, and sorting out the fantasy from the reality is an important problem in itself. Since we can't accurately anticipate the direction in which a discussion will go, we need to be prepared to handle confusions or unusual ideas as they come. Controlling our attitude is more critical than controlling the literature. In this case, Bobby became quite frustrated because none of us granted much credence to his ideas. They had some validity, particularly in light of the whimsy of the story, and provided a colorful turn to the discussion. It would have been valuable for all of us had I placed more value on his philosophical thought at the time and somehow indicated this during the discussion.

Not only would we have had a greater appreciation of Bobby, but we might also have appreciated a different angle to the story.

These are but a few examples of critical thought displayed by the children during our study sessions, but they illustrate the variety of thinking skills already in use by the ages of six and seven. With the exception of some specific instances of naïveté and lack of experience, I can distinguish no qualitative differences between the way these children think and the way adults think. While there were cases in which the children seemed to be tied to their immediate observations, when they were hypothesizing, comparing, explaining cause and effect, or whatever, these cases all had a physical base. There were cases as well that dealt entirely with abstract concepts that the children were able to handle: Laurence in transferring the concept of evidence from the discussion to the story or in classifying colors, warmth, and ideas all together; Tommy's connection between motivation and blame or Bobby's between motivation and the rabbi's instructions; the children's understanding of language, particularly in interpreting another child's idea, or in clarifying an idea for the benefit of another child; and the ability to hypothesize, as in Laurence's explanation of why the house seemed smaller or Bobby's figuring out why the rabbi gave the instructions that he did.

The children were able to imagine differences both physical and not: differences between the house with and without animals; the differences between reality and fantasy as expressed in Donald Duck; the difference between lying and exaggerating. They were able to see cause and effect: if Bear woke up in the snow that would cause him to believe he was on the moon. They imagined alternative possibilities: even though there are square pies, perhaps Bradley hasn't seen one; if one lived as high as the moon, certain things would be impossible; a robber might steal the mice rather than a child. They were able to mesh information: on the one hand, the house got bigger, on the other, the man had to go see the rabbi, therefore something is wrong; bears hibernate in winter and snow falls in winter, therefore bears do not see snow; the sun warms the inside of your body by one method and the outside by another. They were able to maintain a logical thread of thought over time. And above all, they were able to see many things from another's point of view: how one could feel like eating a horse; how the world must look to the sun; how Bradley could see things differently than the rest of us; why the animals in the mosquito story believed and acted as they did; how it wouldn't be fair to someone to vote on his guilt.

The children were able to assess the situation and judge how to think and behave accordingly. They knew that critical thinking was expected of them, and though they didn't know the term "critical thinking," they understood much of its meaning. They understood that it meant to look carefully and judge conscientiously, which they did. Their thought sprung directly from the stories and wove around the contents of the stories in a completely relevant way, dealing with its concrete events and abstract concepts in the concrete or abstract ways for which they called.

The children often lacked facility with language and many of my interpretations were based on inferential judgement of what they meant. I do not consider this dangerous ground on which to judge, however. To make certain that I had interpreted correctly, I frequently restated or clarified for a child, checking with her or him on my interpretation. Furthermore, every statement implies a store of background knowledge and understandings which have not been expressed. Indeed, conversations would be unbearably tedious, if they could exist at all, were we required to explain the background behind every statement we made. My interpretations of the children's meanings have come directly from the context of the discussions in which we all took part honestly and freely. The children have shown themselves very capable of philosophical thinking even though their lack of facility with language sometimes impedes their expression.

Thus, using several critical thinking skills, the children proved themselves remarkably capable of reasonable and conscientious treatment of the subject matter, considering the evidence and presenting it carefully in a kind and dignified way.

References

Aardema, V. (1975). *Why mosquitoes buzz in people's ears.* New York: Scholastic Book Services.

Asch, F. (1983). *Mooncake.* Englewood Cliffs, NJ: Prentice Hall, Inc.

Cohen, M. (1985). *Liar, liar, pants on fire!* New York: Greenwillow Books.

Lionni, L. (1967). *Frederick.* New York: Pantheon Books.

Palermo, S. G. *Bradley and the clock.* Unpublished.

Wildsmith, B. (1978). *What the moon saw.* New York: Oxford University Press.

Zemach, M. (1976). *It could always be worse.* New York: Scholastic, Inc.